Praise for
The Art of Digital Music

"Let's suppose I wanted to invite almost every leading mind in the field of digital music over to my house for an evening dedicated to the exchange of new ideas. The list would include many of my friends, contemporaries, and professional heroes. I would make it very informal—cushy chairs, good food, great conversation. And I would be sure to have David Battino and Kelli Richards send out the invitations, for obviously no one can resist them. Here is your chance to join the party."

—Jack Douglas, producer (Aerosmith, John Lennon, Cheap Trick)

"If you're making music today, read this book by tomorrow!"

—Bruce Haring, Managing Director, the DIY Convention;
author of *Beyond the Charts: MP3 and the Digital Music Revolution*

"Astonishing depth and variety—there's some real inside information here, and what an impressive mix of interviewees!"

—Eliot Van Buskirk, Editor, MP3.com; author of
Burning Down the House: Ripping, Recording, Remixing, and More!

"Despite having a thorough technical background, this book never forgets that 'art' is the key word in 'state of the art.'"

—Craig Anderton, author, performer, and music technology guru

"Usually books on music technology are about as dry as database manuals. But reading this one is like eavesdropping on great artists and creative tech geniuses. Just about everybody has something interesting to say."

—Mark Mothersbaugh (Devo, film and TV composer)

"You interview like Woody Allen used to do standup—you've prepared your questions but make it seem like a spontaneous conversation with a friend."

—Roger Linn, drum machine inventor

THE ART OF
DIGITAL MUSIC

56 Visionary Artists & Insiders
Reveal Their Creative Secrets

by David Battino & Kelli Richards

Backbeat
Books

San Francisco

Published by Backbeat Books
600 Harrison Street, San Francisco, CA 94107
www.backbeatbooks.com
email: books@musicplayer.com

An imprint of CMP Information
Publishers of *Guitar Player*, *Bass Player*, *Keyboard*, and *EQ* magazines

CMP
United Business Media

Distributed to the book trade in the US and Canada by
Publishers Group West, 1700 Fourth Street, Berkeley, CA 94710

Distributed to the music trade in the US and Canada by
Hal Leonard Publishing, P.O. Box 13819, Milwaukee, WI 53213

Cover Design by Richard Leeds — bigwigdesign.com
Back cover photo (Alan Parsons) courtesy of *Tape Op* magazine
Composition by Michael Cutter

Library of Congress Cataloging-in-Publication Data

The art of digital music : 56 visionary artists and insiders reveal their creative secrets /
[edited] by David Battino and Kelli Richards.
    p. cm.
Includes bibliographical references (p.) and index.
ISBN 0-87930-830-3 (alk. paper)
1. Sound recording executives and producers—Interviews. 2. Musicians—Interviews.
3. Digital audio editors. I. Battino, David. II. Richards, Kelli.

ML74.A78 2005
786.7—dc22
                       2004025015

Printed in the United States of America

05 06 07 08 09 5 4 3 2 1

Contents

Foreword

I'm sitting here in the machine room of my studio, in the warm embrace of the whirring hard drives. For me, film composing is all about computers. Drumming is all about blood and guts, snot and fingernails.

But sometimes they come together. With our first bit of money in the Police, we went to Manny's Music in New York City and bought all kinds of crap. I got a Fender Stratocaster, a cool Roland amp, and a Roland Space Echo tape delay. At the sound-check that night, I plugged a microphone into the amp and got this echo response going with the snare drum where I could get these cool rhythms bouncing back off my amp. One of the techniques I discovered was the dotted-eighth-note delay, which creates that swinging "dugga-*dugga*-dugga" sound. For that to work, you have to be pretty exact with your tempo, which was tough with tape.

When digital delay lines appeared, you could just set the number and it could be the same every night. In fact, I would almost use it as a metronome. I'd go *bap* on the snare drum and wait for the response, and then I could figure out what the tempo was supposed to be. It almost made an honest man of me.

Drummer Stewart Copeland founded the Police and recorded five multiplatinum albums in a row. As a film, TV, and opera composer, he has more than 60 soundtrack credits and Golden Globe and Emmy nominations.

I was already a home recording enthusiast. I had a Revox tape recorder and one of those drum boxes made for lounge artists. It only had five rhythms, but I'd use that as a backing track and then overdub my guitars. Eventually I realized that it had a cool sound of its own.

One day, someone lent me an E-mu Emulator with all of those orchestral samples in it, and I thought, "Oh my *god*, this is incredible!" and I started recording that. And then someone said, "Look, there's this Fairlight [Computer Musical Instrument]; you can actually tell it what notes to play and look at the notes on a screen, and fiddle around with them."

That's about when I started scoring *The Equalizer*. I had to turn over a show every week, and I did the first half of the first season with just the eight monophonic, 8-bit voices on that Fairlight. It was a *chunky* kind of sound, but it was one that most people hadn't heard before. So it registered as fresh, even though it had its drawbacks. With just eight simultaneous notes, it was very difficult to have wafting chords or pads.

The Fairlight was very unfriendly for players. It was more something that you programmed. But that was perfect for me, because I'm not a keyboard player. With the graphic representation, I could create the notes I needed and put 'em on the page. The reason I'm a composer is because the music is in my head, and all I have to do is figure out a way of getting it out.

One of the anomalies in life is that the Good Lord hands out His gifts erratically. I got a gift for playing drums; I got a shine for the guitar. The piano was not given to me. I spend all day, every day, doing my work on a keyboard, entering notes into MOTU Performer. And I *still* cannot play the simplest thing: "I need to trigger this sample on beat 1." One, two, three, four—*baadada!* I hit two notes! "Okay; let me try it again." One, two, three, four—*whadadawhak!* I missed again.

If I'm doing an orchestra date now, I go straight to Finale, my notation program, and print it out. But for soloists in the studio, I just have them play it right off the screen. In fact, one of my crucial musicians is an Electronic Valve Instrument (EVI) player, Judd Miller. I use him for everything—guitar solos, woodwinds, strange drones. The EVI doesn't make sound itself; it outputs MIDI control data to the computer and samplers. So Judd can play a solo, and—Hey, look; we've got a complete score on the screen. We can see musically on staves what he just did. And then he can do a solo in harmony with it.

So the art of digital music is advancing. What's still very frustrating is the number of different formats. At any given time, I can have *six* programs running—Performer, Pro Tools, Final Cut Pro, After Effects, DVD Studio Pro, and Photoshop or Quark. How do I advance the sample one frame to the right? Where's "Play"? What we need is another breakthrough like MIDI, which is a great blessing in that it was a standard that everybody adopted. I wish that idea could somehow apply to screens and to the divide between Windows and Macintosh and all of these different formats.

But the overwhelmingly positive side to this revolution is that achieving great things—or even making a living as a musician—no longer requires training. I had a decent music education, but I've only ever used what I learned on the job. I'm fascinated by chordal structure and harmony theory, but it's *completely* academic. I don't need any of it. And neither does any computer composer, because you use your ears.

You no longer need a big investment in equipment, either. The original Fairlight cost about $120,000. When I was a lad, if I wanted to make a record, I had to go to somebody to get money because a studio was way outside my means. Today, the difference between the $49 GarageBand and my fancy Digital Performer is getting smaller and smaller. It's *really* egalitarian. Marx would have loved this. If you have the talent, you can do it.

For more on Stewart Copeland, visit www.stewartcopeland.it.

Introduction

Some of the best music comes from pushing instruments and equipment to their limits—and in the process discovering something about ourselves.

In the timeless "mockumentary" *This Is Spinal Tap*, there's a scene where guitarist Nigel Tufnel explains that his amp is great because it "goes to 11." In the digital world, of course, everything is ones and zeros, so you might say the goal is to crank it up to 1. The computer's combination of fantastic power and rigid "zero or one" personality makes it an especially dramatic creative partner. It enables almost *anyone* to unleash the music that's within them, yet requires a radically different approach.

How, we wondered, are world-class artists dealing with that simultaneous freedom and challenge? We drew up a list of artists and producers we thought were especially successful at making technology serve their vision—whatever style of music they produced. (Digital music is not necessarily synthetic.) For another perspective, we included designers and software wizards who create pioneering instruments. Because digital technology also has a profound effect on the ways music is distributed and experienced, we added Internet visionaries, wireless experts, record-label insiders, and educators. Then we posted the list to a private Web site.

"That's a great cocktail party list!" exclaimed one visitor. As the interviews progressed, the party metaphor proved to be increasingly apt. Instead of the usual "What plug-in did you use on song X?" inquisition, we discovered it was more fun to talk about how and why people make their creative choices. (You'll notice the comment "[*laughs*]" comes up a lot.)

Most interviews lasted 45–70 minutes and covered both universal and interviewee-specific questions. After editing the transcripts, we sent them to the interviewees for fact-checking and clarification. (That's an unusual step, but we saw the interviews as collaborations rather than interrogations.) The more personal responses went into the first half of the book, where they serve to introduce the participants. We then extracted common themes from the remaining text and arranged them into topical chapters in the second half of the book. Due to space constraints, we still had to cut a lot of interesting material. Please check www.ArtOfDigitalMusic.com periodically for outtakes and updates.

We're often asked how we were able to get access to so

We recorded most interviews through a JK Audio QuickTap into a Korg PXR4 flash-RAM recorder. The Korg's built-in mic and battery power worked well for live interviews, too.

Digital Is As Digital Does

We recorded the majority of the interviews with a tiny Korg PXR4 digital multitrack recorder (see photo). The PXR4 stores audio in MP2 format, which uses less data compression and processor power than MP3. For telephone interviews, we used a JK Audio QuickTap, which connects between the handset and the phone's base, providing a mix of both sides of the conversation. For live interviews, we used the PXR4's built-in condenser mic and ran the recorder on two AA batteries.

Ideally, we would have used dual lavaliere mics for the live interviews and an advanced telephone tap—such as JK Audio's Inline Patch—that could output both sides of the conversation independently. When both parties spoke at once, it was sometimes tough to make out the words. And the PXR4's mic picked up room reverberation, blurring the voices.

I also wish I'd heeded Phil Ramone's advice not to worry about "using all the bits" when recording; the PXR4 sometimes distorted even when its meters were in the safe zone. However, this system had some tremendous benefits. After recording each interview, I could connect the PXR4 to my computer with a USB cable and drag the file over for safekeeping.

To help transcribe the files, I wrote some software that turned my word processor's function keys into Dictaphone-style playback controls. Pressing F10 would rewind the audio slightly and then resume playing, pressing F11 would stop it, and pressing F8 would copy the current playback location (in minutes and seconds) to the computer's clipboard so I could paste it into the transcript. You can download the software from www.ArtOfDigitalMusic.com.

As I listened to each file, I used the F8 technique to mark locations I thought would make good sound bites for the DVD. Later, I simply typed those values into my software and jumped to the relevant word.

—*David Battino*

many accomplished people. The lion's share of the credit goes to Kelli, who as president of the All Access Group connects the dots between artists and technology daily. As co-authors, we had an unusual "words and music" collaboration on this project. Kelli came up with the idea, lined up most of the interviews, compiled the bios, and chased down the photos and DVD materials. I conducted and edited the interviews and produced the DVD.

We'd like to thank the interviewees and Stewart Copeland for so graciously sharing their time and insights; Richard, Amy, Gino, Kevin, Kate, and Nina at Backbeat for giving us so much leeway on the book's design; Jeffrey Brandstetter, Esq., for brokering the deal; Todd Spencer for help with the bios; Tim Tully and Jim Reekes for help with the DVD; Julie duBrow; the tireless transcribers (Shelley Chance, Elisabeth Luu, Kami Nguyen, and Karen Shibata); and Mark Vail for his advice on structuring the interviews. Mark's book *Vintage Synthesizers* (also from Backbeat) was an inspiration, showing that it's the people behind the technology who are the most important part.

I'm grateful to my family—Hazuki, Toma, and Miaki—for their extraordinary support, and to my parents, Rubin and Charlotte, for all of the music lessons. Kelli thanks her friends, family, and industry colleagues too numerous to name.

Whether you crank it up to 1 or 11, here's hoping you'll have as good a time as we did while writing this book.

—*David Battino and Kelli Richards*
Cupertino, California
www.ArtOfDigitalMusic.com

Profiles

Ableton Software

(Robert Henke & Gerhard Behles)

www.ableton.com, www.monolake.de

Growing up in Munich, Robert Henke was inspired to buy a Roland Juno-6 after hearing Jean Michel Jarre's epic album *Oxygene*. In 1990, Henke moved to Berlin to study sound engineering, and formed the electronic music group Monolake with Gerhard Behles. The duo began writing its own software to facilitate its live performances. Finally, a colleague at software developer Native Instruments convinced Behles to launch Ableton, and Henke joined as a conceptual advisor. Monolake eventually became a Henke solo project; he continues to tour the globe and release albums.

Robert Henke, aka Monolake: "One reason computers are for control freaks is because it's way too complicated to use them."

Ableton Live is a brilliantly twisted concept—an audio sequencer you can play like an instrument. Where did the idea come from?

Robert Henke: We both made music with computers for many years. And we realized that there was no tool that solved the essential question of musicians on stage: How can I perform and interact with my tools in a spontaneous way, and at the same time retain complex structure? The closest alternative was drum machines, which provide an easy-to-use interface that allows for rapid changes like changing the pattern and programming a new pattern. But you're pretty limited if you use only an 808 [*the classic Roland TR-808 drum machine*] on stage.

The other approach would have been to use [Emagic] Logic or a hard-disk recording system, which basically allows for playing back an existing track and doing some overdubs or mutes.

So we developed our own applications using [Cycling '74] Max/MSP. Then when Gerhard finally concluded that it was time to start his own company, it was obvious that the tool that should come out was exactly what we personally were looking for.

Gerhard Behles, Ableton CEO: "The studio has been used as an instrument since the '60s, but these days you can have it on the stage as well."

Gerhard Behles: I would add that it wasn't only the stage aspect. What happens on stage is similar to what happens in the studio: In many situations you're thinking in a realtime mode, tweaking the knobs while you're recording. So you experience those same limitations while you're working with a strictly timeline-based sequencer like [Steinberg] Cubase, Logic, [Digidesign] Pro Tools, and so on: You're always confined to thinking in terms of a song.

Robert Henke: Sequencers are not very flow-oriented. It's more like sculpting versus playing. So Live is a product that came from a playful approach toward making music.

Gerhard Behles: Computer editors had limitations as well. When editing in Pro Tools, you completely lose the sync information, because you constantly have to zoom in and out to find the downbeats and the proper points to edit. So that also was unsatisfying.

As software designers, how do you get around the dilemma of wanting to add more features and consequently making the program harder to use?

Gerhard Behles: Being a small company definitely helps [*laughs*], because you understand that even the tiniest feature is something you need to plan, allocate resources to, and monitor in terms of *everything*. We have to be completely aware that every feature costs us money. You have to have very tight control by many people about what gets in.

That question you just raised is so fundamental to us because we only have one product, and the one unique selling proposition we have is that Live is *not* complicated. Of course, you can

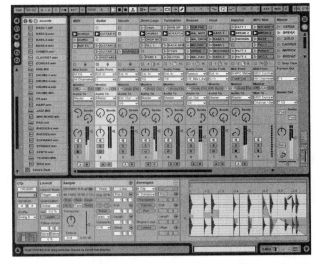

Ableton Live is a sequencer that's designed to be played like an instrument.

play with Logic on a stage. And of course, you can time-stretch a loop in whatever program. So the one thing we are completely focused on is making the access as easy as we can.

And that's why we don't have one person jumping in and saying, "Hey, here is a cool feature I just built." We talk about everything at length, and that is a very tedious and often frustrating experience, because you come in with the impetus of, "Hey, cool idea; let's do it." And you get out with, "Well, I guess I have to think about that again."

Robert Henke: It's better to have a feature *not* implemented than to have a feature implemented in an unsatisfying way. Because if something is not there, there's always the prospect to say that it will come. When something *is* there and it's unsatisfying, it's like buying furniture you don't like. The best thing you could do is to realize that in the first week and dump it. The longer you have it in your room, the more likely it will be there forever. And it always disturbs you, but it's *there.*

Gerhard Behles: That's the *most* difficult part of the whole thing: Technically, everything is possible. And in fact, if you walk into that hall [at the NAMM show], you *will* see everything. Everybody has done everything in some way. Except it's maybe not the way you would like it to be.

Glen Ballard

www.glenballard.com

T he winner of five Grammy Awards, Glen Ballard has worked with a staggering number of artists, from Aretha Franklin to Van Halen. As a staff producer, arranger, and songwriter for Quincy Jones, Ballard broke through with Jack Wagner's 1984 album *All I Need*, whose title song hit No. 2. He also wrote Michael Jackson's "Man in the Mirror" and played synthesizer on several of Jackson's albums. His two biggest productions, Wilson Phillips's self-titled debut and Alanis Morissette's *Jagged Little Pill,* sold 10 million and 33 million copies respectively. Ballard also runs his own record label, Java, and wrote and produced the feature film *Clubland.*

How has computer production affected your music?

It's been the single most empowering epiphany I've had. It allowed me the freedom to very quickly, on my own, express an idea and know whether it's worth spending more days and weeks on. It used to be that you'd have to go into the studio, put it on analog tape, and, after a huge commitment of time and money, wait for the verdict. The fact that you can now just sketch in your own environment—and actually *use* a lot of it because it's of such good quality—has been enormously empowering.

I think we all went through a moment in the analog-to-digital transition when we felt obligated to record something on analog first and then transfer it. I disabused myself of the need to do that after doing some blindfold tests of hearing the same material going to analog and digital, and then really not finding a distinguishing characteristic between them other than the most esoteric thing.

I think we were doing due diligence, because superb analog recording is a fantastic and wonderful art. And I don't think we want to lose the elements of that, but we were spending five times as much time doing it that way [*laughs*] than if we had just gone straight to analog or straight to Pro Tools.

The sound has *changed* slightly, but I don't think it's been this great loss of authenticity. It's what's happening in the room where you store it that matters. It's the song, the voice, the band, the performance—the *emotion.* There are plenty of records that sound really scratchy. The stuff from Billie Holiday, from the '30s especially, is really poorly recorded. It's nothing but midrange, but it's so arrestingly fantastic.

What types of experiments are you tempted to try now that you have extra time and capabilities?

More than anything, I still try to focus on the music side of it, and on creating interesting themes and variations. Digital allows time to concentrate more on the *writing,* as far as I'm concerned, because you can get a track together and get really inspired very quickly.

I do understand that some people have the opposite experience. They have so many options available to them on Pro Tools that they may record a hundred or 200 separate tracks on one song, and then not know what to do with them at the end. So it can be a debilitating way to procrastinate on making certain arrangement decisions.

"I'm always learning from the visual side and trying to use the lessons of good filmmaking in record-making: keeping it interesting, keeping the right dynamics."

Do you find that you're amassing many more tracks now that you aren't limited by tape?

No, I'm very disciplined. I take some pride in never giving a mixer a song without having some sense that it's already been arranged. I wouldn't just dump a hundred tracks on an engineer and say, "Okay, sort this out." And there *are* people who do that. Some people just aren't good editors of their own work. I like to have it airtight and then let a mixer really have creative fun with it. That said, I still like dense harmonic structures, so I'm always having to make sure that I don't put too much *music* in.

The fun thing for me, as a record producer, is that I get to be able to open the toolbox at any point and try anything. If I want to try a tuba part, I can at least play a sample first and then call the real tuba player in. But I'm enormously happy with the tools that are available. There are good instruments being made by everyone—new guitars, new compressors, new preamps. I just got the *Vienna Symphonic Library* [orchestral sample collection], and these samples are *so* exquisite, it's like, "Oh my gosh, we just took *that* to a whole other level."

Jack Blades

www.jackblades.net

"Sometimes my wife puts on music just to relax. But there's no relaxing for me because I'm analyzing the bass line against the melody line against the keyboard part."

Besides fronting Night Ranger, one of the most successful arena rock bands of the '80s, Jack Blades has produced and penned songs for some of rock's biggest names. This former pre-med student played in Damn Yankees with Ted Nugent; wrote songs for Aerosmith, Cher, Alice Cooper, Roger Daltrey, Journey, Vince Neil, Ozzy Osbourne, and Styx; and produced albums for Great White and Samantha 7. Blades released a self-titled solo CD in 2004, on Sanctuary.

What have you learned from setting up your own digital studio?

Back in '98, I bought a full-on Pro Tools setup just for the expedience factor. I'd been using a two-inch Studer [analog tape] machine for years, and the change to digital really was stunning because suddenly it was, "No more rewind." [*Laughs.*] No *waiting* for everything.

For the songwriter, it's *really* amazing. It's so much *easier* to be able to go, "Maybe this doesn't *need* a B section. Well . . . here." Two seconds later there's no B section. Then you hear it and you go, "No, it needs a B section." So you just hit the Undo button. To have the ability to instantly do things like that is really something else.

But you have to be careful; otherwise, you fall into the trap of, "Why sing anything more than once?" I try to sing all the choruses in a song, just to make 'em a *little* bit different, because otherwise it's so easy to just copy and paste—boom, boom, boom—and it's done. Then you lose that feeling of the second and third choruses, how it builds up.

Another big change in moving from tape to hard disk is that you aren't limited by tracks anymore. So you end up keeping all 50 guitar solos . . . or do you?

Well, it's interesting. A friend of mine, Ron Nevison, has produced everyone—he was the engineer with Led Zeppelin on *Physical Graffiti,* all the way through Bad Company, the Babies, and Heart; he did Damn Yankees, Ozzy. . . . And he really hipped me to something: You can get hung up on that. With some hard-disk systems, there are over 190 tracks. That's insane.

So I always just save one solo and *get it right.* I'm sure somebody could recover the other ones because we back up everything on an AIT tape drive. And I QuickPunch everywhere. [*That is, rerecord just a phrase rather than the whole solo.*] I *live* by Quick-Punch. But after a while it's like, "Come on, man, just *decide* what you're gonna do here." [*Laughs.*] You *decide,* and *move,* and that can be *great.* If you don't, it can be paralyzing because you're just kicking the can down the hill, man. You're making it so when you're mixing, you now have 95 solos to figure out. And what good is that?

Now that everyone has Pro Tools—there's even a free version—how do you make your own music stand out?

You can do all you want with Pro Tools, but at the end of the day, if you've got a shitty song, it's going to be a shitty song. I learned that a long time ago when I was co-writing with Steven Tyler. He can make a *shit* song sound like the next big Aerosmith smash. Do you know what I mean? By singing it with his, "*Aaack, kya, kya, kya, kya.* . . ." [*Laughs.*]

You don't make your song stand out with a cooler loop, because someone can always trump you on that kind of thing. But who can write a better chorus? It *always* comes down to that. People *try* to change it with computers. But you can't, man.

You know, Pro Tools is a tool. Hey, let's go over the name of it: "Pro . . . Tools." Whoa! It's a *tool* to make your business easier and your music better. You've always got to remember that.

Do you think there's a way that computers themselves could be more musical?

That would be a scary thought. You don't want HAL. [*Adopts creepy robot voice*]: "I don't know, Jack. I don't like the way that verse goes into that chorus."

"Hey, fuck off! *I'm* writing the song!"

"I won't let you do that then."

"Hey, fuck *off!*"

You know what I mean? That would be the most frightening, horrifying thing in the world.

BT

www.btmusic.com

lthough his most recent album hit No. 1 on the *Billboard* dance music chart, Brian "BT" Transeau has been an innovator in electronic music for more than a decade. He has remixed or produced Tori Amos, Sarah McLachlan, Madonna, *NSYNC, Seal, and Britney Spears. Moving deftly from progressive house to trance, to breakbeat, to film scores such as *The Fast and the Furious, Under Suspicion,* and *Monster,* Transeau wields astonishing creativity and technical skills. Collaborator Peter Gabriel said, "BT mounts mesmerizing journeys with his compositions. He is not only a virtuoso programmer, but an extremely gifted musician."

Peter Gabriel once spoke about the two main creative modes: playing and editing. Many people see that as a left-brain/right-brain competition. But for you it seems like the editing is wildly creative.

It is, man. Just to preface this with who I am as a human being, the two things that have always been riveting to me have been math and science, and music. However, I'm someone who failed algebra but could have taught the class in non-euclidean geometry.

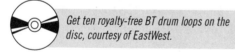

Get ten royalty-free BT drum loops on the disc, courtesy of EastWest.

So the process of editing for me is very mathematical, but it's like conceptual math, where there might not even be a right answer, or if there is, there's 50 different ways to get there. And it's just another part of the creative process to me.

The editing process has as much to do with the final impact of a piece of music as the core piece of music itself. And I think that's also why different kinds of people respond differently to my music. I mean, with "Somnambulist," the first single we've got out from the record, a friend of mine who has a radio station in Florida called me and said, "Dude, every time I play this song, guys call in and they go, 'The beats and the edits to this shit are so dope,' and the girls call in and go, 'I love the lyrics.'" [*Laughs.*] It's so where I'm at as a person, it cracked me up.

The press release said that song had 6,178 edits on the vocal track. How did you keep track of that? And why?

I made a point of keeping track of this one, because I really wanted to outdo myself. And it's a perfect example: In "Somnambulist"—sleepwalker—the person singing it is saying, "I've been sleepwalking my whole life and have finally realized that once you're loved, that's all you need." It's a very simple thought, but I wanted to take a simple thought—and a simple melody, too—and make them not only cutting-edge but fall in line with the subject material.

You're kind of walking around in a haze, confused, and so the edits to the vocals are symbolic in many ways. There's this sort of confusion, and coming out of confusion, in the lyrics. So I really wanted to make a point by making something *very* complicated out of a very simple idea yet retaining its simplicity. That was really hard to do. When it first started, the entire thing sounded like Max Headroom on *crank.*

"One of my barometers for whether I'm really enjoying something is to think about how my 13-year-old self would feel doing whatever I'm doing at any particular moment."

I've interviewed about 45 people so far for the book, and lots of them have disparaged Britney Spears. So I'm assuming you saw your work with her as another creative challenge.

I'm going to give her mad props, man, because I can't *imagine* that anybody who's worked closely with Britney would ever try to knock her. She's an *amazing* combination of commercial prowess and a real gift. She's got a *great* voice. I did *so* little work on her vocals when I tracked her. And I have no reason to defend her. It's not like she's a close friend or anything.

And the thing that sucks is that she's easy to knock, because on every vocal she's done that's come out, you've got producers like Max Martin getting her to sing in this really *nasal* spot of her voice. She has a *really* rich instrument, and she's encouraged to sing in that nasal area, I guess because people think that sounds sexy. I actually think it sounds like *ass.*

[Antares] Auto-Tune was never turned on, ever, in working with her. She's got *great* intonation and great phrasing. It's *confusing* doing her vocal comps, because she would sing lines the same, over and over, a hundred takes. So [*laughs*] I've got nothing bad to say. I mean, you could ask me about some other people and I would have talked *big* shit. She's not one of them.

LTJ Bukem

www.glo.uk.com

D anny "LTJ Bukem" Williamson is one of the most influential figures in the techno styles of jungle, drum 'n' bass, and breakbeat. (His nickname derives from the Spanish phrase for "the DJ" and the *Hawaii Five-O* quip "Book 'em, Danno.") Drawing on jazz and fusion, Bukem's lush, melodic productions bring some much-needed soul to electronic music. *The All Music Guide* called his double CD *Journey Inwards* "an album of pure brilliance." Today, Bukem balances life as a musician, DJ, producer, and head of England's Good Looking Records, which he founded in 1991.

"I love constructive criticism about my own music. I mean, I'm my own worst critic, so I definitely take on board people who, in my eyes, make good music."

Because you're involved in so many areas of music production, the Internet must have had a profound impact on you.

The Internet has as much helped as hindered us as independents. I was doing a *mad* tour, doing ten, 12 days in a row, like Singapore, Kuala Lumpur, Japan, New Zealand, Australia—everywhere. We come to Singapore, and when I finish DJing, I always want to talk to the whole club. I don't mind; I'll stay for the end, shake some hands, sign a few CDs, talk to some kids—just to get a feel for what the people who come support me are about. And I got talking to these six, seven kids, and they're saying—it's 6:00 in the morning—"Why don't you come down to this marketplace where everyone goes after the clubs and we'll just talk, and eat, and have a drink?"

And I was like, "Yeah, why not?" Then it got from there to the guy's house. He wanted to show me his LTJ Bukem collection of CDs. And I thought he meant original CDs. But this guy brought me home to his house, with three computers, and he's sitting there going, "What d'you want to hear?"

And I'm like, "Uhhh . . . nothing. [*Laughs.*] I hear it too much." And he goes, "There's *every* tune by you, *everything* on your label—"

So I think, here's some guys who haven't paid a penny for my music, but would they have heard of us if they hadn't been passed the music? It's similar to the early days, when promoters recorded your set and then sold it and paid you nothing. I was angry sometimes, but had to understand how that also helped my career. It's hard. I'm not with piracy, but you can't stop it.

What's another way computers have surprised you?

Another example of that was Conrad, my MC. He came 'round my house and I went to show him [Propellerhead] ReCycle—this was '97, '98, and he hadn't gotten into it. And I said, "Look—let's just try it out. Just put *anything* through it and have some fun. It's so quick." So I found this old soul loop, probably about 80, 90 bpm. I chopped it into 16 bits [slices] and started playing around with it on the keyboard, and couldn't *believe* what I'd just created—just in showing him how ReCycle worked. And that became one of my favorite tunes on *Journey Inwards,* two years later. At a tempo of about 130 bpm, even though those bits were originally at 80 bpm. It's mad.

There's a fine line between repetition and boredom. How do you warp loops to keep them interesting?

I think that, basically, *you* know as a producer when you've found the loop. And if you've found the loop, then you can hear that for ten minutes, 20 minutes, half an hour, an hour, and you haven't got to do much to that loop, because the loop is saying everything to you. No matter what you put around it, as long as it's not hideous or stupid, it's going to enhance that loop and the whole track you were doing. I think it's a whole world in itself, just *finding* a loop.

But that's hard, because music is so personal. What I'll sit here and play you in my record room and go, "That makes me want to have a wank," you're going to go, "Okay. Yeah. Fair enough. Strange guy." [*Laughs.*] I play in clubs for a thousand people, and a thousand people will take every tune you play in a different way.

I hate all these *rules* that people have set themselves in music. I *hate* them. I think you should always make what turns *you* on, and then go on and get it to someone else and hopefully you can touch someone else's heart and mind.

Joe Chiccarelli

www.artistpro.com (Joe's Garage forum)

Grammy Award–winning producer and engineer Joe Chiccarelli has completed projects with Herb Alpert, Tori Amos, Joan Baez, the Bangles, Beck, Bon Jovi, Michelle Branch, Café Tacuba, Counting Crows, Melissa Etheridge, Hanson, Rickie Lee Jones, Elton John, Journey, the Kronos Quartet, Offspring, Oingo Boingo, Poco, George Thorogood, U2, Brian Wilson, Frank Zappa, and legions more. Chiccarelli is also a music supervisor for film and TV, a moderator for the Music Production forum at ArtistPro.com, and adjunct professor at Ex'pression Center for New Media.

"I've always tried to do whatever I could to bring the listener closer to the artist, to remove those walls."

Many of the tracks you work on must have started in home studios. How do you deal with the handoff?

For everything that I work on nowadays, some percentage of it is done in a personal studio. Sometimes I as producer decide to use some portion of their demo tapes because they captured a spirit or had some clever parts that were very well done. Or perhaps we decide we'd like to be in an environment that's a little more laid back and where the artist can work at his own pace.

In fact, I just mixed an album for Sophie B. Hawkins, and she's most comfortable doing all the vocals by herself at home. She comps them, and tunes them, and does the whole thing all on her own. [*"Comp" refers to creating a composite performance from pieces of individual performances.*] And she does a *great* job. She seems to do better at that stage without having a producer hovering over her with a lot of other ideas. She just likes to focus, and she's fully capable of delivering great performances on her own.

For a project I did last year—a new artist for Warner Brothers—he did all these *great* sequences and layering at home. And on some of his recordings, because he did it in his bedroom with really cheap microphones and everything else, the fidelity was substandard.

But the *performances* and the ideas in the way that he layered things and sequenced things, and even some of the cheap VST plug-ins he used to get some of the sounds. . . . He came up with such a unique sound and heart that even though the fidelity wasn't ideal, we had to use them. There was no way we could even look into duplicating them.

Do you end up taking a contrast approach in that case, where you add some really sparkly sounds or effects to complement the lo-fi tracks?

Yeah. And when you think of a painting or any piece of art, usually it's the contrast between the dark and light things that makes it more exciting and alive.

What about the situations where someone just goes overboard?

Any *time* a new technology comes out, people get crazy with it. They go full on, and overindulge, and explore the technology to the most absurd degree. [*Laughs.*] If you remember the '80s, when drum machines and digital reverbs and digital delays came out, every recording was just chock-full of all that stuff. If you think back to the '70s and '60s, when multitrack recording came around, everybody went track-crazy and overdubbed everywhere.

I think it's just the nature of creativity that we're going to go a little nuts with all the digital possibilities now. And I already see it settling down. I see people still incorporating analog recording with digital. A lot of bands realized that the sound of analog tape really does something for rock and roll, so they'll record their bed tracks on analog tape and then dump them into the computer, and then edit and process them from there. So you're starting to see people realize what the benefits of workstations are, and what the overindulgences can lead to.

There are obviously some sonic benefits to digital, such as the lack of noise and the lack of generation loss. And the convenience and "recall-ability" are *fantastic.* You can do pretty much the same things in the analog world, but it takes you four to ten times the amount of time and aggravation. The sound quality in some cases is better in the analog world, but digital is getting *so good* that the concept of even *comparing* analog to digital will just go away any day now.

Dr. Elizabeth Cohen

www.gseis.ucla.edu/faculty/pages/eacohen.html

Elizabeth Cohen is a professor of Information Sciences at UCLA. She holds a Ph.D. in acoustics and an MS in engineering, both from Stanford. Her areas of interest include digital libraries for music and media, communications systems for the arts, music perception, and information policy. Her current projects include realtime collaborative performance over high-speed networks, scalable business models for music archives, media retrieval systems, and intelligent systems for data migration of digital media.

"I want to make sure people realize that they are deeply affected by information policy."

You gave a fascinating talk at an Audio Engineering Society conference about "metadata"—information in a media file about the file's content. Why is metadata so important for music?

There's a *desperate* need for metadata. Think about how many times you've been traveling in your car, the announcer doesn't give you the name of the tune, and you're dying to know what it is. So in that sense, it's a user need.

On the other hand, think about all the production and post-production studios for film and television. Say you create a film, but it's going to be repurposed into a TV series, a CD, a DVD, and an interactive game. So all of those elements, all of those sound effects, may go from one place to another. How do you make each component sound file accessible to all these derivative projects?

There are ongoing efforts to do this; in the post-production community, there's AAF [the Advanced Authoring Format; www.aaforganization.org]. But the need for metadata exists throughout the entire audio life cycle. By the time the media get all the way to the library or the archive—now we've gone through production, post-production, and the consumer—we *really* need all the information that goes with the creative experience or product.

That information would also be useful for the re-creative experience, wouldn't it?

Exactly. Look at this whole idea of garage media. That's the term of a colleague of mine, Marc Davis at UC Berkeley. [*Davis's technology uses metadata to make it easy for people to create their own multimedia from preexisting sources; see http://garage.sims.berkeley.edu.*] If, to paraphrase what Isaac Newton said, our creative work stands on the shoulders of people who came before us, then the whole cultural motivation is to be able to absorb and then create based on all of this input we've experienced.

There is metadata that allows you to identify and locate an object, metadata that defines user access and artists' rights and encryption, and what's called *interpretive* metadata, which makes sure that the artist's name goes with it. Then you can also have technical metadata—signal coding or device-storage information or streaming parameters. And then you can have all of the process information—was something edited, what version it is.

And then there are *relational* types of metadata—how all of the information is related. It's sort of the verbs of the metadata sentence. And finally, what are all the space and time coordinates? What were the creation times?

Once you have all of that information traveling with a piece, you have all sorts of opportunities to do new things with it—either in a workgroup or on a planetary scale.

But won't it be overwhelming for musicians to have to embed all that information as they create files?

No. The whole idea is to have all of this done automatically. So that's what people are working on, so that a lot of these parameters will just be acquired.

You've also studied the effect of information technology on society. What are some of your concerns?

There's of course the issue of the digital divide. And I don't mean just access to the Internet, but that people actually can create content for it—that they have the technical education, the chops, to *participate* in what's going on rather than just be passive consumers.

That's a very big concern of mine, because I've always believed that as many people as possible should be involved in making music. If you just consume software and you can't write it, you don't *understand*. You can't develop a sense of confidence and a sense of power if you feel you're at the mercy of all the machines.

We have to teach people who were not traditionally active in these fields of information. You're seeing a new generation of activist librarians, for instance, because many aspects of information-policy legislation impact what they're able to deliver. With copyright being [*laughs*] life plus 95 years, you now have the issue of, "How do we meet our access mandate when most of the cutting-edge stuff is tied up?"

Ted Cohen

www.emigroup.com

As the vice president of Digital Development and Distribution for EMI Recorded Music, Ted Cohen is one of the key figures in advancing digital music distribution. *Wired* named him one of eight "hypernetworked nodes who secretly run the world," noting that in 1999 both the RIAA and Napster asked him to help them reach a compromise. Cohen co-founded and chaired the initial Webnoize conferences, and has held senior management positions for Warner Bros. Records and Philips Media. He also ran two highly successful new-media consulting operations, attracting clients such as Amazon.com, Microsoft, DreamWorks Records, Universal Studios, and Wherehouse Music.

You were one of the first people to have an MP3 wristwatch. What's on it now?

My emergency Beach Boys music, "Hello, It's Me" by Todd Rundgren—literally the five songs that if I went down on a plane, and I had to listen to the same songs over and over again on an island until the battery died, these are the songs I want to be trapped with. But now in addition, I'm carrying a 20-gig iPod; I'm carrying a T-Mobile PocketPC phone that has five or six of my favorite videos on it; and I'm carrying a little Nomad MuVo, that little 128-meg USB stick MP3 player.

So gadgets are still my life, and I like having my music with me. I think the portability is critical. So whether we go to copy-protected CDs or digital initiatives, we've got to get it off the desktop.

That's been one of the big criticisms of online music subscription services, hasn't it?

Well, if you let people do anything they want with their downloads, how personal will they be about it? Does someone's giving you 99 cents to buy a track give them unlimited rights? If so, for 99 cents you're buying the right to make a million of them. And *that's* the tough one. When they say the music industry doesn't get it—we *get* it. We totally get it. But the question is, is it reasonable to put speed bumps at a point where it's obvious that you're exceeding rational, reasonable personal use?

And my definition of reasonable personal use is you need to burn two or three copies so you have one in the car, one at home, and one at work—fine. You need to put it on your home server so you can listen to it anywhere in the house—*fine*. You need to move it onto two or three portable devices—fine, except for me; I need 20 portable devices. I need an exemption.

That's the only exemption I want. I don't want to be part of creating any rule set that would prohibit me from doing what I normally do, which is most of that stuff. What I *don't* think is reasonable is for someone to assume that if they want to burn 200 copies of it for their sister's wedding, that that's reasonable personal use.

People say, "I should be able to do anything I want with it; I bought it." No, you bought a *copy* of it. Then it got extended through the Home Recording Act that you could make a copy for personal use. And then a copy became multiple copies. So now we're up to, "If I want to give it to 200 of my friends, and I didn't *sell* it to them, that's personal use."

"My having 6,000 CDs in my living room—I'm a nut case. I said ten years ago that I would trade all of them for *access* to all of them wherever I go."

But it seems like there are so many challenges with the idea of selling music as a service rather than as a product.

Yeah, but we're getting there. We've got five or six services up right now. They're getting better and better. You could say, "Well, it's not as good as Kazaa, man. I've got to pay for it and it doesn't have everything."

Yeah, it's because of that really awkward, stupid thing called "getting the rights and compensating people." And yes, there's a lot of people that think you should ask their permission, my company included. It's just that we've spent hundreds of millions of dollars to bring this art to market and it might be nice to just say to us, "Hi. Is this okay with you? Can we work out a deal here?" instead of going into business and then going to court.

I want this all to work. I mean, this is my 21st year in all this. I really am *tired* of the litigation. I'm tired of all the fighting. There's a lot of issues we have to deal with to make it work, but the list is getting shorter and shorter. If it isn't done and settled by the end of this year, it's within the next 18 months. [*Indeed, shortly after this interview, Cohen brokered the deal with Apple that helped to launch the wildly successful iTunes Music Store.*]

The Crystal Method

(Ken Jordan & Scott Kirkland)

www.thecrystalmethod.com

Fusing enormous, distorted beats and bass lines with rock, soul, hip-hop and techno sensibilities, Ken Jordan and Scott Kirkland, aka the Crystal Method, have inspired the electronic dance music scene for a decade. The duo crafts songs in its computer-packed L.A. garage studio, collaborating with artists ranging from Limp Bizkit guitarist Wes Borland to rapper Rahzel of the Roots. Estimating it would take 15 musicians to perform its intricately layered music live, TCM tours extensively as a duo, augmented by pounding electronics. Its 2004 album, *Legion of Boom*, hit No. 1 on *Billboard*'s Top Electronic Albums chart.

Scott Kirkland (L) and Ken Jordan, aka the Crystal Method: "Even when we're just working on a two-bar or four-bar loop-based track, we're still always thinking whole-song."

Your grooves are so powerful and sonically intriguing. How do you process loops to make them come alive?

Scott Kirkland: One way is with the REX technology that Propellerhead came up with in their program ReCycle. Being able to extract the hits from a loop, import them into a [Propellerhead] Reason track, and have them adjust to the tempo—or even adjust to the rhythm—has helped quite a bit in giving our loops that human, non-repetitive feel we look for.

With [MOTU] Digital Performer, you can drop a REX sample right onto a track and Performer will split up the component beats so it locks with the tempo of your sequence. And then you can do a Groove Quantize or a Human Quantize to an eight-bar section of that repeated loop, and adjust it to where it doesn't sound like the same loop over and over again.

Very few loops we find are perfect. So another thing we've always done, even before we've been able to import REXs, has been to go in and take the hi-hats out, or take the snare out. So there are lots of combinations that are thrown together to create a rhythm pattern in a song. You have to be creative and find different ways to get around that simplistic sort of repetition that bores the hell out of you.

But then a lot of dance music, a lot of techno, a lot of house is simply some sort of [Roland TR-]909-type kick drum hitting four on the floor. So it is a fine line. What's so wonderful about electronic music sometimes *is* that consistent rhythm. But then it's up to you to make it more human, to throw some percussion or some other element on top of it that has the real feel or life.

Do you like to keep a steady tempo throughout the song?

Ken Jordan: Yes. A bad drummer is a drummer that drifts. [*Laughs.*] But we program tempo changes for effect a lot of times. We do a lot of things where we go to half-time or double-time but get there gradually, over four bars or eight bars. And a lot of times we'll go from one tempo to three-fourths of that tempo, or from one tempo up to 150 percent of that tempo. That can work out well, because you can do things with 6/8 time and eighth-notes and it will all match up once you get to that eventual tempo. But we won't *gradually* change a track from beginning to end; we won't make it end two beats faster or anything like that. That just sounds cheap to us.

How are you balancing the recent transition from hardware to software?

Scott Kirkland: I can't imagine the day when we're working exclusively in the soft-synth world. When we're on the road, or away from our studio, that's all we *have.* But when we're in our studio, from the very beginning we've wanted to experiment, to run things through outboard gear, and play used synthesizers that we've collected over the years. So making that transition would really set us back.

You've been working out of your garage studio for quite a while. What have you learned by setting that up, and what would you like to do differently?

Ken Jordan: [*Sighs.*] Everything. I'd like to do everything differently. Maybe a brighter room with a window to the outside. [*Laughs.*]

Scott Kirkland: When we set up our studio about seven years ago, we thought it was great. Our only concern was getting some sort of soundproofed room inside this garage and finding a place where we could put all of our stuff and just start working on music. As we look back, there are many things that we would like to adjust and fix and do better, but, again, that takes away from the art of working on music.

So many times we've played with the idea of relocating our studio and taking the time to do it right, but that takes you out of your studio for three to four months, and that's something that we just haven't been able to do yet. I imagine that at some point we will, but it's a big deal.

Chuck D

www.publicenemy.com, www.rapstation.com

As the leader of Public Enemy, Carlton "Chuck D" Ridenhour redefined rap music and hip-hop culture, blending explosive political insights with masterfully arranged samples. *The All Music Guide* called *It Takes a Nation of Millions to Hold Us Back* "arguably the best hip-hop album ever made." Chuck D has hosted his own segment on Fox News, published the best-selling autobiography *Fight the Power*, and spoken extensively on the college circuit, often about digital music delivery. He currently oversees rapstation.com and has a second book, a pair of albums, and a new record label in the works.

You recently put out a construction-kit CD called Welcome to the Sampledome. *How do you feel about other artists sampling your work?*

I don't have a problem with artists sampling my work. But if it's used for something that goes against my philosophy, like selling *crack*, or [*laughs*] murdering scores of innocent people, we got to reconsider.

Have you been surprised by the remixes you've heard of your music?

Yes. There were 11,000 downloads of the *a cappella* we did on the last Public Enemy album, *Revolverlution*. Four hundred and seventy-four mixes came back. Even the evaluation process was innovative—I think we had the world's first record company with a virtual staff. About 50 people, many of whom I've never met, evaluated the 474 mixes by making their top 10, top 20. And that's how we scaled down to pick the four winners.

Did you find the mixes sonically surprising as well?

Oh yeah. And diverse. The first-place winner was a guy who did a combination of club, hip-hop, and house—and he was from Buenos Aires, Argentina. And the guys who were second came from Madison, Wisconsin. Their mix was like sonic shrapnel—going about five or six different places but still sharp enough to win.

What needs to happen for digital music distribution to really take off?

[*Laughs.*] It depends on how you look at it. For it to *really* take off, the five major labels would have to stop attacking the innovations that come from outside. But it already *took* off. You have billions of downloads. Taking off *legally* is a whole other story.

One of the things that's needed is accessibility to the out-of-print albums that the majors have rights to but can't physically create. Record companies really have to figure out what to do with all the content they own. And the obvious choice is digital distribution.

That in turn can bring a lot of young people and older people in, exposing younger people to a bigger world of music and letting older people know that the thing they were into back in the day isn't lost forever. It's not feasible to get the fifth song on a lost Sam Cooke album in the store, but you could order that as a digital file. Once people figure out that their *needs* are all similar, it just makes it so much more feasible than trying *not* to do it.

"For years I used to hear people talking about, 'Oh, we need distribution. We need distribution.' And then when it pops up, people don't recognize it."

Sonically, I know there's a slight difference between an MP3 and a .WAV file, but in rock and rap music, the difference is really thin. There was a *drastic* difference between AM and FM radio, but there was a beauty to the AM sound as well. It was an introduction to your possibly getting a *higher* level of sound on your own.

MP3 is a fantastic-sounding radio. MP3 players are small and portable, and people are thinking this is the first time it's ever happened. But 40 years ago, transistor radios had millions of songs on them, too. It's just that you couldn't program them. Still, they turned on a whole world and they were portable, so you could put them underneath your pillow at night.

Audio has a fantastic place in our lives. It's just that now it has to be accessible when we *want* to get it. Radio today is almost like waiting for the steak that might never come.

I wonder if we'll start seeing CDs that are sponsored in a much more obvious way—covered with "Intel Inside" logos, perhaps.

Well, I wouldn't be opposed to that in certain instances, because everything that goes across the counter is commercial. It's commercial the minute you sell it. [*Laughs.*]

But that's the beautiful aspect about MP3: It's more for the fans. It's like a bartering system. So if you can give away a file that can get downloaded a million times, then you actually are building a bridge to a consumer base. And not just consumers, but fanatics of the art. That's very important. How do you first build a bridge to a fan? Do you trick them? That's basically how the CD era was built.

Thomas Dolby

www.thomasdolby.com,
www.beatnik.com,
www.retroringtones.co.uk

As a London teenager, Thomas Robertson experimented so enthusiastically with synthesizers and cassette recorders that his friends nicknamed him "Dolby." His superbly crafted electronic productions like "She Blinded Me with Science" have won him five Grammy nominations. He has played keyboards for Foreigner (4), Def Leppard (*Pyromania*), and Roger Waters (*The Wall Live in Berlin*). In 1996, Dolby founded Headspace—now called Beatnik—to develop interactive audio technology for the Web; the company is now a leader in synthesizers for cell phones. Dolby also works with Retro Ringtones, developing custom sounds for European phone companies.

You've coaxed some very evocative music out of digital electronics. Is there something almost metaphysical about certain instruments that makes you want to hold on to them even though they're technologically obsolete?

Definitely. I'm very reluctant to get rid of my Fairlight. I don't know if I'll ever use it again, in terms of sampling something into it, because it's sort of like a black hole. But I have a definite soft spot for it. And in a way, you feel you'd be amputating a limb if you've been *that* attached to something. On the other hand, my studio setup now is *tiny* compared to the one I had 15 years ago. And that's a real blessing.

Hear Thomas Dolby's ringtones and two songs from his private birthday concert on the disc.

But the other thing is that—and I'm sure you hear this all the time—when I'm getting creative, the *last* place I want to be is in front of a computer screen. I think the way you relate to technology changes over the course of a career as a musician. You start out with this tremendous sense of adventure: "If I just combine what's in my imagination with this fantastic roomful of gear, then something amazing and *new* is going to come out of it." And over time, as you mature, it's kind of, "Well, how can this *serve* me to get the job done?" I think there's a very small handful of musicians who, ten albums into their career, are still able to be as adventurous with technology as they were when they started out.

Some musicians achieve that by swapping around the people they work with. Think of Madonna going to William Orbit, or Björk going to Matmos, the duo that put microphones inside balloons and things like that. [*Laughs.*]

Do you think that diving into that kind of experimentation could get you excited about technology again?

Well, I don't want to give you the impression that I'm not excited by technology. I do remain excited by technology. I just don't relish the thought of spending months with my face in my laptop.

I think what I really crave is live tracking dates. You go into a slightly unfamiliar studio, you get a bunch of musicians in, and you mic them up. Then the first run-through sounds absolutely dreadful, and you're cursing and just wishing that you'd done it with a sampler instead.

"I just love the way the Nord 3 [synthesizer] works, with all of the LEDs on the knobs. You can *feel* the parameters affecting the thing. I wish Nord would design my life."

But every time you run it, it will improve in a hundred ways and maybe deteriorate in a dozen. So you gradually get to that magic moment where you turn around and make sure that you're really recording, because *this could be the take.* There's a slight bit more urgency and anticipation in the way you talk to the musicians. You've basically got an hour's window to get the take, and then it's going to be diminishing returns again, and no amount of retaking is really going to fix it.

So there's a certain magic to that, because it's really alive. And the nice thing is that once you get *the take,* you stop focusing on any of those details, and what is communicated through the speakers is just the magic of the music. At that point, you become less critical of whether a note is slightly out of tune, or whether the timing is quite perfect. You're just expressing the music.

And in a way, if you're doing everything on a computer, you *never* have that magical window, because all of those elements have no knowledge of each other. There's never really a synergy or a perfect balance between them. They're just dumb elements that you're pushing around in different combinations.

So what I find myself craving is those live tracking dates, and *then* going back to Pro Tools or whatever and using those real performances as my building blocks, as opposed to individual *notes* or individual samples. And then you just use a gentle touch. You have to try not to destroy the magic that was there, just light it nicely and put it in a good context.

Bob Ezrin

www.bobezrin.com

One of the most influential record producers of all time, Bob Ezrin has produced multiplatinum albums and live events for Alice Cooper, Peter Gabriel, Jane's Addiction, Kiss, Nine Inch Nails, Pink Floyd (Ezrin put the children's chorus on "Another Brick in the Wall"), Porno for Pyros, Lou Reed, and Rod Stewart. He also founded 7th Level, a computer game pioneer, and co-founded Enigma Digital, which operates the Internet's most successful live radio stations, KNAC.com and Grooveradio.com. Ezrin also served as vice chairman of Clear Channel Interactive, responsible for new strategies and technologies.

"One of the things I say to everybody when I go into a project is, 'I'll *fight* for my ideas like crazy, but don't *back down* if you don't think I'm right, because I *love* to be wrong.' Every time I'm wrong, something wonderful happens."

You're heavily involved with online music. What is up with this adversarial relationship between record labels and music fans?

Well, that's new. That's a very bad, ill-conceived, and arrogant reaction to the *audience's* reaction to our mistakes. How stupid are we? We made the mistake; they didn't. We had a shot at Napster before *anything* happened. Napster went to everybody and said, "Give me licenses." And everybody said, "Are you out of your *mind*? You're illegal." And any *idiot* could have said to them, "You can't *stop* this, so you'd better get on board." In fact, I was on a Webnoize panel the day the RIAA lawsuit was filed against Napster [December 1999]. And Napster was on the same panel and so was the Electronic Frontier Foundation.

People were bouncing back and forth, talking about the *philosophy,* and how this is unfair to the artists, and so on. And I said, "Wait a minute. I'm the *only* one on this stage that this is really about, because I *am* a producer whose stuff gets played and bought, and that's how I make my living. I'd like *all* the record companies to grant Napster a blanket license for the next 18 months and have an agreement to agree thereafter. And *let's see what happens.* Because the marketplace will *tell* us what we need to do with our stuff. And then—*together*—we can work on a great model."

Instead of that, the record companies said, "We're not going to bow to extortion. We've got *500* engineers who are going to work on this for three months straight and we're going to have *bulletproof* copy protection software." And I said, "Well, guess what? There are 40 million *really* smart kids—as smart as any of those engineers—whose *life-work* it's going to be to undo anything they do. Who wins?"

You can't *make* a technology that isn't crackable. Microsoft knows that; they stopped putting copy protection on their shit. They concluded, and correctly so, that the way they're going to save their industry is by making all the other things that relate to their software available only for a price. So go ahead—steal the software. If you want all these other *features*, you get them from us. And you know what? It's *far* more convenient to work with Microsoft than to try to find a crack for every single one of the things they're offering.

How would you extend that to music?
We have to find something that people pay for because it's more convenient. In our case, we should be looking at how we get that stuff to them. If we provided a service that was just easy, worked everywhere, gave you what you want whenever you wanted it, and charged a monthly fee like we pay for EarthLink, I think that just out of a sense of convenience people would subscribe.

I may be naïve, but it's a pain in the ass to go on Kazaa right now and find what I want all the time. And *I'm* looking for it because I want to license the song or because I want to hear what this person does because I'm thinking of using them. *I* want to do it because I want to make that person money, and I can't find the shit.

So I would make a delivery system that was an all-label, all-material, no-restrictions, one-price, all-you-can-eat model. All this multi-tiered pricing [*adopts lilting salesman's voice*]: "O-kaay, you can have 15 songs for $10 and *30* songs for—" Give me a fuckin' break. I can't keep *track* of what I'm consuming. I don't want to have to think about that. And I also don't want to be in *love* with a piece of music and be just about to transfer it to my personal player as I'm about to go out running, only to find out that I'd exceeded my quota or that my license doesn't apply to 5 o'clock on Sunday afternoons. That would *really piss me off* as a consumer. I'd just go back to downloading, because it may be a pain in the ass, but at least nobody's looking over my shoulder.

David Fagin

www.therosenbergsband.com

"Not only is allowing [media] companies to basically own everything killing the music industry, but it's also killing the journalism industry, the television industry, and the movie industry."

David Fagin is the lead singer and songwriter for the New York guitar-pop band the Rosenbergs, which rose to fame after turning down a potential record deal with Farmclub.com. (Farmclub, an Internet label backed by giant Universal Music, had presented the Rosenbergs with a big label's typically exploitative contract.) The experience turned Fagin into a crusader for artists' rights in the digital age. The band signed instead with Robert Fripp's label, DGM, which allowed them to retain ownership of their master recordings. Later, they even teamed with the outlaw Napster for tour sponsorship.

You recently did a panel discussion at South by Southwest [www.sxsw.com] that almost erupted into a fistfight. What was that all about?

[*Laughs.*] It was about the future of the music business. I threw out the idea that *nobody* is going to pay $19.95 for CDs anymore—*period.* End of story. With file-sharing and the crappy music the record labels are dealing out on a daily basis, there's no way anybody is going to pay more than eight or nine bucks for a CD.

So if labels were smart, which they're *not,* they would partner up with the artists. Everybody can make a record from their home now, so labels are going to have to start taking a percentage of live performances—concert tickets, merchandising, and all that stuff—in order to survive. And that will help both sides, because the label gets more money and the artists get more promotion for their shows.

Greg Latterman from Aware Records was totally behind me, and Dave Marsh, the journalist, was like, "It's ludicrous; the labels are never going to give you a correct *accounting* statement," this and that. And he has a point, but they just started going back and forth. [*Laughs.*] It wasn't so much a fistfight, but it was a really heated discussion. It was pretty funny.

Actually, the role of record critics is probably changing as well.

Yeah, I think everybody does feel threatened. At the same time there's a sense of some sort of miniscule change happening, of certain bands making it through to the other side. I'm working with AFTRA [American Federation of Television and Radio Artists; www.aftra.org] and a couple big sites like CorporateWatch.com to organize a million-band march in Washington during the FCC hearings on media consolidation. We want to use the voice of the independent artist to say, "Hey—we're unknowns, but there's a hundred thousand of us here and you can't ignore that." Because every town we go to we see 100 or so little songwriters, indie musicians, and *everybody* is fed up with the radio.

The thing that's scaring us the most right now is the Clear Channel situation. A few giant corporations own the venues, and the promoting, and the management companies, and the radio stations, and the television stations, and the billboards, and the tracking magazines. That's complete monopolization of the music industry.

Are CDs doomed, or could cutting the price in half or adding multimedia help?

I think if you add multimedia and you lower the price you'll be okay. For the most part *lots* of people still don't use file-sharing. Anybody who's over the age of 30 still loves that you used to be able to open up the CD, see the artwork, check out all the stuff that the band put in there and the CD itself; it was kind of like a little *event,* buying your album. And now it's like there's *nothing;* it's just *air.* And numbers and zeros and ones.

But for the most part Kazaa is *amazing.* I mean, when Napster [the original illegal version] sponsored our tour, I didn't even *use* Napster. And then a couple weeks ago while we were making our record, I was bored off my ass and I went on Kazaa, and I started to learn how to use it, and I'll *never go back.* I had *a thousand dollars'* worth of CDs stolen out of our van and I replaced every single one of the songs that I lost, but *only* the good ones from the bands that I like. [*Laughs.*] It took me *minutes* and I had 300 songs. You can't beat that.

Have you been surprised at some of the ways your music is moving around?

[*Laughs.*] Sure—Kazaa especially. I'm like, "Holy shit. Someone has a song of ours that wasn't even *released.*" It's like *demos* from 1995 and it's on Kazaa. I was just like, "How the hell did someone get *that?*"

The Fat Man

www.fatman.com, www.projectbarbq.com

The Fat Man, George Alistair Sanger, has been creating video game music and sound since 1983. His credits include *Loom, NASCAR Racing, Putt Putt Saves the Zoo, The 7th Guest I* and *II, Wing Commander I* and *II*, and more than 200 others. Sanger composed the first General MIDI soundtrack for a game, the first soundtrack included with a game as a separate audio CD, the first music for a game that was considered a

 Hear the Fat Man's music and MIDI ferret on the disc.

"work of art," and the first soundtrack that was considered a selling point for a game. He hosts the annual Texas Interactive Music Conference and Barbecue (aka Project Bar-B-Q), a think tank for influencing the future of music on computers. His rollicking book, *The Fat Man on Game Audio: Tasty Morsels of Sonic Goodness,* came out in 2003.

Project Bar-B-Q is designed to influence music hardware and software. What do you think its greatest contributions have been?

The most valuable results have come when companies put features second and compatibility first. When one thing talks to another, it makes all *kinds* of magical, unforeseen things happen. One of the greatest examples is MIDI.

And that magic can happen when things are even slightly compatible. Because every music program or piece of gear has some form of audio output, you can always plug one of those outputs into the input of something else. Whether it's digital or not, you can run the output of [Propellerhead] Reason into [Sony] Acid; you can run the output of Acid into [Sony] Vegas Video; you can run the output of Vegas Video into an ADAT [Alesis digital tape recorder]; you can run the output of the ADAT into [MOTU Digital] Performer; and you can run the output of Performer into your [TASCAM] GigaSampler. And then you can save those things off as a sound-effects library and cue it from Reason. [*Laughs.*]

There's always a stereo cable that can go out of one and into the other. Whether it's synchronized or not, whether it's digital or not, don't *worry* so much about it.

And I'm here to tell ya, because I was recording back in the day, the degradation you get between generations of dumping the output from one computer into the input of another is *nothing* compared to what people did on 24-track tape to create some of the world's best music. I did all of the *7th Guest* music on one ADAT, and I did enormous amounts of analog dumping through the mixer and then back onto two tracks. I must have gone eight generations in, because I only had one ADAT.

And you *never* hear it. Nobody ever listens to that and says it's a little muddy. Because it's *not.* If you had done that on 24-track you'd be sunk. Yet people still do it on 24-track. Because muddiness is not the important thing—by a long shot. What's important is that you are freer to create than any one user manual would imply. And the way to free yourself is to think of each of these tools as something that will take sound in and spit sound out.

"None of the computer tools has rounded the corner to where it's worth dedicating one's life to. But *all* of 'em put *together—yes!*"

If you *happen* to get two things to talk to each other fluently, then you have better possibilities for creativity. For instance, Digital Performer hooks up to an ADAT extremely well. The sync is perfect. And that's a fantastic environment to do certain things. But if you spend your life trying to get Performer and the ADAT to then synchronize to your PC, you'll just cry a river. That's what Bar-B-Q's working on. We'll make the synchronization easier. Hell, you won't even need *cables.*

And what you can do as a user is meet these efforts halfway by lowering your expectation of what compatibility is. Don't wait for somebody to come out with an ad that says, "Now you can plug your [Electro-Harmonix] Golden Throat Mouth Tube into your computer." Get that Golden Throat Mouth Tube out of your closet, run the speaker output of [Sony] Sound Forge into it, move your mouth around, and then mic that. ·

Albhy Galuten

www.galuten.com

A lbhy Galuten is a Grammy-winning record producer, songwriter, and arranger who works as a consultant in technology and digital policy. Until recently, Galuten was Senior Vice President of Advanced Technology for Universal Music Group, performing technical due diligence of software, hardware, and business systems; inventing technology; filing patents; and managing standards participation for DVD, MPEG, OMA, and more. Before working at Universal, Galuten was vice president at ION, where he co-created and developed the Enhanced CD format. During his music career, Galuten worked with numerous multiplatinum artists, produced 18 No. 1 singles, and generated sales of more than 100 million records.

Where is the fight against Internet music piracy leading, legally and technologically?

We won the Napster case, in many ways, because they were stupid. The discovery [process] was terrific. They had said awful things like, "We're going to take down the music industry." And I think [it was] the same thing for AIMster. They had a lot of hubris, and they're arrogant and thoughtless.

But you could make the argument, "Well, I'm just distributing things on a peer-to-peer network and I don't know what they are." You could say, "Sometimes I have to go over 55 because I might have an emergency. Therefore, you can't have a speed limit." Well, no. You have speed limits, and then if there are extenuating circumstances, maybe the policeman will cut you a break. In the same way, you have to say sharing is illegal and the government has to have a means of doing that. Saying that driving over 55 was illegal was meaningless unless you had a police force.

So unless you're going to have some sort of monitoring mechanism in the networks—and there are now *lots* of technologies that monitor packets—you're going to end up at the point where there's no music left to buy. And the same thing will happen to books and movies.

You'll still have people who make music in their spare time. Or people who are in touring bands, who make their money some other way. You'll have people who make their money doing car commercials and hit shows like *American Idol*, and who do it on the weekend and maybe write a great song. But it will be more difficult to support the Beatles or the Bob Dylans.

Hopefully, we will soon have the tools—such as DRM—for artists to package their own material for sale, and the viral marketplace will assure that if the next Paul Simon writes the next *Bookends,* word of mouth will make it a success just as word of mouth made ICQ [*the pioneering instant messaging service*] a tremendous hit. [*DRM, digital rights management, is an electronic way to control how and where someone plays a file.*] I think that society will eventually find a way to support the arts, and hopefully it will require as little government intervention as possible.

I *hate* to be Draconian. I'm mostly focused on generating *positive* reinforcement for good behavior more than negative enforcement of bad behavior. But the reality is there are hundreds of millions of people using Kazaa, and Pressplay is a better service. It just costs money. [*After this interview, Pressplay was acquired by Roxio and relaunched as Napster 2.0, a paid download service.*] There's *no* question. I ask for a song, I can search on a name, it downloads instantly, it's easy for me to use, the quality is there, and there are no ads.

"If you really are a great artist and you have great music, then before you're discovered on the Internet you're discovered by somebody locally."

Do you think the popularity of those music subscription services would increase if the price went down?

Well, the price for what? As it is, for ten dollars a month, you can listen to any of 300,000 tracks. The only thing that's missing is the dozen major artists who are not allowing their material on those services. That will settle out eventually. That's just their managers negotiating for more leverage. *Ten dollars a month* for access to all the recorded music! Is that too much? Does that need to go down to five dollars?

The reason the price seems high is that there's a free alternative—albeit not legal. If you'd said three years ago, before Napster, "Hey, you can burn any ten songs you want onto a CD for ten bucks," people would have gone, "That's great. What a *bargain.*" The reality is that we have had competition from the free services, and they've set the price at a place that doesn't pay for the music.

Marc Geiger

www.artistdirect.com, www.wma.com

Marc Geiger has been a concert promoter, talent agent, record company executive, and computer whiz. He co-created the Lollapalooza tour in 1991 and subsequently became executive vice president of A&R, marketing, and new media at Rick Rubin's American Recordings. Recognizing the Web's potential to link artists and consumers, Geiger co-founded Artist-Direct in 1994. The organization grew to house a talent agency, two record labels, a marketing solutions division, and one of the most popular music destinations on the Web. While there, Geiger signed more than 130 artists to e-commerce deals. I interviewed him shortly before he left; he is now a senior vice president at the William Morris Agency.

"If you don't value the news enough, you'll unsubscribe. The bottom line is that keeping the consumer on the hook is the job of the programmer."

The concept of ArtistDirect.com was to foster more interaction between artists and fans. How's that going?

We were too far ahead of the curve. Artists still don't understand the responsibility to communicate with the fans the way a magazine publisher would. But as the world changes and the artist community, management community, and supplier community understand what it takes to keep loyalty and sell products, they will get better at it.

ArtistDirect was the facilitator—the enabler—for the artists, and they were not very good partners. We had some of the biggest artists in the world. And it's hard to do with the biggest artists in the world because the system is working for them already. So we're continuing to forge ahead, but I can't say it's a massive success.

Well, what do you ask the artists to do?

Just give a little content. There is a natural evolution that needs to take place with the artist evolving from a blind supplier to a connected supplier. The blind supplier is: I make a record in my studio, I give it to my record company, and my record company gives it to middlemen or filters—radio, retail, MTV. I don't have to know anything about either of those two handoffs, and the end consumer and I have zero interaction, except at a concert when they're cheering and holding up lighters.

A connected artist is communicating directly to fans. They might talk about their favorite records or their favorite books, how they make their music, what their tour dates are . . . or sell tickets. There are a lot of pieces in place now—e-commerce, advance ticket sales, Web sites where a consumer can get recent information. But it's Neanderthal in terms of the sophistication I believe will come.

There's millions of artists around the world—lots of music. And most artists believe the consumer should come to them. And the truth is that consumers couldn't give a fuck unless they already love the artist. The artist does not *understand* yet that it is the artist's responsibility to get it to the consumer. Because the artist had a record company who did it—and that's all changing. The artist has to get *savvy* in capturing their audience and then communicating with them on an ongoing basis.

The artist can't say, "Hey, David Battino, I know you listened to my record 32 times; what song is your favorite?" because this is a one-to-many model. But they can certainly say, "Hey, Dave Battino, look at what I've been doing this month, and by the way, there's a new song I recorded, and here's the tour schedule. On April 5th, I'm putting tickets on sale for my real fans, who are you guys who subscribe. And if you go to this hidden URL, you'll be able to see the video that's in the works because it's not going to MTV for another 30 days." And you're going to feel like you're inside his world. That's what we were trying to do.

Do you think mystique is overrated, then?

People ask me that all the time, and it's the wrong question, because you can make the *communication* mystical. You can have an all-black e-mail that just has two words on it, but if it comes from Radiohead, *that's* mystique.

Are there any other underexploited Internet opportunities out there now for musicians?

All of the avenues on the Web are underexploited, but the important thing is that once you make a fan—they call it "customer acquisition" in the rest of the world—you can't let them go. What happens now is the song gets played on the radio and there's no connection. When somebody buys a record, there's no lasting connection. Even if somebody goes to a concert, there's no lasting connection. Every single time the music industry catches the fish, it lets it go right then. You can't do that. If the fan chooses not to buy something, that's okay, but at least they knew about it or listened.

Dr. Patrick Gleeson

A pioneering synthesizer performer, Dr. Patrick Gleeson dropped out of academia to tour and record with Herbie Hancock and run his own recording studio, Different Fur. Besides playing keys, writing, engineering, and producing for Devo, Joe Henderson, the Kronos Quartet, and Meat Beat Manifesto, among many others, Gleeson composed for television (*Knots Landing, Hard Copy, Unsolved Mysteries*) and feature films. He's credited as a "master synthesist" on *Apocalypse Now*. Gleeson continues to score film and produce jazz. He is also working on his own book, *Orchestration for Electronic Instruments*.

You were one of the world's top analog synthesizer players when you abruptly switched to digital, becoming one of the first [New England Digital] Synclavier owners. Digital audio was so primitive then that a megabyte of RAM cost $3,000. So, what intrigued you?

"I clung to the Synclavier until amazingly late—until about '89 or '90—just because it was so wonderful. *Everything* could be done in one program."

I had started on the scene playing for Herbie Hancock in the early '70s. And of course, Herbie is an *incredible* musician—maybe even better than people think. I always felt that because he had this incredible facility with the piano, he relied on the fact that he could always go to the piano and sound great. That's probably okay, but I think it also made it hard for him to put in the time learning this new synthesizer technology at first. And so I thought, "I've spent ten years playing analog instruments, and the same thing's going to happen to me if I don't do something about it." So I sold all my stuff.

Of course, I regret it now, but it was probably still the right move because it forced me to learn the Synclavier. And I did what I did when I first was learning the E-mu modular

Hear "Void When We Want," Gleeson and Jim Lang's amazing piece that resulted from mutilating an obnoxious client's CD, on the disc.

[analog synth]—I got a record project with a deadline so I'd have to learn it. I did a rendition of *The Four Seasons* for Varèse Sarabande.

When the Synclavier first came out with sampling, they needed a disk drive. And the price was just astounding. I think it was $12,500 for ten megabytes. And we thought that was amazing. Ten megabytes! I remember [former Tangerine Dream member] Michael Hoenig saying, "You'll never use all of it." [*Laughs.*]

It's amazing you stuck with digital instruments, given the barriers.

Well, it was quite a step up from the barriers with analog. I played the first small synthesizer ever built by anybody: Don Buchla's first analog modular. You *could not* keep it in tune. You had to wrestle with incompatible voltages and patch cords. And Don always had an attitude about the synthesizer being used as a keyboard instrument. [*He equipped it with a touch plate instead.*] Not that there's not an argument to be made about that; the keyboard is a shitty interface for a synthesizer. But if you wanted to play melodic music on the Buchla, it was pretty tough. Needless to say, it did not lend itself to virtuosity. In comparison to that, the digital stuff was a dream.

You're doing really complex computer music production now. Where is all this music technology heading?

It's funny—the longer I make music, the more in love with the process I am. I *never* loved music this much in the '70s. There's absolutely *nothing* I would rather do than just get here in the studio and stay.

Why do you think that is?

[*Long pause.*] I don't know. I didn't become a professional musician until I was in my thirties. I took piano when I was a child, but then I wanted to play jazz, and of course it was the '50s and my parents did not think this was going to lead to a living. [*Laughs.*] So I was a good boy and I went to college and got a Ph.D. in English literature, and taught until 1968.

I started making music pretty seriously in the '60s, but I was still teaching, so I was very frustrated. My one night a week over at Mills College [electronic music studio] was more exciting than my whole rest of the week over at San Francisco State. So I was just so goddamn grateful. You would think that the gratitude would wear off, but I just enjoy it more and more.

Maybe it's like when you're little and you think that one day you'll know everything. And then you walk into a library and realize that you'll never possibly be able to read all those books, and you really start to appreciate the vast number of choices there are. I think music is like that. On the surface it seems so simple, but it's endlessly deep.

Fortunately, we don't understand the real complexity until we've been making it long enough that it's too late to stop. [*Laughs.*]

Peter Gotcher

www.digidesign.com

D rummer and sampling expert Peter Gotcher founded Digidrums in 1983. The company, re-named Digidesign, is now the world's leading manufacturer of digital audio workstations with its ubiquitous Pro Tools systems. At the 2000 Grammy Awards, Gotcher accepted the Technical Achievement Grammy in honor of Digidesign's contributions to the recording industry. Digidesign also won a Technical Achievement Oscar in 2004. Gotcher is currently a technology-focused venture capitalist who serves on the boards of directors of Dolby Laboratories, Line 6, and MusicMatch.

"One of the things I really enjoyed about my whole Digidesign experience is I felt like we were democratizing the recording process."

What did you learn during the amazing odyssey from Digidrums to Pro Tools?

Evan Brooks and I had no intention of starting a company. I was working for Dolby Labs and had a great job; I was 23 years old. Evan was working as a hardware and software designer. We were playing in a band, and I'd always wanted a Linn drum [*i.e., an LM-1*], but they were $5,000.

The [E-mu] Drumulator came out and it was a thousand-dollar digital drum machine. So I scraped some money together, bought one, and brought it to a rehearsal. And 20 minutes into it, everybody was screaming at me to turn the thing off. [*Laughs.*]

I'm sure it had a lot to do with my programming, but the original sounds were pretty lifeless and dry and dull. So we ended up reverse-engineering it. I was doing a lot of recording, so I had a bunch of sounds. So we created our alternate sets of sounds and we took them down to Santa Cruz, really just to show the folks at E-mu what we had done with the machine. Their VP of sales left the room in the middle of the demo, came back about 15 minutes later, and told us she'd called Sam Ash and Manny's and had a bunch of orders for us.

I didn't want to quit my job until I knew this was going to work out. So we spent the first six months recording, editing, and burning drum chips all night, and then taking a big pile of boxes to UPS in the morning and going to our jobs—classic bootstrap startup scenario.

Back then [early 1980s], there were hardly any digital recorders. We had to hack a Sony PCM-F1 video tape recorder to get digital data out. And there were really no commercial digital audio-editing systems. We were using a home-brew S100-bus computer, and I did all the editing by looking at screens of hexadecimal sample measurements. [*Laughs.*]

About that time, the Macintosh came out. The bitmap display made a lot of sense as a way to visually edit sound, so we got busy on Sound Designer. And really, the original idea was that it was going to be an in-house editing tool for doing these drum sounds.

But right about the same time, the drum-chip market cratered. Yamaha had come out with a drum machine where all of the sounds were on one chip. And E-mu came out with the SP-12, which could sample—in fact, we did all the stock sounds for that machine. So the market was clearly going towards either cheaper drum machines with a lot of preset sounds, or towards the drum machines you could sample your own sounds on. We'd had a great run for a couple of years—we sold over 100,000 alternate drum chip sets—and it really provided the seed capital for Digidesign.

The whole road map for Pro Tools has been in place for probably a decade. We knew about things like the TDM [Time Division Multiplexing] bus, plug-ins, and DAE [Digidesign Audio Engine] that other applications could take advantage of. And we knew that we'd need more inputs and outputs, and more DSP [digital signal processing]. Things like ProControl [a remote hardware control surface] and software instruments were obviously coming down the pike a good five years ago.

If I look back at the other really pivotal point for Digidesign, back around '91, we'd just brought out Pro Tools—the 4-track version. I was looking at companies like Sun, which was really taking off then. And I felt very strongly that their whole success was based on open standards and open APIs and a lot of third-party development—as was Microsoft's stronghold on the PC market. [*APIs—application programming interfaces— are software systems that enable programs to communicate with each other.*]

The problem was that for a company of Digidesign's size, it was a *very* expensive investment, because to develop an open system we had to develop things like DAE, a distributed DSP architecture, and TDM.

There was a lot of controversy inside the company about investing a huge amount of R&D into these architectural features when all that money could be invested in more user features and more short-term products. And if I look back, the best decision we made was to stay the course. Because I don't think Pro Tools would have the dominant position it does today if it weren't for the third-party support.

Jim Griffin

www.62chevy.com

Jim Griffin founded the technology department at Geffen Records, leading a team that in 1994 distributed the first full-length commercial song online (Aerosmith's "Head First"). Currently the CEO of Cherry Lane Digital, he consults on wireless technology and the digital delivery of art, and has testified before the U.S. Senate Judiciary Committee on file sharing. Griffin is also the co-founder of the Pho group (www.pholist.org). Pho's thousands of members meet online and in noodle restaurants to discuss the convergence of entertainment and technology.

"If you talk to the Book Publishers' Association, it's like talking to the RIAA about music. They say, 'Those librarians are terrible. What are they doing, lending out books for free?' It's almost unbelievable."

The Pho list has been buzzing about something called "actuarial compensation" for musicians. How would that work?

It's essentially an acknowledgment that people will be anarchistic in their use of music—they will resist control. And the price for that could be seen as a kind of insurance.

Look at the roads as an example. They're quite imperfect. And the vehicles that use them—well, they're kind of designed to kill people. In the advertisements, you don't see huge, puffy objects; you in fact see them flying down the roads. You see them weaving and dodging and spinning, and they really show you that, hey, you can do whatever you want. This is freedom.

And that freedom means that you can swerve into the oncoming lane and kill a school bus full of children. Essentially, the control system we've built for the roads is five feet and a white line. And we leave it to the driver to do a damn good job, but how do we monetize that behavior? We use a pool of money—insurance—and a relatively fair way of splitting it up, which is actuarial economics. And that's how the modern transportation industry came about: It became possible to insure against risk.

In fact, school buses do plunge over cliffs. And so it is with digits: The rising tide of digitization has an effect on the rights surrounding creative things that we could interpret as damage. We can insure against that risk by creating a pool of money, and that money can be divvied up to those rights holders based on roughly the sampling that shows their success on a particular network—the "damage" that occurred.

So everyone with an Internet connection or a cell phone would pay a buck or two a month into that pool of money. But how would the people who write the checks identify all the songs that were played?

For the most part I'm for taking a rough sample—say, an hour's worth of stuff in a day—and setting it aside and analyzing it to find out what it really is. I think that you can do some of that automatically, but you still need to use your ears, because watermarks and [audio] fingerprinting fail under traditional media usage.

And that's how we've always *done* it. When radio came out in the 1920s, we moved from a world where you could count all of the people in the room to one where you didn't know how many people were listening. So what did we do? We created ASCAP, BMI, and SESAC [performance rights organizations], and we treated performance differently. We said, "If you, as a radio operator or restaurant owner, want to use music without asking permission, then there's a price for you to pay." And so it is with cable, satellite, and Web-casting. We essentially come up with a fee because we lose control of the music.

Actuarial economics is not so much my prediction as it is a *real* acknowledgment of how we got to where we are. Let's acknowledge that anarchy is and *always will be* a part of our business, and that it's actually one of the great blessings of our business. Instead of trying to stop it, monetize it. Don't tell me it can't be split up; it's split up by radio today. It can *easily* be done.

It's just *so* very important because the alternative—controlling the quantity and the destiny of art, of knowledge, of music—is scary. And if you go a step further and condition access to art and knowledge on one's ability to pay, then you've just done a terrible thing. If I think about the libraries and what they meant to me as a kid, I can't *imagine* living in a world where your ability to hear a song or read a book or watch a movie depends upon the size of your parents' wallet.

Nothing would be more destructive of our society than to create a world like that, because it really is the "have-nots" who create some of the greatest art and who will be less inspired. It's just critical for us to understand that we can hold so much more in an open hand than we can in a closed fist.

Herbie Hancock

www.herbiehancock.com

"If we're just thinking about sliders and knobs and building on what we've constructed in the past, then we'll still be inside that box."

Virtuoso keyboardist Herbie Hancock has moved fluidly between almost every development in acoustic and electronic jazz and R&B since 1960. He played in the Miles Davis Quintet for five years. By the mid-'70s, Hancock was playing to stadium-size crowds all over the world, and had four albums on the pop charts at once. He won the 1987 Academy Award for his soundtrack to the film *'Round Midnight*. He has also won nine Grammy Awards. Since the '70s, he has incorporated the latest technology in his music. Still touring extensively, he has built a live show featuring dynamic surround sound and a bevy of virtual instruments.

You've made heavy use of the Korg Karma synthesizer live. Are you using it to trigger some unexpected patterns that you then react to?

Oh *yeah*. It's really great. Actually, you know how we were using it? As a surround sound–producing synthesizer, because it has not only a left and a right, but two auxiliary outputs. We'd construct certain sounds so that we were sending some components to the third output, and we sent that to the surround engineer. Then he would place them wherever he wanted in the rear speakers and the side speakers. It made the instruments sound *huge*.

We can also manipulate the sounds ourselves with the Karma's sliders. That's a *great* feature in a surround environment, because we're able to *move* the sounds from the stage and create an experience of sonic mobility for the audience.

What types of sounds would you send to the surround speakers?

For the most part, I would have the attack of a note come from the front and the body of the sound spread out in the sides and the rear. But it could be the opposite. First, I have to know the direction of the music. Then I select sounds that I think might have a *place* in that atmosphere. And then I decide which ones would best serve as a surround kind of sound. In a lot of cases in the past tour, because I was promoting this record *Future 2 Future* that I did a couple of years ago, the sounds were ambient types. But I also created a surround environment for some of the brass sounds, to give them that body.

From your position on stage, though, you'd have the opposite perspective from the audience, right? The surrounds would almost be like the front speakers.

Right. On stage, we couldn't hear it as surround at all. That's something I'm working on now—having surround headphones so that we can hear what the output is on stage.

You're also using software instruments extensively on stage. How has that worked out?

You know, I've dreamed about being able to have one instrument that plays them all. For a long time I thought there would be hardware cards, and each one would be a particular synthesizer, and they'd all fit in one card cage or something. I never thought they'd be able to use instrument modeling and other techniques to reproduce pretty much the exact sound of either acoustic instruments *or* synthesizers. It kind of freaks me out that it's gone that far.

We're already starting to go beyond remaking instruments of the past. Emagic has a bunch of virtual instruments that are nothing like physical instruments. There are also a bunch of things for the PC that are pretty interesting.

I'm mostly a Mac guy, so I don't have all of those. But I actually bought a Carillon rackmount PC to run [TASCAM] GigaStudio, and that's what I'm going to load the *Vienna Symphonic Library* [orchestral sample set] into. I had a chance to experience their demo and . . . [*whispers*], "Wow!" What a fantastic sound you get. So I'm really looking forward to using this stuff.

Actually, I tried to load it last night and couldn't figure out how to do it. [*Laughs.*] So I may have to make a phone call. For the most part, I don't really *do* this stuff myself anymore. I hire people to do it. So I wish I could provide you with the kind of answers I was able to provide in the beginning of this modern venture into the use of electronics and instruments, but I had to make a decision some time ago that I was either going to conceive of the music or spend the time putting the sounds together, because I couldn't do both. Conceiving of the music is more a linear, horizontal concept and constructing the sounds is a vertical one. You have to stop time to do that. It was slowing me down. [*Laughs.*]

Steve Horowitz

www.thecodeinternational.com

Steve Horowitz is the audio director for Nickelodeon Online (www.nick.com), where he creates music and sound for children's games. He also wrote the original score for the 2004 hit Sundance documentary *Super Size Me*, and was the lead composer for the reality television show *I Bet You Will* (as seen on MTV.com). Horowitz won a Grammy Award for his production work on the bluegrass compilation *True Life Blues: The Songs of Bill Monroe*. He also served as chairman of the Interactive Audio Special Interest Group (www.iasig.org). Horowitz plays the bass and tours frequently with his eclectic, progressive band, the Code International, which has released three CDs.

"You've got to design your own quirks into using the tools."

What's behind the scenes of creating soundtracks for Nickelodeon's online games?

Most of the time, it's pretty much as it would be in a regular recording studio. I'll create the music and sound effects in Pro Tools or with sequencers, and then mix down to DAT or CD or bounce directly to disk. And then it's a matter of bringing them into [Macromedia] Flash, making them interactive to picture, choosing data compression schemes, and making sure everything sounds good for the different compressions. All the interactive stuff takes place within Flash.

If you want to get into some *really* trippy stuff, check out Marty Wilde's articles at Sonify.org. He's trying to build MIDI sequencers in Flash and has come up with some techniques for doing reverb and delay. A lot of it we don't incorporate because it tends to pump up the file size, and our games are already pretty big.

Some games we're working on are site-wide, where you're collecting what we call Nick Points from all areas of the site, and then within the game you can spend those points. So now we have these Flash sessions that have all this back-end to the servers as well—collecting user names and passwords, keeping track of points and where people are on the site. And that sometimes makes it difficult for me; I can't incorporate really tricky audio stuff into games like that, because there's just *too* much going on as people hit the servers. [*Laughs.*] They'll get like 100,000 users on a weekend, and they just *melt down*, man. From the user experience, everything starts to go *really slow*.

Do visitors hear audio dropouts or lose synchronization between the audio and visuals when that happens?

Not so much. That used to happen more with Flash. Flash is pretty good now. You can set certain elements to stream in and then sync, so if one element's not there, the other usually won't go.

I have no complaints, because I came from the world of CD-ROM, where I was doing a lot of 8-bit conversion [*crunching pristine 16-bit sounds into gritty 8-bit ones to make the files smaller*], and I don't have to *do* that anymore. It's nice that the MP3 compression schemes are built into Flash. The only thing that would be nice in terms of bells and whistles would be if they included pitch-shifting and reverb, or some sort of effects algorithm. And Flash doesn't incorporate the MIDI paradigm at all. If it did, it would be a 200 percent improvement.

Do you think Flash will eventually support soft-synth plug-ins?

Oh, God! [*Laughs.*] I'd love it! I don't see much of a reason why they couldn't. But I can't see it in the near future.

They've done some nice things in the latest versions, though. It used to be you had one iteration of a sound that would just play. Now they've made it so you can start from the middle of a sound. So it makes it easier for me to use smaller assets to create multiple sound effects.

It seems like pitch-shifting is one of the major tools that sound designers use.

Yeah. That's what makes Flash—and Web audio right now—so frustrating. I mean, Beatnik [www.beatnik.com] was really on the right track—*really* on the right track, and then it looked for a while like [Microsoft] DirectMusic Producer was going to step in. And it's just too bad that those both died, because that's the biggest shortcoming in Flash—that you can't pitch-shift. Which means you're stuck with constantly increasing file size, which kind of bites.

But these are pretty amazing times. Somewhere in the mid-'90s, a hurdle was overcome in digital audio, and the terrain is super-interesting now. It's *amazing* what I'm doing with just a Mac, one MIDI cable going in [*laughs*], and that's *it*.

Jennifer Hruska

www.sonicimplants.com, www.sonicnetworkinc.com

Sonic Network President Jennifer Hruska has been in the audio engineering business since 1984. As senior sound designer for Kurzweil Music Systems, she voiced the company's award-winning K2500-series synthesizers and digital home pianos. Today, Sonic Network develops the Sonic Implants line of sample libraries for professional samplers, and licenses software synthesizers and wavetable files to cell phone manufacturers. Hruska is also a composer, working currently on a performance piece involving sending specialized audio signals into modified televisions.

Your GigaSampler orchestral string library fills 20 CD-ROMs, whereas your cell phone wavetables have to fit into a few hundred kilobytes. How does designing sounds on each end of the sampling spectrum influence the other end?

I guess the main way it overlaps is that I'm always trying to improve the quality on the low-end stuff. Even though you don't have hardly anything to work with, you still know what it's supposed to sound like, because it's the same set of ears going into it. So I think the little sets we've been doing actually sound pretty good because of that. Quality-wise, it folds over and keeps making us polish and polish. Going the other direction, there's probably not so much of an overlap.

Hear Jennifer Hruska's music, Sonic Implants ringtones, and sample library demos—and get royalty-free Sonic Implants SoundFonts—on the disc.

But it must be strange after so many years of being really constrained on memory to suddenly have so much space to stretch out.

Definitely. And every time I see [GigaSampler creator] Jim Van Buskirk, I say to him, "I don't know whether to hug you or kill you." [*Laughs.*] Because it *really* did change everything. It changed sampling. Now there's just *so* much data that you need to get through that you don't have time to do a lot with the individual samples. And that was sort of okay for us, because we just like to get a really good recording and then leave them alone as much as possible. That's how we get our organic sound.

But it also created this phenomenon where you have a lot of sound developers out there who don't really *know* how to do anything small. If you can throw a lot of memory at it, it is somewhat easier to get a good quality output. But as soon as you have to make things small, that's where a different set of skills comes into play.

"What you really should be using these tools for is trying to *break* them and get happy accidents out of them."

I imagine you can get sloppy when developing the large samples.

Yeah, you can. And then it's the marketing thing, too: A bigger number on your advertisement looks better, whereas it's *not* necessarily better. And in some cases, it makes it a lot harder for the composer or the musician to deal with. We actually heard from a lot of composers, "I don't have time to go *through* all that. I just need 20 really great, playable string patches."

As a sound developer, how are you dealing with sample piracy?

It's a *real* problem. Our samples are getting pirated like mad, just like everybody else's. And we're a small company; we don't have lot of money to invest in lots of copy protection and encryption. So we're somewhat vulnerable.

But now you're starting to see a lot of sample libraries, like Eric Persing's stuff, come out as plug-in synthesizers. It's a cool way to work, and it's a somewhat easier way to work, but it's also popular because when you package your samples with a software synthesizer it's much more difficult for those samples to be stolen. You've got some copy protection built in.

What about discouraging piracy by providing more utility? If your samples came with a much better manual or a tutorial or something, would that be enough?

You mean, overcomplicate the product so you require a manual? [*Laughs.*] I *hope* I don't have to do that. But we're definitely going to move into packaging our stuff with a synthesizer to reduce some of the piracy.

We're also looking at going back to a hardware sampler. It would interface with the PC and Mac environment, so it wouldn't be entirely a standalone hardware sampler like you might normally think of. But it would be off-loading the synthesis to a black box and the samples would only play on that black box. And it's not only for copy protection: Since we're selling synthesizer code to cell phone manufacturers and embedded systems, obviously we're building up our synthesizer technology.

Mark Isham

www.isham.com

Trumpeter and synthesist Mark Isham has composed more than 65 film scores and many albums of electric jazz, acoustic jazz, and new age music. He has won a Grammy, an Emmy, and a Clio in addition to multiple Grammy, Academy Award, and Golden Globe nominations. His evocative scores grace such films as *A River Runs Through It, The Moderns,* and *Men of Honor.* Isham also performs live with his band on the Los Angeles club circuit and at national festivals.

"One of the great compositional elements a composer has to work with is harmonic strength—chords that go *exactly* where they need to go, and go there with purpose and direction and with satisfaction."

Ableton's Robert Henke had a great story about captivating an entire club with just his laptop and a reverb. [See the "Success Through Failure" chapter.] Musical tools are really changing, aren't they?

That's what's beautiful about Ableton Live—they're actually turning the computer into a musical instrument. We *love* that program. I've been trying to get somebody to do something like that for years. In the early '80s, Sequential Circuits rewrote the firmware in some little analog sequencers for me so I could call up patterns in time and turn them into performance instruments.

As MIDI evolved, that got harder to do, and then when the computer entered, nobody was thinking of the computer in that way. It really hasn't been until Ableton that the whole concept of being able to control things and maintain that constant point of sync has existed. They've done a brilliant job. My new band has a DJ based around a Titanium [Macintosh laptop] running Live.

The band receives the MIDI Time Code so anybody can lock on with delay lines or triggers. And we've got the songs split up in sections so that any section can be open-ended.

Having a jazz background, the idea of pushing Go and then having to stick to the same form just doesn't excite me. As we get to know the program, we're discovering we can actually start to create new textures and new rhythmic patterns on the fly that we've never even rehearsed.

Has technology always worked so smoothly for you?

No, it doesn't always work smoothly. It *never* has always worked smoothly. [*Laughs.*] We spent the last 48 hours in computer *hell* trying to get this video card to work right. That's the *one* downside when you embrace this much technology at a professional level. I don't care how great the concept behind most of these programs is; by their very nature, you've got the potential of computer hell.

A stable datum around here is that if it's working, don't change it. Because you may say, "Well, we're just going to change this one *thing*. We'll have it done in a couple hours." I don't care—it's four days. That's just the nature of computers.

Yet you keep coming back for more.

I've always embraced the stuff. Back in the late '70s, I was carrying around an ARP 2600 and an Oberheim Four Voice [analog synthesizers], and we used to carry two Revoxes [reel-to-reel tape recorders] and do Frippertronics live. [*See the "Fripp It Good" sidebar.*] I've always *thoroughly* embraced all this technology and gone through whatever battles one has to do to get it to work.

And in the last five, six, seven years I've actually had several different setups that have tried to use the technology to the greatest degree I can to *get* interactive and to be a real performance instrument. Part of the problem for me was that if I'm a trumpet player also, I was like this raving lunatic on the stage. I had buttons here, and knobs *there*, and a mixing console there, and then I'd pick up the trumpet and blow a little, and then I'd go back to it because I had to get the drum fill in. My wife would come to the shows and say, "I can't even *look* at you. It's like watching a crazy person up there." So I finally just said, "I'm going to get somebody who will take on that role so I can relax and not have to do everything myself."

Fripp It Good

Frippertronics is the term guitarist Robert Fripp coined to describe his technique of creating realtime rhythmic echoes. He ran a tape between two Revox recorders, with the first set to record and the second set to play. Fripp then mixed the playback signal—delayed by its journey between the machines—back into the first machine, along with his live guitar signal. There's a diagram of this setup on Brian Eno's *Discreet Music* album. Eno, who himself had been inspired by Steve Reich's tape music, taught Fripp the technique.

Jimmy Jam

www.flytetyme.com

Producer/songwriter Jimmy "Jam" Harris and his partner Terry Lewis have contributed to more than 100 gold and platinum albums, including four multiplatinum albums for Janet Jackson. They've also worked with Mary J. Blige, Mariah Carey, Boyz II Men, Michael Jackson, Gladys Knight, Patti LaBelle, Lionel Richie, Rod Stewart, Luther Vandross, and Barry White. Jam and Lewis won their first Producer of the Year Grammy Award back in 1986, and have been nominated for it again the last four years straight. They work principally out of FlyteTyme, their well-appointed studio. (Take a virtual tour online.)

You said your iPod MP3 player was "the greatest thing ever." Do you use it to audition song sequences for albums?

No. I just use it for storing ideas. I used to walk around with one of those little digital voice recorders just to put ideas in. Olympus makes one that's compatible with Macs, which is nice. Once I have my sound files, I download them into my computer, drag 'em into my iTunes jukebox program, and then I put 'em on my iPod. I basically then have a library of a million ideas, because the ideas come much faster than the ability to record them in finished form. So that way, I can put everything in a folder and have all these 30-second or one-minute ideas that are organized. The coolest thing is the organization. Every time you plug it in, it updates whatever's not in there.

So to me, that's as *simple* as it gets. Actually, Terry gave my iPod to me, because he's much more the computer guy. And I said, "What do I *do* with it?" And he said, "Just plug it into your FireWire and it does everything *for* you." And I plugged it in and it downloaded all of my playlists, and I was like, "This is great!" Then the other day I heard a song I liked, went to the Apple music store, found it, downloaded it for 99 cents—I'm like, "Wow! I love it." So for a slow guy like me, the simplicity of it was really the key.

So with the voice recorder, you're just compiling a huge database of dum-da-dum-da-dums?

Yeah, sometimes it's *dum-da-dum-da-dums.* [*Laughs.*] Usually I come up with a lot of track ideas before I come up with melody ideas. Sometimes when I'm listening to a track, though, I'll come up with a melody idea that I don't want to lose, and that's usually what I'll sing in. Usually those are a chorus or a melody for a song, or maybe a lyric idea. But they're generally no more than about a minute. If I walk into the studio and I'm stuck, because inspiration doesn't strike every day, I'll go back and say, "Hmm. Maybe I've marked something. . . ."

Jimmy Jam (L) with Terry Lewis. "I love when someone samples our songs. Particularly now that I've been in the business for so long, it's all about legacy and hoping that the music has a life and can touch people again. I feel that way when *we* sample."

Or a lot of times I'll have an idea for a song for an artist we have absolutely no connection with. And who knows, three or four years down the line, all of a sudden we're working with that artist, and it's like, "Oh! Wait a minute. I had a great idea. Let me see if it's *still* a great idea." For organizational stuff, it just makes it easier, because I used to have everything on a million cassettes. [*Laughs.*]

It's funny, because now that we all have the [Macintosh] G4 laptops, we don't even use CDs much anymore. When we walk into the studio now, all of the songs are on our laptop hard drives. We're working on Janet's project now, and we've been collaborating with a bunch of writers on songs and they've been sending us stuff. I'll put the CD in my G4, we'll play everything from there, and the songs that she likes, I'll download into a folder called Janet Potentials. Then we'll go back two or three weeks later and run through 'em, and the ones she doesn't like, I'll delete. But the organizational part of it is *great*, because you're dealing with so many songs—at any given time, Terry and I could be working on five or six different projects.

We did a Bryan Adams record last year for the animated movie *Spirit*, and I still haven't met Bryan Adams. We did it all over the Internet—everything from FTPing final files to just MP3ing ideas back and forth. And there's no way we could have done the project physically, because he couldn't come to Minneapolis, we couldn't go to L.A., and it needed to be done in four days. But we had a record that got Golden Globe-nominated and was pretty successful.

Leslie Ann Jones

www.skysound.com

eslie Ann Jones is the director of scoring at Skywalker Sound, the award-winning audio post-production facility owned by George Lucas. In 1975, she became the first female recording engineer ever hired at ABC Recording Studios in Los Angeles. Later she became a staffer at the Automatt Recording Studios, starting her film-score mixing career with *Apocalypse Now.* As staff engineer with Capitol Studios in Hollywood, she recorded Rosemary Clooney, Michael Feinstein, MC Hammer, Marcus Miller, Michelle Shocked, and BeBe & CeCe Winans. She joined Skywalker Sound in 1997, working on *Forrest Gump, Hercules, Jurassic Park, Mrs. Doubtfire,* and *Toy Story,* among many others.

"I mix on a set of Tannoy PBM 8s, and here at Skywalker we have B&W Nautilus 802s. But I try not to worry about too many different kinds of speakers. I'm not making records for 16-year-olds who have 18-inch woofers in their trunks."

Mix magazine praised your "educated ears." What do you listen for?

I think I listen for something that's *different.* You have to listen to a lot of things at the same time, and the more comfortable you get as a recording engineer or producer, the more easily you can move things to the background and start to concentrate on certain aspects. So you might be listening to how the snare drum sounds in the context of not only the drum kit, but also the *weight* that it carries with the rest of the rhythm track—and whether the reverb on it is appropriate.

Right. In many recordings, reverb is applied so specifically that it seems like there's one drum that's way down the hall.

Yeah! [*Laughs.*] When I'm working with singers, I'm listening a lot to phrasing and pitch, because the nature of recording vocals is that they're always going to be fixed afterwards, and you're always going to have to punch in. So you start to listen in terms of *how* you're going to be able to do that, and whether somebody's phrasing things the right way, because that could mean you won't be able to punch in on that track, or that if you tried to put together a composite vocal later, that you might not have the pieces you need.

There are some songs I hear on the radio where it's *clear* that somebody held a note longer than they could have had they sung it live. So I'm very mindful of that, because the illusion that someone actually sang it all at the same time is very important to me.

How granular do you get when you're doing punches? Do they start to lose their personality as they get shorter than a whole phrase?

They *can*, and I try not to let that happen. I think it's probably a *good* thing that I don't do a lot of digital editing myself, because I still try to take things a little more holistically instead of trying to think that I can make anything work because I have the power of Pro Tools behind me. It *has* to work for me in the context of the song and the performance—as opposed to the other side, which goes, "I can do anything now. I can tune it; I can move it wherever I want." I think people *hear* that on records. There's a lack of something that touches you on an emotional level. So the better you can take whole performances, the better off you are.

Do you use any psychological tricks when listening, like plugging an ear, or turning around, or walking down the hall?

Sometimes if I'm playing a mix back for somebody, I'll walk outside of the room a little—just to get a sense, particularly on the volume of the vocal. I don't mix for radio, because I don't make those kinds of records, so I'm not particularly concerned with what it's going to sound like on a pair of Auratones [*very small speakers used by many recording engineers to estimate what a mix will sound like on cheap consumer radios*].

I will play things at a low volume. I try not to mix too loud so I don't get ear fatigue. And sometimes I'll make CDs and play them in my car, just to take it out of the element of the studio and see how the homogenization of the mixes is sounding. But I don't really care how it *sounds* when I'm driving. It's more about having a different listening environment to see if anything sticks out tonally or balance-wise. And I just have this stock car stereo, so it's not anything that sounds particularly great.

I still find in the records that I make that I'm looking for the perfect bass sound. Particularly on the records that have acoustic bass, there's a sound I hear in my head from old Billie Holiday records that I want to emulate. And I haven't quite gotten there yet. In some ways, it's good to never be able to meet that, because it makes me keep trying.

Ikutaro Kakehashi

www.rolandus.com

As an orphaned teenager in postwar Japan, Ikutaro Kakehashi supported himself by repairing watches, radios, and musical instruments. His love of music—especially organ music—prompted him to launch Ace Electronics in 1958, where he developed the world's first transistorized manual percussion instrument, the Rhythm Ace R-1. In 1972, Kakehashi founded Roland Corporation, one of the largest yet most innovative musical instrument manufacturers. Roland was also one of the first companies to support computer music production. Kakehashi says his life's goal is to bring the joy of creating music to as many people as possible.

Several years ago, you said that music-making seemed like an exclusive club—as if ordinary people were not able to join.

It's partially true that musicians are a kind of club. But everybody *appreciates* music. It's just that when they cannot play, they say, "I'm a little bit . . ."

Hazukashii? [*shy or embarrassed*]

Hazukashii, yeah. So there's no way to express what's inside.

So how can we get people involved with music without feeling embarrassed or awkward?

For example: karaoke. In Japan, as you know, it's very popular. And in the beginning, it was only done by "singer people." But now young people, even families, visit karaoke places. It's quite different from Western society.

There's a nearly 30-year history of karaoke. But the early stage and today are quite different. Actually, karaoke started from professional singers. They needed a backing band, but it's not so easy to travel with one. So they prepared a tape. Then this idea went to nightclubs, bars, and finally to separate karaoke rooms.

Today, most people are not so shy. It used to be you'd give them a microphone and everybody said, "Oh no, no, no! Not me. I cannot sing." But today, if you give them a microphone, the mic will never come back! When I discuss karaoke with Western people, they say, "No, no, no, no. Not me." But it's exactly the same as the early stage in Japan.

*t it also takes a lot of effort to play traditional musical instruments
'l enough to enjoy what you're hearing. Perhaps technology could
ke it easier to cross that barrier. Many people who pick up a tradi-
nal instrument get frustrated and give up quickly.*

My explanation is that the music society used to be a school.
ere was only one entrance. But now with digital and computer
usic, hobbyists also can approach this—we call it Music Paradise.
ce you join, you still need a push. It used to be that parents pushed:
ou must play; you must do more exercises." But once people enter
usic Paradise, they have a built-in engine, because they enjoy it. We
ust give people many chances to reach Music Paradise. This is a *big*
ance for us. Even for other businesses.

"There's hardware and software. But
[for] music, we need *artware*. Without
artware, digital instruments will
never create good music. You must
understand the artist."

*fascinating to play the keyboards in your booth here at the NAMM
w that are filled with sounds and styles from all over the planet. But
you think world music is becoming less distinct because of that?*

No. There are two types of musical artists. One type—for exam-
e, classical musicians—tries to recreate music. They follow the score exactly, as if they wanted
reach a target. But other musicians want to create something new. Electronic musical instru-
nts are perfect for them. One group wants to escape the fixed mind, and the other is chasing
hat is the best music?" Both are very pure people [*laughs*], but different ones.

*e of the unique things Roland does is integrate video features with music hardware. That's an excit-
 direction, especially for electronic music, which is often dull to watch. Where do you see video going?*

If you look at my idea, it's like this [*draws a circuit diagram with video and audio sections*]:
n or 15 years ago, recording studios were very popular. But today, many people can make
usic in their own rooms. Our recording equipment, like the VS recorder, has become very pop-
ar, so even the average student can make a CD by himself.

But video equipment is also very inexpensive now, thanks to software. This camera, a Sony
oints to his camcorder], is $1,500. This DV quality already can be used for broadcasting. So
en amateurs can create good video.

For video people, though, it's not so easy to enter music. But musicians, if they understand
deo, they can go this way. [*Moves finger from audio to video side of diagram.*] It's just like—do
u know diodes? One way.

Also, musicians understand synchronization. Video people are only 30 frames per second. So
turally, sound and video must be combined. That's why I started with video. Because the future
music—DJ people, they don't care about history. They touch LP records like *this* [*pantomimes
atching a record*]. It's the same thing—they have non-fixed minds.

Stephen Kay

www.karma-lab.com

Stephen Kay has produced music for commercials and TV, sampled symphony orchestras, and worked as a musician in everything from prog-rock bands to cruise-ship piano bars. He has been closely associated with musical instrument manufacturer Korg, providing demos and programming for many of their products. For the past ten years, Kay has been developing the patented algorithmic music generation technology KARMA (Kay Algorithmic Realtime Music Architecture), which is featured in the Korg Karma Music Workstation and available in software form.

To what extent do you think technology can help non-musicians make music?

Anyone can make musical *sounds*, but does that make them a musician? Software can't necessarily give you a good ear for what goes together, what bass line fits with what drum groove. Those are things you develop.

"I want to see instruments that allow you to make interesting music with gestures, like sculpting sound with your hands. I envision a floating three-dimensional construct, and you poke holes in it and stretch it and shape it, and the music changes instantly."

KARMA lets people do things they wouldn't normally be able to do. If you *are* a good musician to begin with, and you have a certain knowledge of chord structure and rhythmic patterns, you can use software to enhance what you can create, but it's still based on your own skill level. It's like the cyborg body armor that amplifies your normal movements into something with the force of a sledgehammer.

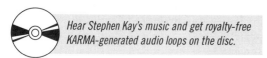

Hear Stephen Kay's music and get royalty-free KARMA-generated audio loops on the disc.

For example, I feel that I have really good keyboard skills, but if I can generate something with software that sounds as good or better, and saves time to boot, then I'll use it. In any case, I'm looking for the inspirational edge, the ability to generate something I wouldn't have thought of. I don't feel threatened by software that can generate things I wouldn't normally play.

Don't forget that the end result is listened to by people who have no idea how you created it. They won't know if a riff came from KARMA, or an arpeggiator, or a sample CD, or if you worked three days on it until you could play it manually. Either they like it or they don't.

Do you feel a different mindset when you're interacting with KARMA versus another musician? Someone said that having a Karma keyboard was like having another band member who always suggested cool ideas.

[*Laughs.*] Those are some of the good comments. On the other side of the camp, you get comments like, "KARMA? That's not really music. You just press a *button* and stuff comes out"—which misses the whole point. I don't think software can really take the place of interacting with another human yet, but that's not to say it's not *good*. It's a different way of getting new input.

When I was reviewing the Karma keyboard, I was struck by how the patterns evolved in response to my playing. How did you get the musicality in there?

As a musician, one of the things that bugs me the most about loops, arpeggiators, phrase factories, and auto-accompaniment schemes is the almost overwhelming boredom factor you get when you hear them repeat more than a few times. That's why I prefer MIDI-based phrase generators, so that the notes can be easily manipulated. And that's why I've tried to program many *musically useful* randomly variable parameters into KARMA.

Simply hooking up a random-number generator doesn't ensure musically useful results. In fact, most often the results are non-musical, mechanical, or plain stupid-sounding. For example, almost all standard arpeggiators have a mode that chooses notes at random, and you will quite often get the same note two or three times in a row, which immediately sounds mechanical. KARMA's random index choices will purposely *not* allow duplicate notes in a row by default. That immediately sounds more satisfying for some reason. I sprinkled many of those sorts of decisions throughout the software.

Another key factor to making randomness sound musical is the ability to repeat a series of random choices, like a musician getting an idea and vamping on it. If you are constantly randomizing things with no repetition, it becomes more like avant-garde jazz than a groove. With KARMA, you can repeat the same series of note and rhythm choices, but have a slight randomization of the velocities [*i.e., volume and brightness*], as if the musician played the same notes but was unable to play them with exactly the same accents.

It would be nice to be able to dial in the amount of attitude, or even ego, because you can certainly design software to be unpredictable. [*Laughs.*] That's not a problem. It's the human characteristic that's tricky.

Ray Kurzweil

www.kurzweilAI.net

Inventor, scientist, and author Ray Kurzweil was the principal developer of the first text-to-speech synthesizer, prompting customer Stevie Wonder to challenge him to create a keyboard synthesizer with rich acoustic sound. The result was the Kurzweil K250, one of the first (and most highly regarded) sampling synthesizers. Kurzweil received the Lemelson-MIT Prize (America's largest award in invention and innovation) and the National Medal of Technology (the nation's highest honor in technology). His best-selling book, *The Age of Spiritual Machines: When Computers Exceed Human Intelligence,* was the No. 1 book on Amazon in the categories of science and artificial intelligence. Upcoming books include *The Singularity Is Near: When Humans Transcend Biology.*

As computers start to exceed human intelligence, how will it affect music-making?

Music in general requires the full range of human intelligence. I think you can build a lot of intelligence into software today, but it's not going to be at a human level of musicianship until computers achieve human levels of intelligence—which I believe they will by 2029. In my view, the heart of human intelligence, 99 percent of it, is the recognition of patterns. And that's always been a weak area for computers.

See Ray Kurzweil's virtual-reality musical performance video on the disc.

That may be why someone said the problem with computers is that they don't laugh: They can't consistently juxtapose elements into something surprising and pleasing.

Well, I think that gets back to the question, "What is music?" Music is human communication using the highest level of human thought. And what is the highest level of human thought? It's basically human emotion, which includes humor.

Computers already can greatly exceed humans at doing mathematics and other types of analytical thinking. But mastering our emotions is something they're just beginning to do. So when I talk about machines exceeding human intelligence by 2029, I'm talking specifically about these kinds of things—being able to get the joke, and be funny.

And music is a language or a set of languages where you can express these kinds of concepts. Music definitely can be funny. People have to understand the vocabulary and the allusions in the music to get the joke, but that's true of any joke in any language.

But the way that human intelligence does that is through our recognition of patterns. We actually understand now *why* that is from looking at our efforts to understand how the human brain works. The activity in the brain principally takes place in the connections between the neurons. Those connections compute only about two hundred transactions per second. That's about ten million times slower than electronic circuits. However, unlike today's computers, we have a hundred trillion of them, and they're all potentially doing something at the same time. And that massively parallel architecture is an ideal paradigm for recognizing patterns.

"I think it would be motivational for people to be able to create interesting and complex music before they'd fully developed their playing skills, because right now, there are a lot of dues to pay before music-playing sounds like *anything.*"

Our emotions are very much based on patterns. We have a whole hierarchy. We start with our senses, and then we do basic recognition. We recognize lines and circles, and we recognize objects like faces and trees and leaves, and we put them together in scenes. We recognize situations, and then at the very highest level of this hierarchy we recognize sadness, or humor, or joy.

And music, through aspects of our brain that respond to things like rhythm and tone color, is able to generate this whole elaborate hierarchy leading up to the most profound human emotions. The ability to recognize a sequence of sounds that expresses musical ideas is a deep pattern-recognition task. It's very hard to express in if-then logic rules what makes a good melody.

As we learn more about how pattern recognition works—and I've been studying it for 40 years—we'll have greater insight as to how the human brain can recognize patterns in music. And then we can create programs that can write music, or, more important, interact with human musicians to be more intelligent accompanists.

My father used to accompany singers, and he always used to say the hardest thing for a musician is to be an accompanist. To be an intelligent accompanist means really understanding what the singer or violinist or whoever you're accompanying is doing, and then trying to strengthen them if they're reaching a weak point.

You want these cybernetic accompanists to similarly bring out the best in the human musician. I think we can already do a pretty good job of that, but that's going to get better and better as we go forward, and I think we will routinely be jamming with our cybernetic musicians.

Roger Linn

www.rogerlinndesign.com

Roger Linn is best known for inventing the first programmable, sampled-sound drum machine, the LM-1 Drum Computer, in 1979. The LM-1 and its successors, the LinnDrum and Linn9000, have propelled countless hit records. Linn later partnered with Akai to create the MPC60 and MPC3000 MIDI Production Centers, sampling drum machine/sequencers that became industry standards in rap, hip-hop, and dance music. His latest product, the AdrenaLinn, is a rhythmic digital sound processor for guitar. A guitarist himself, Linn toured with Leon Russell and co-wrote hits for Eric Clapton ("Promises") and Mary Chapin Carpenter ("Quittin' Time").

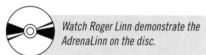

Watch Roger Linn demonstrate the AdrenaLinn on the disc.

You've been programming computers for decades. Why didn't you design the AdrenaLinn as a software plug-in?

One of the biggest problems with audio on most computers is realtime latency. Plug-ins are realtime on *playback,* but not from audio input to output. And some plug-ins really have to be used as you're playing. Amp modeling is one of them and the beat-synched modulation effects in the AdrenaLinn are another. They're intended to *change* the way you play, not just alter it after you played. So we couldn't make a plug-in that would guarantee low latency on every computer. Latency is coming down, so we may make a plug-in version in the future, but for now we had to make an actual hardware product to get it right.

And actually, the AdrenaLinn is just two very high-speed computers inside—one DSP computer and one microcontroller for the displays and housekeeping. The analog gets converted to digital and everything happens in the digital domain. Then it gets spat back out as analog. It's all invisible to the user.

You built your first drum machine to help with your songwriting. As technology spawns more one-man bands, how can they replace the creative dialog that drives real bands?

It seems to me that technology tools help us generate ideas when we work alone. An imported loop, or a sequencer that lets us play lines we otherwise couldn't, or an AdrenaLinn or other creativity tool can all lead us in new musical directions.

That said, there's nothing like playing with other musicians. I play in four different bands now. And I *love* jamming with people. I've been jamming with Peter Gotcher, the Digidesign founder, who's a great drummer. It's us, a guitar player, and a bass player. It's *loud,* and it's fun, and it's among the world's oldest garage bands.

"A creative mind, in my experience, is a *loud* mind. It has lots of thoughts popping up in all directions."

It's interesting that the drum-machine guy should be praising a live drummer.

[*Laughs.*] He's a *great* drummer, man. He can play great grooves. My point is that both human interaction and composing alone on computer have their merits. What I like about composing on computer is that sometimes it's good not to have my original idea changed by the styles of other musicians. What I don't like is that I end up altering my compositions to fit how the computer wants to work. We're basically changing our music to adapt to what's great and not great about computers and software. And to me, what is not great is that you sit by yourself at a desk. That's what people normally call *work.*

It's funny—I went to a Peter Gabriel concert a couple of months ago because his guitar player uses an AdrenaLinn. And in the middle of the stage, there was a *desk* with a computer on it. And I thought, "Is Peter Gabriel going to check his *e-mail* during the show?" It's just so counterintuitive to what we expect music to be.

What would you like to see in new musical instruments?

One thing I'd love to do is create a new musical instrument that combines the best parts of computers and traditional instruments. I'd take lots of ideas from new music software and put them into a beautiful, handcrafted instrument that has an organic shape and conforms to the body, so you could stand up and move around while you played it, and you'd *feel* like being on stage playing instead of sitting at a computer. You'd be able to play chords, and fully expressive melodies, and rhythm simultaneously through body gestures. And at the same time, it could interact wirelessly with other musicians playing the same instrument or variations of it.

When musicians played together, they would automatically fall into sync with each other over a wireless network. There'd be rhythmic sync, as well as perhaps dynamic and harmonic sync to the other musicians, in ways that you don't have enough body parts to control. But that's too expensive for a little company to build, so I just enjoy brainstorming about it with a few bright friends.

David Mash

www.mashine.com

David Mash is Vice President of Information Technology at Berklee College of Music in Boston. He was also the founding chair of Berklee's Music Synthesis Department, the first degree program in MIDI and music synthesis in the United States, which is now internationally recognized as the premier music technology program of its kind. (In fact, *all* Berklee students are now required to study some music technology.)

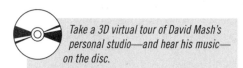 *Take a 3D virtual tour of David Mash's personal studio—and hear his music—on the disc.*

Mash has collaborated on development and artistic projects with companies including Adobe, Digidesign, Kodak, Korg, and Opcode. *Rolling Stone* called him "the industry's leading evangelist for the marriage of music and technology."

A few years ago, Berklee added Propellerhead Reason to the curriculum in a big way. How have virtual studios affected the way students learn music production?

Actually, Reason is later in the curriculum, but we put it on all the computers that students have access to. So a lot of times the students will go to those machines and use Reason just because they want to play with it. It's great; it's like having a store where you can buy yourself as many devices as you need to make music.

We originally started using Reason because we had a class in our music synthesis major that focused on building a system. And for the final exam, we would take one of the workstations completely apart and the students would have to assemble it and get all the cables in the right places. The downside was when the students don't get it back together the right way [*laughs*], you have a mess that you have to clean up in time for the next class.

So Reason is great because it lets you do that in the virtual world. You can put all the gear you want in the rack and give specific instructions as to how you want it to function. And then the students have to configure it, and you can very easily find if it works.

I think it's a really important transitional product from the perspectives of understanding how things work in the real world and being able to work in the virtual world. It's an interesting time in our society, because we live in both worlds now.

What are some surprising things you've discovered as you guide students and faculty through the new techniques of music production?

The surprising thing is just how *fast* the technology is advancing. Just two years ago, there were very few software synthesizers that actually worked. You walk around the NAMM show here, and now there are too many to even look at. I don't think there's a way that a human being can possibly look at *every* one of the software samplers that's available today and carefully evaluate the feature sets against one another—and more important, what the *sound* differences are.

Of course, there's a distinct difference between the music-products industry and the music-making public. I think that the artists are quite a bit behind the curve in terms of where things are at, let alone where they can go.

And it's a little confusing right now. I spend my life looking at this stuff and making music with this stuff and thinking about how to teach with these things, and I'm *overwhelmed* by what's here at the show. I'm happy I have a lot of colleagues who can help me look at the things in a parallel fashion. [*Laughs.*]

"We've changed our core curriculum so that every entering freshman takes Introduction to Music Technology. The idea is that everybody has to get over that hurdle right away. And then it's a constant learning process."

With the amount that music technology changes in a four-year span, you must have to be refreshing the curriculum constantly. And still, your seniors will be out of sync with your freshmen.

Yeah, but that's just the way of the world. Things are going to continue to advance and change. And one of the most important things we have to teach students is how to adapt to change.

Learning is all *about* change. When you pay tuition to go to a school, you're saying, "Change me. I want to change. I want to *learn* more. I want to *become* something that I'm not today." So our job is to teach people not only how to change through what we know, but how to adapt and change with the things that we *don't* know yet. To be a lifelong learner and a functional member of society, you have to cope with change. And that goes beyond music. That's just being a productive member of the 21st century.

Douglas Morton

www.quparts.com

Douglas Morton has created and published over 300 CD and CD-ROM sample libraries. His groundbreaking work at Optical Media International resulted in the world's first sampling CD-ROM. (Back then, CD-ROM drives cost $2,500.) In 1992, Morton and his wife Susan formed Q Up Arts, a content provider and publisher of sample libraries. He recently formed a new company called Mortronix, which specializes in sound design, music composition, and special sampling projects. Morton composes and plays keyboards for many CDs, television shows, and exhibits. His credits include *The X-Files,* Toyota, BMW, Michael Jackson, Electronic Arts, Microsoft, the Cure, and Yes.

Your soundtracks play throughout the Monterey Bay Aquarium. What was going through your mind as you composed them?

Well, I've done a lot of scuba diving. I actually learned how to dive in Monterey. When I was under the water, I always looked at all the elements down there as an orchestra piece. You can attach different parts of what you're seeing to different instruments. You see a school of fish—*boom!* There's some flutes. You see a pinnacle coming up, that could be a low, sustained thing. I had some real revelations when I was diving. [*Laughs.*] It changed the way I looked at composing. I realized that nature had everything I *needed* to interpolate into music.

Hear Douglas Morton's underwater soundtracks—and grab some royalty-free Q Up Arts samples—on the disc.

The Monterey Bay Aquarium gig was ideal for me because it's a very musical *world* under there. Sampling can get a little dry and clinical, so it's been a really nice outlet. When I walk through there now, almost all the exhibits have my stuff.

What is the production process like?

I basically watch videos and have a couple of meetings. The video producer describes what the exhibit's going to look like, so I don't have to go out there very much.

We created some new ways to do exhibit scoring, because in the early days there wasn't a lot of consideration to the audio. They had those little round speakers that were all *mono,* so I suggested we do surround.

The first exhibit I did was "Mysteries of the Deep." They had five zones that descend to different areas of the ocean, each of which contains different lifeforms. So I decided to compose several pieces of music that could crossfade harmonically. [*For example, if one zone was in C major, the next zone might be in A minor, because the scales contain the same notes, but start in a different place.*] As you walk through the exhibit, you hear a little bit of the last one as you walk into the next one.

So the sounds are mixing in the air, rather than electronically?

Right. And then we went to some 6/8s from 4/4s [*i.e., six beats per bar rather than four, which produces a wavelike feeling*]. It's dreamy, watery stuff, but there are subtle shifts, and suddenly you're in a new zone with new animals and it's a different aural experience. We did a lot of experimentation to determine what keys can sit together, what instruments are not going to collide. I learned a lot.

How did you test that in your own studio?

We had this big room with five speakers, and I just routed one song to each speaker so you could walk through. I was doing everything in MIDI then, so it was easy to go, "Let's change the keys of Zones 3 and 5," for instance. It was a lot of trial and error, but it was *really* fun.

And it turned out well. You walk into one area and there's a surround zone, and a big wall of video screens, and a subwoofer down behind. We didn't do any head-spinning surround stuff, but I positioned instruments in different parts of the sound field. I've snuck in there and watched people, and their jaws were hanging open.

What's it playing back on? DVDs?

PCs. On the video wall, the servers that were feeding the video had all the audio tracks synchronized. There were something like six screens with different things on them. And then all the videos were synchronized. We had to do a lot of research to make that happen. That was a big year!

"The access to cultural music through sampling and computer music is awesome. To take some Turkish material and send it to a musician in Japan—that's magical to me."

Amy X Neuburg

www.isproductions.com/amy

Amy X Neuburg tours the country performing her "avant-cabaret" works for voice, electronic percussion, and live looping and processing. She also composes for dance and visual media. The *Village Voice* called her "far more musical than Laurie Anderson"; the *San Francisco Classical Voice* said she's "nothing less than brilliant." Neuburg has performed at the Other Minds and Bang on a Can festivals, toured internationally with Robert Ashley's operas, composed for the cult-hit Web animation *Piki & Poko in Starland,* and fronted the band Amy X Neuburg & Men. In 2004, she released her fourth CD, *Residue,* on Other Minds Records.

One of your songs starts with your brushing your teeth into the mic and forming a rhythmic loop out of that, which you then sing over.

"Experiencing my music is really all about seeing a live performance, because watching me build up the loops in real time and hit drum pads and deliver my songs theatrically is how my music was designed."

It's called "Every Little Stain." It's about brushing a person out of my brain. [*Laughs.*] In my live shows, I try to keep a chatty, informal feel. I blab at the audience and invite them to ask questions, which seems to relax everybody without them taking me any less seriously.

In fact, this has become a whole stage persona I've inadvertently built up over the years—intense and professional interspersed with slightly inept and self-deprecating. It seems to work. People often tell me they love the parts in which something goes wrong technically and I make jokes about it, which seems to happen on a regular basis. In fact, after my last show a friend overheard someone saying, "She always includes a part where things go wrong; it's part of her schtick." Well, it's not, but I was tickled by the comment.

I've just gotten used to things going wrong and having the confidence that eventually they'll go right. I've never had anything as bad as a piece of equipment crashing and ending the show. But I've had a *song* that doesn't work, and I've simply had to go to the next song.

Or often I'll hit the wrong pad, or I'll hit a pad too many times in a row. Instead of stopping a loop, I'll accidentally start overdubbing again, so whatever I say gets into the loop—that kind of thing. Either you just go with it, or you stop the song and start over, or you turn it into something else. I just try not to let it bother me too much, and I think that relaxes the audience and allows them to just enjoy the process.

Hear Amy X Neuburg's music and see her performance video on the disc.

I've even had people come up and tell me, "It's nice to see you make mistakes because it lets us know that you're human." And I'm like, "Okay . . . I didn't know that was up for questioning, but [*laughs*] it's nice to hear that."

Do you think that comment comes up because they're at a looping festival and expect to be grooving on the technology?

No, I think it's just that they see what they might perceive as perfection, because my songs are very tightly composed; I'm not just screwing around and seeing what happens. I've got everything under control, so it's nice when things go bit awry and they can say, "Oh, look—things are out of control! Ooh! What's going to happen next?" That adds an element of entertainment or excitement to it. And that's what they mean by "It's nice to see that you're human."

Professor X

Perhaps the most inspiring teacher I've had was composer Conrad Cummings (www.conradcummings.com), who specializes in modern opera and electronically enhanced chamber music. When I asked him who was doing the most interesting high-tech vocal music these days, he cited Amy X Neuburg, not realizing I'd already interviewed her—or that she and I actually met in his Music Technology 101 class at the Oberlin Conservatory. (Cummings now teaches at Juilliard.) I asked him to reflect on her work.—David Battino

"Some singers lean forward when they need to get close to you," Cummings wrote. "Some step back, because what they've got to deliver is going to come at you like a major-league pitch, and they need some room to wind up. That's Amy. Her voice is amazing: complete technical freedom through a two-octave range, effortless vocal production, perfectly smooth melding of registers as she moves up and down through it. How often do you find that in a singer who is free of every affectation associated with classical voice training? I think I could list such singers on one hand. It's daunting how Amy deploys her realtime sampling, with her red drumsticks flailing on MIDI pads. Her intonation is so perfect that she can effortlessly assemble a six-voice counterpoint with herself in harmonies of celestial purity—and then smash through it with something monstrous."

Marty O'Donnell

www.bungie.net

Marty O'Donnell is the audio director for Bungie Studios at Microsoft, where he produced the sound and music for the revered Xbox games *Halo* and *Halo 2*. His work on *Halo* received numerous awards, including Best Soundtrack of 2002 from *Rolling Stone*. O'Donnell also produced the sound design, foley, and final mixes for Cyan's *Riven: the Sequel to Myst,* and all the original music, voices, and sound design for Bungie's award-winning *Myth: The Fallen Lords.* He has a Masters degree in composition from USC, and has also written and produced scores for TV, radio, film, and advertising, including the Flintstones Vitamins jingle.

 Hear Marty's Halo *music on the disc.*

As a game composer, you have a unique advantage in that you can use both sound effects and music to underscore your scenes.

Right. Have you heard my quote on that? [*Laughs.*] "Sound makes it real and music makes you feel." It's corny, but it really is true. Especially in games or animations, really good sound design brings it completely to life. But all that means is that it's now a living thing. It doesn't necessarily tell you if you're supposed to feel happy, or sad, or scared.

What would happen if you tried reversing those roles?

I'm not sure exactly how I'd do it, because people always have an emotional response to music. But sound design actually is much more powerful than just realism. You can *easily* use sound to make people feel something.

That's something I learned when I was doing music for TV and film. I would go to the final mix and there would be some sound editor there who had already scored the same scene with sound design. And his sound was so great you could play the scene *without* any music. So suddenly we were competing for space.

Or even competing for different emotions.

Exactly. So I didn't want to be just the music guy. I wanted to be able to accentuate one event with a reversed scream and a crashing gate, and the next event with a string swell and a cymbal hit. When I started doing that in commercials and film, it was a lot more creatively challenging. So when I saw the game industry open up to better production, I was hoping to have control over the whole audio space.

Now that you have both sound effects and music at your disposal, what conflicts arise in your mind as you analyze a scene and decide what it needs?

Interesting question. Certain things are decided for you. Most of the time, you know that you're going to have to make something feel real, so that calls for sound effects. But there's a shooting game called [Sega] *Rez* in which almost all of the sound effects are musical. When you're watching somebody play it, you're like, "Yeah, that's kind of cool." But when you're playing it yourself, it really comes alive, because everything you're doing has an instant musical feedback. It's *really* cool.

"One of the things we did in *Halo* was make the ambient sound fill all 360 degrees. Sound design is amazing in 5.1."

And I just was playing [Nintendo] *Zelda*, which produces musical hits that go up the scale as you keep hitting somebody with a sword. I have to say I'm pretty impressed with how that works. [*Laughs.*] There is a sword sound in there, but also the harmonic structures build up until the final killing blow, which goes V–I: dominant-tonic. It's pretty funny.

I remember [Academy Award-winning sound designer] Randy Thom saying that the most effective sound design comes from the main character's perspective.

Exactly. And that's why we've been able to do much more creative stuff with game sound design in 5.1 than most movies do—because most movies are not shot in first-person perspective. That's actually something a sound designer has to decide all the time. Is this sound coming from the hero's position or the camera's position? And if it's coming from the camera's position, who's *that*? The cameraman?

In *Halo,* you're looking out of the character's eyes, so I felt you should be hearing out of his ears. If a rocket is being launched from the left in front of you and it whizzes over your head and explodes behind you, that's the way it should *sound.* And if, while that rocket is traveling, you turn and run away, then the sound should change to match that. But I don't want the music and the ambience to spin around your head as you turn around. We actually tried that and it was almost nauseating.

Dave O'Neal

www.8legged.com

Dave O'Neal's do-it-yourself approach to digital music is epitomized by his *Erratica* album (1997), which he produced entirely on a woefully underpowered desktop computer, documenting the process in a popular series of articles for *Music & Computers* magazine. After several years as a creative audio programmer at video game behemoth Electronic Arts, O'Neal co-founded 8Legged Entertainment to create interactive cartoons. 8Legged's *Deep Fried, Live!* is the Web's only cooking show hosted by an octopus.

Tako the octopus chef bakes some dangerous cookies in *Deep Fried, Live!*, with sounds, music, and programming by Dave O'Neal.

The sounds and music in Deep Fried, Live! *are really fun. How did working in Macromedia Flash affect your composition process?*

What I found really liberating was being able to compose the animation and the music at the same time, which you never get to do in live action. For the cookie episode, Rob [De-Borde, writer/animator] gave me the scene where he had the giant, robotic KitchenAid mixer menacing Tako. It was really interesting the way Rob put it together. But I said, "I hate to be obnoxious, but the music *has* to be what carries this scene. And that just does not fit rhythmically."

So I cut a couple of the animation pieces around what I was doing, and he just flipped: "Yes! That's what I was thinking." I said, "Well, you could have *drawn* it that way." [*Laughs.*]

When the mixer looms up there's a bombastic choral sound. Was that from a sample CD?

No, that was all composed. I sampled three single notes from a choral tune and processed them a bit. And then I threw in a plethora of other things. You've got synth string lines and a couple of big percussion notes. There's actually a little heavy-metal loop in there, pitch-shifted way down.

So I was using other people's notes, but I built my own chords out of them, which is really cool when you have a sample of a fourth interval. *Man,* is that fun to stack! You keep the root, so people perceive it as human voices. But then you add these whacked-out, pitch-shifted harmonies. And since people hear the main voice, they picture these little Munchkins singing and it becomes believable. You can stack up huge chords that way really easily.

What other unexpected sounds do you like to throw into a mix?

I *love* ambience. One of the best things I ever did was back when I was at EA, for *Future Cop.* One day I went on one of those little pedestrian ramps that goes over the freeway. I recorded a

"Humor is juxtaposing incongruous concepts that somehow have a relationship."

bunch of cars coming towards me and going away. So you get the positive Doppler and then you get the negative Doppler.

I stacked that together, alternating positive and negative Doppler, and I had this total eerie *breathing* sound. It's really subtle. You're able to layer everything on top of it and it just hides the vacuum of [*dorky voice*] "computer music." It gave it such an organic feel— but an eerie organic feel because it wasn't a person breathing. It was cars.

There's no such thing as bad noise, just inappropriately placed noise. I actually took a naked quarter-inch plug and ran it around my computer screen. You pick up a lot of the electromagnetic noise; it's like when you hold onto a guitar cord, only more. That can be really effective when you're trying to create ambience; just put it through a little reverb. Although it's out of context, you still recognize it.

See two full episodes of Deep Fried, Live! on the disc.

If you didn't *want someone to feel comfortable, would you simply insert a frightening sound?*

Actually, *no* sound. Make things totally dry. Trent Reznor does that a lot. And one of the classic examples is Pink Floyd's "Money": You've got that screaming sax solo, the reverb's everywhere, then—*pop!*—totally dry. It has such a profound effect.

[*Laughs.*] One of my songs on the *Future Cop* soundtrack was actually written up as a bug by the game tester. This is when [BIAS] Peak first came out and they had that Rappify feature that sounded like you were running a turntable with a bunch of dust underneath it. So I started out with this obnoxious little bass line that I totally munged up. Then everything else comes in so it's got this total groove going on top of it. And one of the testers wrote, "The music sounds like it's falling apart at the beginning."

Alan Parsons

www.alanparsonsmusic.com

Best known for masterminding the conceptual, lushly synthesized Alan Parsons Project albums, this artist, producer, and engineer was one of the first to transform the recording studio into a musical instrument. Parsons worked on both the Beatles' 1969 masterpiece *Abbey Road* and Pink Floyd's legendary *Dark Side of the Moon*. (Although he's credited simply as engineer, Parsons contributed signature compositional elements such as the footsteps in "On the Run" and the clocks in "Time.") As we did this interview, Parsons was working on a new solo album featuring the Crystal Method and Pink Floyd guitarist David Gilmour.

How are you using hard disk recording on your new album?

Well, it's the only medium I'm using; I haven't been near a tape machine. I started the album thinking that I would feel more comfortable backing up to tape, because I certainly used to feel that it's not *real* audio unless it's recorded on some kind of linear format.

I've changed my tune a bit since committing to hard disk recording, but I'm really fussy about backing up at every stage. Ever since I heard a story about the Beach Boys losing a load of priceless master tapes in a fire, I've been very careful to do backups and take them somewhere else. I have a whole bunch of CDs in a safe-deposit box in my bank.

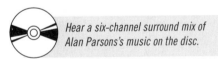
Hear a six-channel surround mix of Alan Parsons's music on the disc.

This album is a series of collaborations. For the track I did with the Crystal Method, I asked them to give me a backup even though it was in Digital Performer. Since I'm using [Steinberg] Nuendo, I can't actually *do* anything with it, but just holding a backup in my hand makes me feel better.

How are computer tools affecting your composition process?

It depends how you define composition these days. On just about everything I've been doing on this electronica record, just the click of a mouse can change the composition in a matter of a microsecond. I mean, it's not as if I sat down at a piano and wrote a verse and then wrote a chorus and then wrote a lyric. [*Laughs.*] It's just not the same way of doing things. The composition comes alive *through* the technology and through the way that you manipulate sounds and the way you overlay things.

You just think in a nonlinear fashion. Nearly everybody in the electronic genre is looping stuff—taking four bars, making it recycle, and adding stuff. And then it's on to the next thing, and let's start taking things away and adding other things. You don't think in terms of structure until almost the last minute.

In dance music, it's important just to keep the build happening. Then, when you've *reached* a climax, you *have* to take things away. And the usual way of doing that is to take it down to almost nothing and then build it back up.

That fine line between repetition and boredom is interesting.

[*Laughs.*] True. I was there in one of the earliest bands to take repetition into an art form: Pink Floyd. And they were very good at it. They taught me a lot about the power of repetition.

"MP3 files *do not* sound good. Period. End of story. And the fact that the public has taken to MP3 in such a big way [when] we've now got SACD and DVD-A, which *do* sound good . . . that's so sad."

What are some other lessons you learned from Pink Floyd?

The power of experimentation, and the determination that there is always a better sound around the corner by experimenting. When I first started working with them, they pushed me very hard. They would imply that things weren't sounding good and that I would have to work hard to make them sound better. But I'm pleased to say that pressure kind of went away, because we started to work well as a team and we were all striving to achieve the same thing, which was a great record.

Speaking of which, your new record should be in the mixing stage soon.

I'm pleased to say that, to a large extent, I'm going to avoid the mix process, because I set good levels as I went along. I've always looked upon mixing as a bit of a formality. [*Laughs.*] I remember on one album I did a rough mix, just a monitor mix or something, and then I spent an entire day and a half doing a precision mix. And then I played the two mixes side by side a couple days later and it was almost impossible to tell the difference between the two. [*Laughs.*] So I think the *soul* of a recording happens when it's made, not when it's mixed.

Jeff Patterson

www.visiblepath.com, www.mugly.com

Jeff Patterson was the co-founder and chief technical officer of the Internet Underground Music Archive (IUMA), the world's first online digital music distribution service. (In a CNN profile of the company in 1993, the reporter had to explain what the Internet *was*.) Patterson started IUMA in his dorm room to publicize the music of his band, the Ugly Mugs, and grew it into the premier forum for independent musicians. In 2001, he was awarded the New York Music Festival's lifetime achievement award. Currently, Patterson is CTO and co-founder of Visible Path, overseeing prototyping of new applications for social networking. He also wrote *Audio on the Web*.

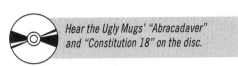
Hear the Ugly Mugs' "Abracadaver" and "Constitution 18" on the disc.

After shaping the online music landscape for almost a decade, you finally walked away from the business. What would it take to bring you back?

[*Laughs.*] That's a good question. I think it would be for the backlash to die down a bit. There's this feeling—especially on the independent music sites—that the artists all want something that the sites aren't providing. And the sites don't want to charge money because everyone else is free. The sites are giving out something for free, and the artists want something solid and reliable, and those two aren't going together very well. So the sites are trying to get out of that hole by using overbearing techniques like pop-up advertising, which only gets the artists to complain more.

People just need to have their expectations reset and all the hype just needs to chill for a little bit. [*Laughs.*] I think it will be possible to come back with a real offering for independent musicians on the Internet. But it won't be this free Web-hosting/serve-up-your-MP3s thing.

I think there are a lot of online collaboration services that could be useful to musicians, whether it's organizing gigs and tours or creating critical mass to get discounts. But I don't see many people organizing them into a unified community.

I've seen a lot of artists get frustrated with the online services and then decide they're going to create their own site. Because "How hard could it be?" [*Laughs.*] Just create a server to host some music and then create a few Perl scripts. But all the grassroots ones like that are usually gone within six months because they don't take support and balance issues into account—and because nobody goes there. [*Laughs.*] I hope I'm not sounding too bitter.

Actually, I've been talking to record company executives lately, and they're definitely on edge.

Yeah, that's the thing. It doesn't seem like a realistic solution has been proposed for digital audio distribution. And it's not something that can come from some little guy, because it's not going to be accepted by the majors. So that's what's been frustrating for me—feeling that, when it comes down to it, I've just got to wait and see what we can play with as an industry.

"I've heard independent bands say they can get their music out through file-sharing applications, but I don't think that's the case, because no one's actually looking for them there."

That's one of the things that's jaded me bit—the fact that ten years ago, Rob Lord and I thought, "Wow, this is going to change things in the next three years. Everyone's going to be distributing music online." We talked with Warner Bros. and Geffen in '94, and we thought, "Wow, they're *on* it. They're going to get it. This is really cool!" And ten years later, we're no closer to actually having a realistic solution in place. [*Laughs.*] I'm feeling like an old man now.

What do you wish you'd done differently at IUMA?

I guess we were too optimistic because the technology was so interesting and the idea of distributing music over the Internet was so powerful. We thought that it would just naturally catch on and we could help guide it with a couple pushes here and there.

We spent a lot of our time in the early years devising these licensing schemes with authentication servers—and this was in '94, '95, when no one was actually on the Net. But we were like, "Well, when they *come*, it needs to be ready." But no one took it seriously, that it was going to be there. So things like that I wish we had been more vocal about.

But I don't think it was possible to understand what we were getting into, because in '93 the Internet wasn't a commercial place; it was all educational. So we were part of that culture and we were playing in that arena. But it was definitely fun.

Eric Persing

www.spectrasonics.net

Eric Persing is the founder and creative director of Spectrasonics, which reviewers have called the Rolls-Royce of sample developers. The company also makes award-winning virtual instruments, including Atmosphere, Stylus, and Trilogy. Persing has served as the chief sound designer for Roland Corporation since 1984, creating the key sounds for many popular Roland synthesizers and samplers. As a studio musician, producer, composer, and arranger, he has contributed to numerous Grammy Award–winning albums and Academy Award–winning film scores.

As a sound designer, you must always be listening for distinctive raw sounds to sample. You've said the Minimoog and Yamaha CS80 are synthesizers that just work *every time. On the software side, would you say U&I MetaSynth is one of those limitless instruments?*

Oh, definitely. That's a program I feel I will never get to the bottom of. I'm sure in 30 or 40 years I'll still be using it and I'll still be learning, because the language is so *foreign.* [*MetaSynth transforms pictures into sound.*]

Hear examples of Eric Persing's sound design and Groove Control technology on the disc.

Basically what I'm trying to do with it is to build a vocabulary. That's what I try to do with each instrument I get, or each device, or each plug-in. I try to build a vocabulary of what that is good for. And what's wonderful is when you can find an instrument that has this really large vocabulary that is all usable. There are very few instruments like that.

There are some instruments that always work for certain things, like the Juno-X from reFX [www.refx.net]. That's a very inexpensive synth, and it has almost no controls. But for the types of sounds that it does, these real aggressive techno sounds, it's *amazing.*

Sometimes you can waste a lot of time on instruments that don't have a lot of personality, but have a lot of parameters. You're thinking that the magic is in the parameters. But it's really *not.* I feel like an instrument either has some magic in it or not. Of course, with a sampler, it's a different story because the magic comes from you. And then hopefully it's got good filters and modulation options. But in terms of instruments that actually create a sound, most of the time, to me they either have it or they don't.

Is that something you can tell right away?

Yeah, right away. Basically every synthesizer can make at least one really good sound. I have *no doubt* about that. So I don't ever say, "Well that instrument's just junk. I'll never go back to that." I try to keep my mind open about it, because invariably when I shut my mind to one particular approach or one sound, somebody will come along later and do something with that instrument that's amazing.

But yeah, generally I do have a visceral reaction one way or another. I can tell within the first minute of trying something whether it's cool or not. I won't pass *judgment* at that point, but that first impression is definitely worth trusting.

I feel the same way about software. I was lucky enough to be one of the first people to find out about Absynth when it was a shareware program, before it was taken over by Native Instruments. And the *first* sound I heard, it was like, "This is *unbelievable.* There's a very musical person behind this." I could sense that right away. And I still have the same feeling whenever I go to it.

"The CS80 [pictured] is a great instrument for pads, string sounds, and leads. But sometimes I'll use it for drums. You end up with something really fresh because you're using something in a way it wasn't intended."

That feeling is what drives me; that's what I want to create in our instruments and in our work. I think a *lot* of instruments aren't made with that intention. A lot of instruments are made from a "Well, gee, what can we do with code?" approach.

Many times I've seen a software guy make a particular algorithm that sounds really good, whereas another algorithm doesn't. And the vast majority of people writing music software can't tell the difference. They are *so* grateful when you tell them, "This filter sucks; this one sounds *great.*" I would say 90 percent, if not higher, of music software coding guys can't tell the difference. They're coming at it from a *completely* different point of view.

I think synthesizer enthusiasts would be surprised if they met many of the people who make these software codes—of how random it is. I mean, the man who made the [Roland] 808 and the 303 and the 909 *still* doesn't want to take credit for it, because he feels they were a failure. It wasn't what he intended them to be. [*Laughs.*]

Roger Powell

www.rogerpowell.com

R oger Powell began programming analog synthesizers for commercials in the late '60s. He then helped design and promote ARP synthesizers, which became the basis for his first solo album, *Cosmic Furnace* (1973). He was keyboardist and synthesist for Todd Rundgren's Utopia, recording ten albums with the band. In 1983, Powell wrote one of the first MIDI sequencers, Texture, used by many top musicians including Jan Hammer and Stevie Wonder. He also wrote audio software for WaveFrame and Silicon Graphics. He is now audio technical lead for Final Cut Pro at Apple Computer.

You've been deep into both computer music and analog synthesizers like the Moog for decades. How do they compare?

Well, I view the Moog as a musical instrument. I'm still having a hard time viewing the computer as a musical instrument because it's meant to emulate everything in a studio, including musical instruments. I find myself feeling the most creative when I just sit down at the piano. That technology has frozen. You're not fighting with something you feel is potentially not up to date and therefore not giving you everything that you would need.

In fact, I've now put together a new analog synthesizer, a Synthesis Technology MOTM [www.synthtech.com]. It has 16 modules or so and I soldered most of them together myself. When I built the first module, an oscillator, I was meticulous. It took me a whole day. And then for about three days, I did nothing but just turn the knob and listen to the sounds. It was like I'd found this old friend again. A lot of that is probably nostalgia, because I've always been pushing computers as assistants to making music.

Hear two tracks from Roger Powell's classic Air Pocket *and* Cosmic Furnace *albums— plus unreleased new material—on the disc.*

But it was magical to realize that you can go out and buy an amazing computer for fifteen hundred bucks and spit out all kinds of noise, but there still is some magic associated with the hands-on experience of (a) building something, and (b) that type of technology, which I view as almost mechanical.

Ironically, computers enabled you to recover your one-of-a-kind analog synth from thieves. What was that story?

Well, it was this huge synthesizer with this custom remote keyboard that I designed. Bob Moog actually hand-built some of the components. We [Utopia] were set up to play two nights someplace and we came in the second night and the keyboard had been stolen.

This was like 1976, so whoever stole the keyboard probably thought it was a home organ. And then they got home and realized that this huge, honking old military Centronics connector was not going to plug into their hi-fi system.

A young Roger Powell with Bob Moog: "I still consider myself a hardcore audio person who is trying to educate the video community about the power of sound."

The synthesizers themselves went through hell. They had whipped cream sprayed on them by the roadies, who thought they were doing a marvelous joke, not realizing that you were supposed to use shaving cream because it washes off. But no—it was whipping cream with [*disgustedly*] *sugar* and everything.

Then we were doing rehearsals in a loft and there was a huge downpour. When we came in the next day, the roof had collapsed and there was two inches of water in the bottoms of the synthesizer cabinets. So I poured that out, got a hair dryer, dried them out, and they still worked.

And just when you think everything is going okay, we had a warehouse fire and all of that stuff burned up.

So then, 26 years later, I get an e-mail from somebody saying, "Hey, take a look at this eBay item." And I knew instantly it was my keyboard. Of course, I had to prove it to the guy. It turns out he was *younger* than the keyboard, so he didn't steal it. But I had to ransom it back. I had to pay five hundred bucks.

And I went through this whole emotional thing like, "Why do I *care* about this? I have nothing to connect it to. It's all beat up. It's *big* and ugly. I've got no place to put it." But ultimately I was like, "You know what? I do have some nostalgia about it." Not the least being it's the only relic that was *left*. The irony is that because it got stolen, it survived. It's actually sitting in my office now.

The prodigal keyboard.

But yeah—it's got big knobs. It's very tactile. That's generally the point I was making about computers. A computer you generally think of as a mirror of your brain, whereas a musical instrument is something that is an extension of your physical and mental energy. There's no computer I've ever operated that I wanted to hug.

Propellerhead Software
(Ernst Nathorst-Böös & Tage Widsell)
www.propellerheads.se

Ernst Nathorst-Böös is the co-founder and CEO of Propellerhead Software, which made the first successful software musical instrument, ReBirth, and followed that with the first successful software studio, Reason. Nathorst-Böös has also worked as a musician, journalist, technical writer, and instrument importer. Tage Widsell joined Propellerhead as the Webmaster and tech support person in 1998 and is now the marketing director. He has a background as a "multi-disciplined university dropout" and naval officer. Widsell found his way to the company through playing music at the club where the Propellerhead crew hung out after work.

Ernst Nathorst-Böös: "I think there are some giant leaps we can take with just the technology we have today—especially in terms of getting people into the process of using this stuff and helping them achieve a good result."

ReBirth was a breakthrough in computer music. Not only did it deliver classic sounds in a fun, affordable package, it spawned a huge community of enthusiastic users. I gather that you were as surprised as anyone by its success.

Ernst Nathorst-Böös: Well, when we did ReBirth, our thought was to do a [Roland TB-]303 [bass synth] emulator. We wanted to do a compact product, but we also needed to get it out quickly. Just doing a 303 wasn't enough, so we did *two* 303s and a drum machine and effects, and we had a little techno studio. But as we saw how people were actually using the program, we realized that there was much more to it than simply recreating hardware instruments in software. It was a way for people who didn't know much about music to get in and program their own stuff. And when it played back, it had the same sound they would hear in the club when they went down on Saturday.

We didn't anticipate that. The second thing that happened was the song-sharing on the Internet. People started collaborating and doing remixes of their songs, and it became this huge culture. And then the mods came, when people started modifying the program with their own skins and samples.

Did you anticipate the mods?

Ernst Nathorst-Böös: No, no, no. Someone just put new resources into the program, and we said, "*Eeew . . .* great idea, but we can't have them redistribute our application in a new format." So we put the mod technology into the program as quickly as we could to accommodate that culture—which we thought was great—without jeopardizing the integrity of the program.

Tage Widsell: "The really successful online sharing takes place when people can get some kind of feeback. It's an ego thing."

ReBirth modding was a milestone in the evolution of virtual instruments. Suddenly computer musicians were able to personalize their instruments, the way someone might repaint a guitar. Were there any mods that surprised you?

Tage Widsell: What was most surprising was the *number* of them, and the amount of work people put into not just getting the sounds they wanted, but also the looks—how they wanted it to feel. We're constantly stunned by the quality.

Another unanticipated development was that people started doing completely modified sound sets. Quite a few of the ReBirth songs that people uploaded didn't have 303 patterns in them at all. Or if they did, it was just as a background, a little bass thing.

ReBirth was a way to make music that people really liked. And the limitations in the application became a fantastic challenge to a lot of people. They really wanted to make the most of it.

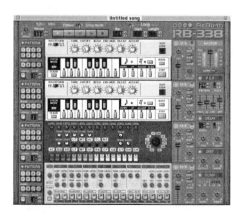

ReBirth and the unauthorized LinnDrum mod, which contains different drum samples.

Often limitations inspire the most creative art, don't they?

Ernst Nathorst-Böös: Absolutely. I think Hegel said freedom is understanding the importance of limitations. We're very much into that idea when we design things. In Propellerhead, flexibility's a bit of a four-letter word. Sometimes flexibility in design is simply someone not daring to put their foot down and say, "We really believe *this* is the best way." So we're trying to do that as much as we can.

Tage Widsell: Someone said that the most flexible software synthesizer would be a C++ compiler. Then you'd have *no* limits. [*Laughs.*]

Still, it seems like you give people quite a few options, especially in the newer versions of Reason.

Ernst Nathorst-Böös: Yeah. Because we're gear junkies. We keep doing all these products because we want them for ourselves. That's what this whole game is about: buying a 19-inch rack and trying to fill it up with as much stuff as you can.

Have you been surprised by the way people use Reason?

Tage Widsell: Not really the *way* it's being used, but we're amazed with how fantastic it can sound. It sometimes sounds like a track has already gone through recording, mixing, mastering, and distribution. It sounds like something you'd buy. The quality of amateur work really can be stunning.

Scotch Ralston

www.scotchralston.com

When Scotch Ralston was growing up, his grandpa gave him a cassette tape recorder as a Christmas present and he proceeded to record everything and everybody. When he eventually used his brother's tape recorder in conjunction with his own and stumbled upon the delay effect, he knew that sound would be his life's work. Scotch has worked with the band 311 as a producer, engineer, mixer, and editor since 1993's *Music*. He has also engineered for Rick James and served as a consulting producer for GarageBand.com, the independent musicians' community site.

What did you learn from working with GarageBand.com?

One thing I learned is that it's neat just to have direct access to an audience with no middleman, no one in between to say, "This sucks," or "No one is going to like this." You can go to GarageBand and hear everything from the raw stuff that people just created to finished songs. Sometimes you can hear some pretty interesting ideas. I've got a little playlist of people's demos that I listen to quite a bit.

Do you find that the GarageBand members support each other?

People are fairly supportive. You have to review a certain number of songs before you can post your own music, and I always try to give a fair critique as well as tips or suggestions. I've posted some music on there, and the reviews have seemed pretty fair. No one just said, "You suck. Quit."

Now that everyone's got their own little Pro Tools setup, how can artists make their music stand out sonically?

Even though you can record something and then tweak it to death, I think people still need to pay attention to the actual

"Use the technology in a really different way, like Aphex Twin. When I heard his stuff, I was like, 'Man—that's technology at its finest.' He just maxes out all of his tools, and it creates a very interesting sound."

recording process. It's still pretty important to have a good microphone and a good mic pre [preamplifier], and try to get a recording that's as close to the final sound you want as you can get. Because I've found that in the digital domain, the more you process something, the more you lose. It starts to sound kind of fuzzy after a while.

Distortion guitars, vocals, and parts like that seem to be fine in the digital domain. But if possible, I still prefer to record drums and bass on analog tape. There's just something more rich-sounding about the low end and the transients.

What tips would you give to artists who are recording at home in preparation for bringing their tracks into a pro studio for overdubbing or mixing?

Try to keep it as simple as possible, but try to get separation on as many instruments as possible. And on vocals, try to have some alternate takes just in case what *you* feel is good isn't good.

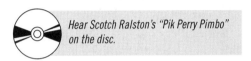
Hear Scotch Ralston's "Pik Perry Pimbo" on the disc.

Some people who aren't familiar with the process will record a track of stereo drums and then when it comes to the mix they'll go, "Can you make the snare brighter or the kick sound better?" Well, no. Sometimes you can tweak the stereo drum mix to be good enough. And sometimes you have to go in and trigger kicks and snares and replace it all. And that's always a drag.

It takes you away from the creative side, doesn't it?

Yeah. And that's another thing I've noticed about the Pro Tools era: You're in the studio and for the longest time it was always the lights were dim, there were no windows anywhere, and you could just close your eyes and *listen*. And now I find that everyone's huddled around the monitor, watching the music go by. And you know how sometimes if you are deprived of one sense it makes your other senses stronger? I feel like since people are *watching* everything, sometimes it's not as much of an *audio* experience.

I've noticed that with a lot of performers. When they see their performance on the screen and there's a grid behind it that represents the bars and beats, they'll be like, "Oh man, I'm late right there. My kick drum's really early right here." If you *didn't* see it, you wouldn't really hear it. I've gotten caught a couple of times when the guy was like, "I really want to do this part over, because look how far off the snare is there." You get a different type of session now that everyone can see the music.

It's funny—I swear to God I thought of digital recording first. In '85 I had an idea; I called it the Track Shooter. I was working on my 4-track cassette recorder, and I accidentally recorded something at the end of the tape that I thought, "Man, this would sound perfect in this song at the beginning. There has *got* to be a way that you can record things and then just tell them when to start." And then years later, there it is.

Phil Ramone

www.philramone.com

Phil Ramone, the "Pope of Pop," is one of the most respected and influential producers in the world. (The groundbreaking punk band the Ramones reportedly named themselves after him.) He has won nine Grammy Awards and an Emmy. A hands-on technology pioneer, Ramone produced the first live digital recording, the first CD (Billy Joel's *52nd Street*), and the first pop DVD, *Dave Grusin Presents West Side Story*. Quincy Jones credits Ramone for introducing him to stereo. Ramone also pioneered remote collaboration, recording Frank Sinatra's hit albums *Duets I* and *Duets II* from different locations in real time.

"No longer do you make a demo as you did 15 years ago—a couple of guitars, a bass, and drums. You now really have to *produce* a demo so that most of the elements can be used again or be the final usage."

Digital audio has gone through so many format changes. There must be real concern among people who are producing timeless records about how their music will be heard in the future.

And be able to be *recalled* [*that is, how future engineers will reload the original multitrack recordings and mixdown settings into a computer.*] I've just been through an interesting conundrum on a picture called *Moulin Rouge* that was made a few years ago. We needed to do something to one of the tracks, and [*laughs regretfully*] there were pieces all over the world. Nobody had thought to *maybe* just dump it onto one old-fashioned piece of tape and store it at Fox Studios.

I encourage Pro Tools, and Nuendo, and any other format that comes along to create a platform that lets us all talk to each other, because at the end of the day, we are only the *transporter* of music. I just started a record in L.A.; took a file to Sydney, Australia; did ten days in Sydney; came back to New York; added some elements; then came to the house and added synths and some guitar work. Next the tapes will end up in London, where we'll do some overdubbing. And then we'll probably mix it in New York. In any of those processes, one of the engineers might like to work in a different way.

And that's okay, provided there is a home base. Fifty years from now, people will want to look at the work of the legends of this business, like George Massenburg, Elliot Scheiner, and Al Schmitt, and they *should* be able to look at it. A lot of us are experiencing it now, because works that we did in the '70s and '80s are being considered for 5.1 DVD or DVD-Audio, and, amazingly enough [*laughs*], bookkeeping in those days was much more strict. Your editing notes had to be very precise, and you wrote them out. Today, the guy assisting could leave you in a shambles unless you read every note he writes into the computer. I always beg them to print it out.

You must get a lot of tracks that start out in personal studios. What advice do you give artists to make sure the transfer goes smoothly as you bring those files into professional studios for overdubbing or mixing?

Well, the files and the words "professional studio" should be synonymous. When somebody sends me something, I tell them to back it up. Because things get lost. People have gotten into an interesting habit in which nothing gets erased; it just gets moved around. Often it gets lost on a hard disk, and they *still* believe they can recover it. And that's like reckless driving, you know? It's like the games you play on Xbox. [*Laughs.*] You drive the car as fast as you want, crash it into a wall, and—oh well, you didn't win that game. But you can't do that with music. At least, I don't recommend it.

Be more meticulous about what you think the best take is, so you don't have endless tracks. Have some kind of *form* to what you're doing. Committing to a good rough mix is probably the best advice I could ever give anybody. Just having endless 100 percent levels of all sounds on your digital meter means it has to come together somewhere. Why not have it come together then? Listen in perspective. Show us what *you* had in mind.

My biggest discussion with engineer/producers is when somebody says you have to use all the bits at all times. Well, if music were written that way, we'd all be playing at full triple-*forte* on every instrument. And it would have no nuance, no flavor.

I highly recommend that you go for the nuance. If a guy says, "I want to play this really soft" and the engineer says, "No, you gotta crank it up; I can't hear it," you have to think about what that means. I look at a lot of the stuff that comes in, and I say, "Well, okay . . . so they used all the bits. [*Laughs.*] Where's the music?"

Jim Reekes

www.reekes.net

A s chief audio architect at Kerbango, Jim Reekes was instrumental in designing the user interface and software architecture of the world's first stand-alone Internet radio, which won "Best of Show" at the Consumer Electronics Show. During his 12 years writing software at Apple Computer, Jim worked at every level of the operating system. As a member of the QuickTime team, he created Apple's high-profile audio technology architecture, earning two patents. Most recently, Reekes worked as VP of Products for Meeting Maker, driving the company's vision and strategy.

You created some of the classic Mac OS sounds. What are your thoughts on audible user interfaces and sonic "branding"?

I think those things are actually much more useful than people suspect. Somebody was calling them "earcons." It's like the Intel Inside logo or the NBC chime logo. I'm surprised more people aren't taking advantage of them. [*The NBC logo sound is actually trademarked. It consists of the notes G, E, and C because at the time the broadcaster was owned by General Electric Corp.*]

I just bought a Minolta digital camera, and you can choose the new electronic sounds or samples of the old mechanical camera. I chose the mechanical set, and it's really cool. It reminds me of TiVo. I *love* the sounds on my TiVo.

"I've seen too many consumer devices overburdened with the need to create or organize the content. That's where they mess up."

Beep Beep, Yeah

Until Jim Reekes created the lush Macintosh startup sound, most computers booted up with a pathetic beep. No wonder they took so long to catch on as musical instruments.

In an interview for *Revolution* magazine, Reekes told me about the origin of his sound, which he produced on a Korg Wavestation synthesizer. "There was this new line of Macs coming out called the Quadra series, and they were going to have much better-quality amplifiers," he explained. "I thought we should make a decent sound that people would hear when they turned the machine on. That was actually a ridiculously controversial issue. Then immediately after it came out, everyone wanted to make their own sounds for every new machine. When Steve Jobs came back, he said, 'Let's go back to the one good one,' which happened to be the one I had made."

Not content to sit by silently, Microsoft soon commissioned Brian Eno to design the Windows 95 startup sound and paid the Rolling Stones $5 million to license their song "Start Me Up."

Do they give you a different feeling about the product?

Definitely. When I try to do something it can't do, it makes a big tympani "*boing!*" Sometimes the screen doesn't update as fast as you want, so when you click something that's in progress, the TiVo plays a little chime so you know, "Oh, it got it." Another really good use of sound in a user interface is Danger Research's little Hiptop [PDA/phone].

So I find interface sounds very helpful. But it's really easy to make them annoying, which is why you want to get somebody artistic involved.

The Kerbango Internet radio.

What makes a good interface sound?

It needs to be non-intrusive yet informative. And that's the trick. You're not trying to spotlight the sound; the sound is trying to spotlight the action. You need an artist involved, but it should also be somebody who understands the technical issues, like how to squeeze sounds into really small files.

It's funny, because realism isn't the best guide. Think of those completely digitally generated spaceship scenes in *Babylon 5* that have lens flare in them. People just don't know what it is until it has those wrong artifacts. [*Laughs.*]

For another example, today's cameras are digital, so they don't make a sound. Yet the screenshot sound on the Mac is still the sample of my old Canon AE that's been in there since System 7. They were doing a new sound for OS X, but they found it wasn't recognizable unless it sounded like the old mechanical power winder.

Tease Tease Me

Jim Reekes has a sly sense of humor. After Apple Computer added music capabilities to the Mac, the Beatles' record company (Apple Corps) complained that having two musical Apples would confuse consumers. The Corps went to court and eventually squeezed $26 million out of the computer maker. But Reekes took revenge by creating an error sound he called Sosumi (pronounced "so sue me"), which is still inside Macs to this day. "My first choice was Let It Beep," he deadpans. "But I thought that was too obvious."

AIFF
Sosumi.aiff

Steve Reich

www.stevereich.com

alled "America's greatest living composer" by the *Village Voice*, Steve Reich has had a profound impact on modern classical and pop music. His early tape-loop pieces "Come Out" and "It's Gonna Rain" revealed the utter beauty in mechanically repeated sounds as they're allowed to drift apart and recombine. Reich later formed a virtuoso ensemble to play the phasing rhythms he'd discovered on machines. His Grammy Award–winning "Different Trains" paired the natural melodies of sampled speech with the Kronos Quartet's strings to haunting effect. Reich's latest opera, *Three Tales,* explores the physical, ethical, and religious impact of technology.

"People have said for many years that any sound can be music. It's *now possible.* Get out your sampler and let's see what you can do."

It's interesting how your early breakthroughs in sampling and looping have been echoed in current pop music, even to the point where people have remixed your work.

Well, in those days it wasn't called sampling; it was called tape recording. And loops were literally pieces of analog tape that were taped together at the ends. I discovered that technique in the late '60s. But I'm aware that those pieces have had quite an impact on a lot of the people in the DJ scene and I think that's *great.*

In a sense, my relationship to the pop world goes back to when I was a teenager and used to come down to Birdland, which was the big jazz club in those days, and hear Miles Davis and the drummer Kenny Clarke. If you cut to 1974, my ensemble was playing in London at Queen Elizabeth Hall, and after the concert, a guy comes up with long hair and lipstick and says, "How are you doing? I'm Brian Eno."

A couple of years later we were playing "Music for 18 Musicians" in Berlin and David

Bowie was there. And I thought to myself, "You know, *this* is poetic justice. I was a kid sitting on a bar stool, listening to Miles Davis and Kenny Clarke, and now these guys are listening to *me*." And you know, that's the way the world *should* be. [*Laughs.*]

It was the same with the *Reich Remixed* album. In fact, even more so because DJ Spooky, and Coldcut, and all those people—I don't think a lot of them were *born* when "Come Out" was done back in the '60s. So it's very gratifying that it meant something to them and they wanted to get involved.

Congress recently extended the copyright limit so it will take far longer for works to fall into the public domain. As someone who's involved with sampling, what do you think of that?

I'm delighted to have copyrights extending, because I depend on written music to make a living. And if there were no copyrights, I would have to sell pencils or something, and survive on concert income, which is not that frequent.

Let's put it this way: In the early '90s, I was doing an interview with a British version of *Keyboard* magazine. And they asked me, "What do you think of the Orb?" And I said, "What's the orb?" So they gave me this CD, which had "Little Fluffy Clouds," which has about 30 seconds of "Electric Counterpoint" on it.

So I brought it home and I thought to myself, "My gosh. Bowie and Eno liked what was I doing, and it influenced them. But these guys are just *taking* it, lock, stock, and barrel." [*Laughs.*]

But I didn't *sue* them. Of course, at that time they weren't a very big act. And I guess the word went out that I wasn't going to do anything about it. Later on, the *Remixed* album happened, and *I* was the beneficiary of a lot of other people's work. So I think there's a line there. I think copyright *definitely* plays a role. And people who pretend it doesn't are just being foolish.

On the other hand, sampling itself is a gray area. *I* don't want to say how much James Brown should get for every "*Whaa!*" [*Laughs.*] There's a place to give stuff away or simply turn your head, and there's a place for saying, "*Hey*, man, you're *stealing*." And that line is hard to draw.

Who should *draw that line? It seems like you, as the original artist, would be the best judge.*

Well, I can draw it in a *certain* sense, and in another sense, I have a publisher, so I simply don't have a say. That's a difficult question. Fundamentally, artists own their own music, and if they choose to be generous, they should be allowed to *be* generous. And if they are very possessive about it, then they should be entitled to whatever fee is legally arrived at. But the laws are being rewritten and rethought, and this is going to take a while to shake out.

Ty Roberts

www.gracenote.com

Ty Roberts is one of the inventors of the enhanced CD (eCD) format, which adds CD-ROM multimedia to a standard audio CD. After founding eCD label ION, he produced a string of innovative discs, including Primus's *Tales from the Punchbowl*, the Residents' *Gingerbread Man*, and Todd Rundgren's *The Individualist*. Roberts joined Gracenote as chief technology strategist in 1998 after the company acquired ION. Gracenote develops music identification technologies such as CDDB, which automatically looks up CD track names, and Link, which enables CDs to unlock online bonuses such as private Web sites.

CD sales are withering and DVDs are the biggest consumer-electronic success in history. Instead of enhancing CDs, why not just shift everything to DVD?

I don't think you'll see the record companies shifting everything over to DVD because there's not yet a portable DVD player that's anywhere near the price of CD Walkmans. So I see them using DVD as a tool to add value to the CD. The thing that happened last week

See a scene from Gingerbread Man on the disc.

with 50 Cent putting a bonus DVD in the CD case and having 300,000 of them fly off the shelves, that's because consumers *perceived* it to be a great value.

This is one of my biggest issues with the recording industry: They've done *nothing* to improve the value of their products. If anything, they've diminished the value of their products in comparison to the competition, which is video games and movies and other things that kids can do with their money, like cell phones. So I do believe that there is some life in enhanced CD for extending the CD platform.

What's an enhanced-CD feature that would really open people's eyes to the possibilities?

What I would love to see put on enhanced CDs are assets that allow the fans to create an experience that goes with the music. Load that disc up with as much stuff as you can and see what the fans can make of it. Give them seed artwork and photos and weird sounds, and even the ability to mix in some of their own stuff.

You should see the alternate covers that fans make for *Dark Side of the Moon*. There are 32-page, high-res color files illustrating every song with amazing artwork that you can download, print out on your little Epson printer, fold up, and put into your jewel case. I hate to say it, but it's way cooler than the black cover with the little triangle.

Tools to do creative work are now in the hands of the masses all over the world. There are tons of people who know how to use those tools on computers and who have talent and passion. And those people could be unlocked to create stuff that other people could consume.

Ty Roberts says the design of Simple Star's EZ-DJ Plus points the way to better music applications.

Every movie needs a theater; every photo needs a frame. So my sense is that the frame for the music could be highly creative and even interactive, so that there's something to explore. Being able to provide some way for people to author the experience in that way would be revolutionary.

As an early example, look at the music-mixer product from Simple Star [EZ-DJ Plus; www.simplestar.com]. The mission of that company is that the *experience* should be the whole thing. The actual process is not the problem anymore; it's making it fun in a way that you'd want to show other people what you're doing. Can you turn the process of listening to music into something that's visual and interesting for the other people sitting in the room?

It's a personal goal of mine that over the next five to ten years I'm going to make that happen somehow. I'm perfectly positioned to do it right now; I have to find a way to make it make business sense, and I have to wait for the tools that make that possible to grow up around what we're doing. I do think it's coming. And when that *can* happen, I believe that will help solve a lot of the piracy problems. Because clearly you're not going to be able to control the audio, but you can very well control access to synchronized online content.

A very interesting thing is happening right now with Pearl Jam. They're putting MP3s of every show on their Web site within a day of the show. And if you buy access to that, then a high-quality, mastered CD version comes in the mail a month later. So they're doing their own bootlegs, essentially. And they're massively successful. So they're a band that's really starting to see the power of what people can do.

"We've actually taken every genre we've ever seen—it's something like 270 genres—and then mapped them as they relate to each other, with weighting."

Bob Rock

www.bruceallen.com/bob_rock.html

Starting out as a session musician and recording engineer, the aptly named Bob Rock has worked production magic with numerous heavy-hitting acts such as Bon Jovi, Mötley Crüe, Skid Row, and Metallica, even playing bass on that band's latest album, the No. 1 smash *St. Anger*. Under his guidance, Metallica's sales exploded from 2.5 million to 14 million copies of a single CD. Rock likes to mix it up between shaping younger bands and extending the range of more established bands. His credits also include Bryan Adams, Cher, the Cult, Loverboy, and Our Lady Peace.

You're using Fibre Channel hard drives now; that must give you an ungodly number of tracks.

*Un*believable. I mean, the Metallica album [*St. Anger*] couldn't have been done without it. I just love them. We had up to six hundred minutes of music on one *song*. And it was all *there*. At your fingertips. While we were working on the last drafts of the song, we could go back to the *conception* of the riff and take something from that and insert it. I mean, the possibilities—we kept *everything*. Every little note that was played with that song. There was *six hundred minutes* of 24-bit audio.

How do you keep track of that?

Notes. [*Laughs.*] Notes!

But talk about option anxiety: It must have been ridiculous trying to wade through all of that.

Well, you kind of don't think about it. We kept it all in one Pro Tools session, so we could

"I think what's really interesting about the reactions to *St. Anger* is that sonically, song structure-wise, in just about *every* way possible, this should not survive a *minute* in the business."

go back if we wanted to. And sometimes we did, but we just made notes of the most important thing, and we could find it. It's pretty easy, really. There were copies of every single edit; everything we did, we just copied it over to a new track. That way you never lose anything, and you can instantly go back and hear how it was. Those kinds of things are great.

But the point is that before we got into this, it was more about, "Okay, what are we going to do musically?" and then, "Oh, great. Here's the technology to make it easier." So in other words, it always *was* about the music and the simplicity of it. If you wanted to get complicated with things, then you could *really* lose your mind.

The whole approach to the album was one of, "This is a simple, back-to-basics thing, but we get to protect ourselves, and we get to experiment." For instance, when the songs were all written in the studio, for me to go out and play bass with the guys and throw down ten minutes of ideas, come in, and then piece together a song in four hours by printing sections and editing—you just couldn't do that before. It would take you *days* of editing and copying and God knows what. So it was *brilliant* to flesh out the best possible ideas.

So you found yourself flying sections around, trying different arrangements of A's and B's, and all that?

Yeah. A few people have gotten it on the *St. Anger* album: We *abused* Pro Tools. We used it almost like a pure artistic tool. We moved sections around and printed things, because everything was recorded live off the floor. Then we'd take a section and use that for a chorus or a verse—we could have taken a section that was recorded half a year later for the chorus, where the sounds are different, or at different levels. And we just cut 'em together.

You could never do that on an analog machine. In Pro Tools, we just change the level. Which is *amazing.* That's what I mean: We abused what Pro Tools does and what computer music does. But in that, there is an art form. And that's what we tried to emphasize: to throw away the rulebook about how everything should blend and should just go right into the next section. We just really cut *hard.* In a lot of cases, there's cymbal cutoffs, tom cutoffs, guitar sounds that go from two tracks to five tracks. And the only way you can make that work is in the confines of a computer.

Nile Rodgers

www.nilerodgers.com

"When I'm making music, I am just *impulsive*. I want to be able to have reliable backup. So in that regard, computers are *fantastic* for me."

Guitarist Nile Rodgers broke through in the disco/funk band Chic in 1977. Soon after, he and bandmate Bernard Edwards began producing chart-topping albums for other artists such as Sister Sledge and Diana Ross. In the '80s, Rodgers produced hits for the B-52s, David Bowie (including "China Girl" and "Let's Dance") and Duran Duran ("The Reflex"). He also produced albums for Eric Clapton, INXS, Madonna, and the Thompson Twins, and won *Billboard*'s "Top Producer in the World" award in 1996. In 2003, his company Sumthing Distribution released the world's first DVD game-soundtrack album in 5.1 surround sound.

What are the best things about working in the digital domain?

Convenience has become an incredibly powerful motivating tool. Ever since I started to record digitally—I think the first thing I did was with Peter Gabriel for the film called *Against All Odds* [1984]—I've never gone back. Because of the convenience, being able to do what I could do on those early Sony machines [the PCM-3324 multitrack digital tape recorders] was just amazing to me. It helped me make better records.

Because I had come from a two-inch, analog-tape world, I was known for cutting up tape. I was working on a record with Paul Simon once, and he went to lunch, and when he came back, he saw me cutting the two-inch tape—the master tape. And he was like [*high-pitched voice*], "What are you doing?! *Garraaagh!*" And I was going, "Man, I just wanted to see what it would *sound* like if we put the piano track backwards just for this one bar. So we've got to figure out *right where it is,* we've got to mark it right on the [play-back] heads. . . ."

I used to do stuff like that all the time. It was fun. And then, all of a sudden in the digital world, I didn't have to *destroy* anything. I could make *non-destructive* edits. I could change my *mind.* Holy cow. That was a dream. It was like finding the Holy Grail. "So you mean to tell me, that all of those things I did last night don't even mean anything today? I can change everything?" [*Laughs.*]

But you also made some very successful music on limited systems.

I know. It's funny. I recorded two of my biggest albums at the exact same time and they were on 24-track analog machines, and they're *dense* with music and loaded with instruments, and have 60 people on them—and it was not even a problem. [*Laughs.*] When I think of a song like "Like a Virgin"—not the biggest song in my life, but the biggest album of my life—you could put it up on a 24-track machine and *still* have five or six tracks open. And nothing is double-tracked. It's just a simple band playing a simple song. The only overdubs are Madonna's voice in the chorus—and that's just one other track— and one synth lick. That's it: 20 million albums later. [*Laughs.*]

Of course, some songs demand *bigger productions.*

They can; look at Pink Floyd's *The Wall.* Look at any symphonic record. But my point is that we did huge productions on 24 tracks. What we call a bigger production now is really just more information—sometimes infinitesimally small amounts. Like, last night, I was working on a song, and I've been working on this *same* song for three days. And just when I think it's done, something new happens that just totally titillates me. But when I go back and listen to the composition, I see that that bit of information is only there for a few seconds. It's a one-time event and I think it's the greatest thing in the world. And most people aren't even going to know it.

So why am I wasting time? Because I can. It's fun; it's exciting; it's great. I love Pro Tools. It's amazing. I love it. All of the stuff that I used to toil over in the old days, now I do with the greatest of ease. But are my compositions any better? I'm not sure. I'm certainly spending more time writing 'em! [*Laughs.*]

This is the age-old question. I love technology and it's wonderful to me. Does it make my life better? Is it more interesting? Do my records sound better? I don't know. They certainly don't sell more, but that could be for many different reasons. But the end justifies the means, and if, at the end of the day, the artistic process is elevated, then that's the answer to that question.

Doug Rogers

www.soundsonline.com, www.eastwestsamples.com

The founder, president, and CEO of EastWest, Doug Rogers has over 25 years of experience in the audio industry and is actively involved in the production of East-West's award-winning sound libraries. In 1987 EastWest developed the world's first drum sample library, and has since amassed a library of over 500,000 sampled sounds, the world's largest sound collection. Artists who have developed sound libraries for EastWest include BT, Jeff "Skunk" Baxter, Bob Clearmountain, Greg Hawkes, Joey Kramer, Prince's rhythm section, Public Enemy, Steve Smith, and Steve Stevens. Rogers is the recipient of many gold and platinum records and a "Recording Engineer of the Year" award.

EastWest is essentially a record company, but you were having problems with piracy and file swapping years before the traditional record companies did.

Any time you get a relatively expensive product—and music software falls into this category as well—there's a tendency for some people to steal it. But there was never any way that we could solve the issue because up until very recently we were dealing with hardware manufacturers that weren't losing the money. They didn't really care about building anything into their [instruments] that would have enabled us to copy-protect the libraries.

Hear a 24-bit EastWest sampled orchestra demo and find ten royalty-free BT drum loops (produced by Doug Rogers) on the disc.

It was only with the introduction of the software sampler that we were able to take advantage of copy protection. The copy-protected libraries we've put out have outsold the others by about ten to one. So we know it's working.

By integrating software with the samples, we also had more control over what we could do with the libraries, as opposed to working within the confines of someone else's idea of what a sampler should do.

So, from your vantage point, what would you recommend to the record industry?

Well, I think they need to do something similar. They need to have something that authorizes an end-user to use a copy of that record. They basically need to take the CD player out of the market and put in something like the DVD player. The hardware technology needs to be changed, and they need to figure out a new delivery method.

EastWest was also one of the first companies to do online sample distribution. What have you learned from that?

I thought it was going to be more successful than it ultimately turned out to be. Back in 1995, when we launched the downloadable sound service, we really thought it was going to take over the whole business and that there wouldn't be CDs in the future. A few years later, the Giga system [TASCAM GigaSampler] came along, and that enabled people to load and play *huge* samples. [*Instead of loading samples into RAM to play them, GigaSampler streams them directly from disk.*]

"With the sample libraries from the past, not many people really *changed* anything. Giving users an interface to manipulate everything that's there really opens up a lot of options that were missing."

If you'd told me in 1995 that we could put out a 1.8-gigabyte piano in 1998, I would have thought you were crazy. In fact, we put out a piano in 1995 that was so "big" it required two networked Akai samplers. It had two velocities, each filling up the maximum 32 megabytes of RAM. Every sample was sample-rate converted to save memory. That was state of the art then. Now it's a complete joke.

What came along and changed our perception of the whole downloadable-sounds idea was the fact that these libraries are now so huge. Our orchestra library is 68 gigabytes—68 *thousand* megabytes. Why? Because there's *so* much expression built into it, so that people can emulate a real orchestra. If you want to have all these articulations and velocities that have been recorded on each note, it all adds up. And then by the time you add the fact that every sample in other libraries is actually three in our library [*because of the multiple miking perspectives*], the data just starts adding up. Plus it's 24-bit, so you've got another 50 percent overhead there. We actually have an 88.2kHz version of the library, too, but we can't put it out right now because computers just can't handle it. So trying to let someone download 68 gigabytes is not realistically going to happen.

So you're safe for a few years.

I actually think that ultimately the connectivity will be so fast that we'll be able to offer the sounds on a rental basis from our server. I see a lot of digital content being delivered that way in the future.

So when you play your keyboard, it would actually pull the sounds off the EastWest server?

Right. You hook up to Soundsonline.com and flick through presets until you find the one you want. I really see that's the way it's going to go, because that would make it a lot more inexpensive for the average musician as well.

Todd Rundgren

www.tr-i.com

www.patronet.com

www.trconnection.com

Todd Rundgren has had massive influence in all three facets of his career: as an artist (the Nazz, solo, Utopia), as a record producer (Grand Funk Railroad, Meatloaf, XTC), and as a technical innovator and digital music futurist. He created the first music video to utilize live action and computer graphics (1981's "Time Heals," the second video ever played on MTV); the world's first interactive record album (*No World Order*, 1992); the first full-length enhanced CD (*The Individualist*, 1994); the first interactive concert tour (1995); and the first direct artist subscription service (PatroNet, 1998). In 2004, Sanctuary Records UK released *Liars*, Rundgren's 18th solo album.

Technology makes it increasingly possible for individuals to produce high-quality recordings at home. But you've been doing that since the beginning. What's your take on technology as a creative assistant?

I didn't immediately adopt at least some of the technology for use in my own creative works. And there are still techniques that I decline to employ—for instance, pitch correction.

That's become a whole industry unto itself.

Yeah, and it doesn't mean that I eschew the technology out of hand; I just don't personally have a use for it yet. Unless I decide I want that effect, I'd much rather try to sing it enough times till I get it in tune. [*Laughs.*]

There are a lot of things that have altered the quality of recorded music compared to music that's performed live. Having said that, I even now go out with an MP3 player and karaoke versions of some of my songs, and I sing over top of 'em.

See a classic Todd Rundgren video and read his provocative editorial about digital music distribution on the disc.

But despite the fact that every other sound is prerecorded, the one line I haven't crossed is lip-syncing my vocal because I'm too busy doing *dance* routines. So in that sense, direct live performance is one of the things that needs to be recovered in the evolution of music in general, now that people think of recorded music as being inextricably connected to performed music.

The idea of recorded music is an anomaly. Previously to Edison discovering how to capture sound, the only way you *ever* heard music was by somebody performing it at the time you were listening to it. And that's been the way it's been for the history of music, except for the past hundred years.

Record labels want to hold on to that model because they don't understand any other way of selling music except as a commodity. But in reality, music is more practically a service. Whatever I feel as a technologist, I have to constantly keep reminding myself of the importance of music in the human sphere, music separate from how it's created or distributed.

"I look at the music industry of the future as being two-tiered. One is that listeners will find someone to whom they feel a connection and would like to offer direct support. That's the kind of subscription model that PatroNet is. Then there are on-demand music services."

Originally, music was considered something mystical, a gift of the gods, and was performed only on the most important occasions. Most people, if they have musical inclinations, they demonstrate them very early on in their lives. And they're not doing it because they're thinking, "Boy, I could make a lot of money." It's because that mystical aspect of music has connected with them. And then there's this long road of technique, and understanding, and learning, and finally, for people who really do achieve the higher levels of musicianship, it evolves into a deeply felt means of personal expression.

And all of the talk about artist rights [*laughs*], and compensation, and digital distribution models to me is so far secondary to reaffirming those primeval priorities in music. It's why I rail against the industry, because it constantly forgets this fact. And why I have to rail against so-called musicians, because often they never knew this fact. [*Laughs.*]

Most people don't remember the moment they bought the song; they remember the first time they *heard* the song. That's when their connection with it started. I believe ethically that the commoditized model we've had over the past 60 years or so really has robbed more from musicians than it's given them.

With the other model, the subscription-based or service-based model, you are free to discover all kinds of music, and that is a direct benefit to musicians. I know it works, because I've been working under that model. And what it's done is enable me to survive, and continue to create, and remain connected to my audience when if I'd had to depend on the record industry I would have had to find another line of work.

As much as I proselytize about PatroNet and what it can do that either a label can't or won't, the message I have for musicians is that the most important and challenging thing they have to do is to get their act together. [*Laughs.*] *Really* play well, go out, and kick ass.

Dave Smith

www.davesmithinstruments.com

Sequential Circuits founder Dave Smith designed the world's first microprocessor-based musical instrument, the revered Prophet-5. Smith later consulted for Yamaha and launched Korg R&D, which developed the popular Wavestation digital vector synthesizer. Moving to Seer Systems as president, he developed the world's first software synthesizer running on a PC. Smith also led the charge in creating the Musical Instrument Digital Interface (MIDI) specification, which enables electronic musical instruments to communicate. Currently he designs hybrid analog/digital synthesizers such as the Evolver at his new one-man company, Dave Smith Instruments.

Your instruments are renowned for having character. Where does that come from?

When you're designing a musical instrument there's a very vague, untouchable part of it, because you don't really know how musical it's going to be when you're done. It's not like designing a disk drive or something where you have a specific functional goal.

Sure, some instruments, especially in the last ten or 20 years, are defined more as pieces of equipment—how many megabytes of samples does it have? How many bits of resolution? How many voices? But I have absolutely no interest in working on instruments that compete in numbers. To me it's a lot more interesting to have an instrument that stands out by having its own sound and feel.

So how do you know when something has that personality?

It's not until the whole instrument is polished up and ready to ship that you really find out what personality it has—what it's good at, what it's not good at, what surprises there are. Quite often, the voicing guys will come up with something twisted that you didn't think about.

"[It's so] silly that we [still] have wires of any kind. You should be able to walk into a studio with your instrument and have it automatically connect to the wireless network."

Eric Persing thought some of the instruments with the most character were the ones that were trying really hard to sound like something else and failed, like the Roland TR-808 and -909.

Yeah. I remember when they came out the rest of us were laughing. We already had sampling drum machines out. And then Roland came out with this thing that was half and half [*the TR-909 had analog drums and a digital cymbal*], and it just sounded absolutely *horrible* compared to everything else.

And so it was dismissed and they laid around forever until you could buy them for a few pennies. And then *because* they were so cheap, people started using them for different things, and lo and behold it becomes the coolest sound ten years later.

Musical instruments are works of art and generate art, and that separates them somewhat from the technical side of things. Yamaha has always had great technology, and yet their instruments for years just never hit the target.

One of the biggest secrets in musical instrument manufacturing is that you don't really *need* that next big piece of equipment to make good music. But everybody thinks they do, and that's what keeps the music instrument industry alive. When the M1 came out, the technology in it had been around for a while; they just put it together the right way and voiced it the right way. [*The Korg M1 (1988) was the best-selling synthesizer keyboard in history, integrating realistic sounds, an 8-track sequencer, and effects processing for the first time.*] My latest instrument [the Evolver] could have been built five years ago. It's just the specific combination of what's in there that gives it a new sound. [*For more on the Evolver, see the "Synth Charming" chapter.*]

See and hear Dave Smith playing the Evolver on the disc.

You're widely known as the father of MIDI. Now that it's old enough to drink, what do you think of its impact?

[*Laughs.*] I always challenge people to come up with anything else that's 20 years old and still in version 1.0. I also challenge them to find something that's in *every* single home studio, every single professional studio, movie studio, and stage—all around the world—and for which something built 20 years ago will work with something that was built yesterday.

It's very rare to have standards that are that ubiquitous and work that well. Even the speed issue, which was always the big complaint, wasn't MIDI's fault for the first ten years. The microprocessors inside the instruments were overtaxed.

And in many cases today, MIDI is virtual anyhow [*i.e., the commands are sent directly between programs on a single computer, not sequentially over cables*], so it's as fast as you want it to be. It's still a limitation if you have one of these silly 128-voice hardware instruments. It can't possibly keep up with all those voices. So there is a need for porting it onto other hardware. And people are putting it on Ethernet and FireWire and USB-2, though nobody has come up with the definitive MIDI 2.0 connector.

But I think it's clearly proved itself and will continue to be around for a long time in different states. I don't want to have anything to do with trying to come up with a MIDI 2.0, because that would be a complete zoo. What it's going to take, again, is the right collection of four or five companies doing something to force everybody else to do it also.

Dr. Fiorella Terenzi

www.fiorella.com

Described by comedian Dennis Miller as "a cross between Carl Sagan and Madonna," astrophysicist, author, and recording artist Fiorella Terenzi received her doctorate in physics from the University of Milan; studied opera and composition at Conservatory G. Verdi; and taught mathematics and physics at Liceo Scientifico, Milan. Her best-selling CD-ROM *Invisible Universe* blends astronomy and music into a voyage through the stars. She has moderated hundreds of panels on science and technology and performed and recorded with artists including Thomas Dolby, Herbie Hancock, and Ornette Coleman.

 Watch two videos and hear two songs by Dr. Terenzi on the disc.

Your Music from the Galaxies *album was a groundbreaking approach to music composition. What was involved?*

It was the first experiment to combine radio astronomy with music, or radio astronomy with the sound of synthesis. It was more than ten years ago, so the computers were totally different. But it will always be up to date, because the music itself won't go out of tune for about 180 million years. [*Laughs.*]

So you rendered the music on a mainframe computer?

Yes. I was working on a Digital VAX workstation with the Unix and C languages. And I was compiling all these radio astronomic data collected by different radio telescopes like the Very Large Array in New Mexico—the one that was featured in *Contact,* the movie with Jodie Foster. It had 27 dish antennae. Then I combined the data with Cmusic, Richard Moorer's sound-synthesis language. [*Cmusic has since evolved into Csound; see www.csounds.com.*]

I had to learn Cmusic, Unix, and C; I had to learn all the different systems and try to combine them, but it worked out beautifully. At least for me, astronomy and science and computers and technology interface almost perfectly.

How much transformation did you have to do on the raw signals?

Actually, I did very little processing on the data from the radio telescopes. I just reduced the frequency from the gigahertz range down into the human hearing range, 20–20,000 Hertz, and then fed the data to Cmusic. I came up with a sonification of celestial data. And I used these raw data coming from a galaxy to match the visual representation of the galaxy. So sound and visuals were analyzed together, just to understand how the visual investigation of the universe can also be done acoustically.

So even a blind person could start to appreciate the cosmos.

Right. Today there are many more experiments that use sound as a way to understand the scientific process. Just a few days ago, these volcanologists on the Discovery Channel were recording the actual sound of the lava passing through volcanoes. And they were able to tell how fast the lava was moving and if there were some obstacles. So from the sound they were deriving scientific information.

"I think we have [become] used to the idea that when we talk about sound we're thinking of the violin or the guitar. But there are sounds that have [such] high complexity that in themselves there is already music."

And then, of course, sound has been used to study pregnant women, so it's a wonderful domain, the acoustic domain. We're at the very beginning of this fantastic universe.

Mainframe computers don't seem very musical. How did working on the VAX affect your composition process?

You ran the processing and then you had to wait for days, sometimes even *weeks,* just to hear a couple of sounds, because there were many other UC San Diego students on the same computer. Today it would be real time.

I describe the process in my book, *Heavenly Knowledge.* You build up a lot of anticipation, sometimes a bit of stress. We want immediate satisfaction. [*Laughs.*] So maybe it would have been happier music if I'd done it today. But the sound itself would not be different, because the sound is a direct representation of the celestial object.

And then with the sound, I composed music. I played all these electromagnetic sounds, different shifting modulations, background noise. So there were three stages: the raw data from the galaxy; the actual sound for scientific research; and then, with that sound, you compose music.

Speaking of found sounds, what's your reaction to hearing other people sample your work?

[*Laughs.*] I'm proud—even if I shouldn't say so. You know the band Massive Attack from England? They did a sample, probably a minute long, from "Sidereal Breath" [from *Music from the Galaxies*]. The song they did is called "Karmacoma." It's fabulous what they did. I love it. Unfortunately, they didn't ask permission, so it is an illegal sample. But I appreciate the creativity. I'm intrigued by that.

David Torn

www.splattercell.com

David Torn (aka Splattercell) is a guitarist, texturalist, composer, writer, producer, and occasional singer. His *Tonal Textures* sampling CD for Q Up Arts was described as the only sampling CD you could listen to as music. Torn also consults for manufacturers including Arboretum Systems, Emagic, Guyatone, Klein Guitars, Lexicon, and TC Electronic. He is often featured as the primary texturalist or soloist on films scored by composers such as Carter Burwell, Lisa Gerrard, Mark Isham, Patrick O'Hearn, Graeme Revell, Michael Shrieve, Ryuichi Sakamoto, and Michael Whalen. Torn won *Guitar Player*'s Readers' Poll Award, in the Experimental category, in both 1994 and 1997.

You said recently that you really wished "more attention would be paid to live looping—by musicians, consumers, and manufacturers alike." What are they missing?

When there is live input, looping is a phenomenally capable musical instrument in its own right. That feeling of instant recording, that feedback loop, is so wonderful for almost any performer, even if it's as simple as a guy playing a little backing track and then playing over it. There was a time when I was very vocal about that. I got pretty deeply involved in the [Lexicon] Jam Man. I proselytized for the damn thing for years, because I think it's such an amazing instrument.

I'm about to get involved with a new secret piece of software that's meant to be a live-performance looping device; it's not unlike [Cycling '74] RadiaL, but with a different set of conceptual paradigms. I keep getting involved in all these damn projects—Jam Man, EDP [Gibson Echoplex Digital Pro], [Electrix] Repeater—because looping has been an *extreme* part of my musical life for so long.

When you're doing live looping, what are some ways you enjoy sculpting the sound?

I've got a pretty simple send-and-return-type setup in which I can manipulate the perspective on any loop. At any time, on the three looping devices that I use live regularly, each can be heard dry, on its own, or processed in a myriad of ways.

And all three of the looping devices are very different in character. The Echoplex is an *amazing* device with what Kim Flint [co-designer; www.loop-ers-delight.com] calls "granular sampling." I use it to build long rhythmic or arrhythmic loops from very tiny bits of sample data, like maybe 12 milliseconds of the simplest brush on the guitar string or a squawk into a microphone. I'll capture that, loop it, and then start multiplying it [pasting copies end to end] and editing out sections.

The Repeater is an archival device, but it's also very good at repeating things in time, and it's very nice for taking timed samples down to *extremely* slow tempos that then become very granular in nature.

And the oldest one, the [Lexicon] PCM 42, sounds warm and wonderful, and it lets you continuously alter the pitch and length of the loop with a footpedal.

When you move to the computer, are you forced to work differently?

Yes, because the toolset is so deep on the computer. I would also say that the user interface for looping on the computer requires a different mindset. The general paradigm is, "Okay, let me drop in this loop from this sample disc," which is basically the [Sony] Acid approach, which became [BitHeadz] Phrazer, which became Ableton Live. They've become super-glorified turntables without the physical response. Nothing bad there, just a different set of expressions of a different need.

I believe that the laptop computer could indeed become the next level of live-performance looping device. But the biggest problem, and the thing that I wish I could convince somebody to do, is to develop a semiconfigurable physical interface for a looping device. That to me is the *nut* of why live looping hasn't really caught the fancy of a manufacturer and, therefore, the public.

When there *is* a physical interface that is more visceral, then the audience can tell that what's happening is happening because the performer is doing it. I did an orchestral tour with Ryuichi Sakamoto a couple of years ago that was one of the most phenomenal multimedia events I've ever seen. In fact, it was *really* hard to play sometimes for wanting to turn around and look at the huge screens behind us. Ryuichi was wearing a special MIDI suit that Yamaha built for him that was velocity-, pressure-, and position-sensitive. It was a very thin suit underneath his tuxedo and there was always an element of the visuals that was manipulated by the movement of his body. It was *incredibly* well done, incredibly aesthetically pleasing—and the audience *got* it.

"One of the problems with software sequencers is that they force you to think in a vertical and horizontal mode. You've got the horizontal timeline and the vertical 'what's available to me.'"

Don Was

www.worldwidewas.com

Best known as the co-founder of the brilliantly quirky band Was (Not Was), bassist Don Was has produced hits for a staggering variety of artists—from pop, rock, and alternative to country, jazz, and Latin. A select list includes Paula Abdul, the B-52s, Jackson Browne, Joe Cocker, Neil Diamond, Bob Dylan, Marianne Faithfull, Glenn Frey, Waylon Jennings, Elton John, B.B. King, Lyle Lovett, Willie Nelson, Stevie Nicks, Roy Orbison, Iggy Pop, Bonnie Raitt, the Rolling Stones, Bob Seger, Carly Simon, Ringo Starr, Travis Tritt, and Brian Wilson.

Do you think computers themselves could be made more musical? It's odd that we're trying to squeeze so much soul out of this overblown calculator.

Well, that's a mistake to be thinking for a minute that you're going to squeeze soul out of anything but yourself. To me, Pro Tools is just a neutral shade. It's really no more than a blank piece of paper. And the crayon or the marker doesn't matter. Even the individual doesn't matter, man. Any individual who thinks that they're coming up with the great ideas is sadly deluded.

"Technology has been a distraction from soulfulness. When you get to the point where people are spending *days* creating a drum sound while the musicians are sitting around, certainly the moment of creativity is going to pass."

One night I was working with Bob Dylan, and I wanted to ask the billion-dollar question: "What do you *go* through when you write a song like 'Gates of Eden?' How do you prepare for that? How do you *do* that? And why can't *I* do it?" And essentially what he said was, "You can believe me or not, but I didn't write that song. I remember moving the pencil over the paper, but I didn't *write* it. It came from without. It came from sources beyond."

Keith Richards will tell you the same thing. In fact, during a session, instead of saying, "I've got an idea," he'll say, "Hold it! Hold it! Incoming." [*Laughs.*] And he never deviates from that. He knows that it's not *his*. So if the best artists are simply conduits for lightning from the creative ether, does it really matter if you're rolling a computer or a Wollensak [old analog tape recorder]?

When you attach importance to the methodology, you're just distracting yourself. To carry forward Keith's metaphor about something incoming, I'd be more concerned with building a really great antenna.

Playwrights often talk about transcribing speech rather than making it up: They invent the characters, and then eavesdrop on their conversations. Perhaps that's something musicians could use as well. Since we're doing so many one-man productions now, there must be some way to have a dialog with yourself.

It's entirely possible. Look, I'm 50 years old, and it took me well into my 40s to discover how to play the bass without thinking about holding a piece of wood. It's like an archer saying, "The arrow comes from my eye. Forget about the *bow*." [*Laughs.*] You stop thinking about holding the piece of wood, you stop thinking about chords, and you just live in the song. You play in the moment. In my life, that's been a far more important development than learning to be agile on the computer keyboard.

I mean, I'm pretty good at Pro Tools now. I'm pretty fast. I don't hold myself up. In a more complicated situation I might hold up a large band, but I'm not an obstacle in Pro Tools any more. But it doesn't matter.

Was Words

At the 2004 NAMM show, Don Was lit up the annual Grammy Producers' panel with his pointed remarks on producing in the digital age. Noting that you couldn't tell the difference in audio quality, he said, "I've recorded the Rolling Stones on an iBook. It's almost returning to the point where it's folk art."

His advice for the record industry: "Make better music; charge less for it. The idea of an industry *suing* its customers is the most absurd idea I've ever heard. If someone's going to steal from you, would you rather it be a multinational corporation or a fan who might then buy a T-shirt?" But he later added, "We've been sitting here vilifying record companies, but my experience is that artists will burn you just as often."

Was also offered this interesting tip for adding impact to songs: "I watch the musicians: No one is allowed to come within a third of where the vocalist is at that moment. If you do that, then the vocals just *leap* out."

David Zicarelli

www.cycling74.com

David Zicarelli has been developing interactive music software for 20 years. In the 1980s, he developed the interactive composition programs M, Jam Factory, and OvalTune. Since 1990, he's been working on the Max graphical programming environment invented by Miller Puckette. In 1997, Zicarelli founded Cycling '74, a San Francisco software company that publishes Max along with its MSP audio extensions and Jitter video extensions. Artists have used Max to do everything from controlling robots to building standalone software synthesizers. Zicarelli's company also has a music label, c74, devoted to works by artists who use its software.

One of the big themes in this book has been option anxiety. Your Max software is like a supertanker of magnetic poetry hitting a mile-wide refrigerator door. How do people deal with that many choices?

"I developed [the Pluggo plug-ins] not by processing raw synthesizer sounds or almost-finished mixes; I just put on my CD collection, which tends toward jazz, and started messing with discs to see if I could mess them up in a way that I thought was cool."

Well, there are two ways people have thought about software for music. One I would call the rationalizing form: "We've made a saxophone; now your job is to operate it." Whereas if you make an infinitely recombinable language [like Max], you're not constraining them in either space or time.

True, you're not *helping* them get started, either. But with the construction-kit approach, you don't focus on making choices. You just start working, and once you've gained some facility one step leads to another based on whatever possibilities you see at any particular time. It's not so conscious.

By rationalizing the task, there's an attempt to make people more aware of the decisions they're making. And that fights against the ability to be spontaneous. I think that in many cases art that's based on conscious decisions is weaker than art that's based on fluid intuition. So the things I do as a programmer are influenced more by improvisation than by overarching intellectual structures.

[Our program] RadiaL puts a priority on being spontaneous and hearing things in combinations that you wouldn't otherwise try. People who use it are always talking in terms of an "experience," and I rarely see that with other software.

How do they describe the RadiaL experience?

The word that comes up a lot is "inspiration." It's reminiscent of M and Jam Factory. Instead of being designed to render preconceived ideas, like sequencers, they were programs you'd use when you didn't *have* any ideas. The goal was that if you gave yourself over to the system, you would come up with something you'd never have imagined.

And to a certain extent, RadiaL is doing that, but instead of using just MIDI notes, it's allowing you to sculpt ideas with loops of audio. You don't have as much control over the details, but it can really change the character of sound in surprising ways. It introduces the notion of mixing and filtering as a compositional strategy. When we play two sounds together, we think we're just adding them, but the ear is not linear. There's a psychoacoustic effect called *masking* where if two sounds are in the same frequency range, one will obscure significant parts of the other.

Read David Zicarelli's "Interactive Music: Standing Up or Sitting Down?" on the disc.

So, what happens when you add two sounds is very unpredictable. If you have controls for being able to filter, time-stretch, and pitch-shift things in drastic and interesting ways and then mix them together, it leads you to try those things and get combinations you wouldn't be able to predict.

Perhaps part of that is due to the difference between a line and a circle. Sequencers and multitrack programs are linear, whereas RadiaL is endless.

I think that *is* part of it. And I know that for many composers, this whole idea of a beginning, middle, and end is really important. But it's less important in electronica and in the music of certain non-Western cultures.

So it could be that the kinds of music software that people have made traditionally are oriented toward the "beginning, middle, and end" assumption. And the things I've been more interested in working on will be more suited to cultural practices in which that's not important. If you give up the beginning, middle, and end, you can have more fun in the endless middle.

Production

Studio Setup Tips

Advice from the pros on gearing up

Today's music-making equipment is better and more affordable than ever, but there are still plenty of issues to consider. Here are some tips from our virtual panel for gearing up.

Joe, you were the co-designer for Hollywood's Royaltone Studios [www.royaltonestudios.com]; what did you learn from that process?

Joe Chiccarelli: What I learned—and what I *still* know—is that for a commercial recording studio, it's all the old-school things that are still the most important. It's a good-sounding recording room, a good acoustic environment with lots of flexibility in the sound, good-sounding microphones, vintage consoles, and everything else.

Of course, Royaltone and every other studio I've worked in has tons of digital gear as well, but the things that were made in the '60s and '70s still hold up because they produced all the recordings that we learned as our standard.

What guidance do you give artists for setting up their home systems so they can harmonize with your setup in the big studios?

Joe Chiccarelli: The *great* thing about this is that everybody has the same technology now. There's a Pro Tools system on every block. Just on my street—I'm only talking about a half-mile stretch—there have to be half a dozen people with [*laughs*] fully professional recording setups in their homes. So everybody can now speak the same language. Whatever walls there were are broken down and now everybody goes about making music.

I personally am a Pro Tools user because I think the interface is easy. It's the current standard. It's the Studer of the times; it's the top of the line. [*Studer multitrack tape recorders have been* the *analog machines to own since the '70s.*] So I recommend artists get involved with the Pro Tools system. There's a certain advantage to a couple of the other systems. [Emagic] Logic is great if you're MIDI intensive. But for the professional world, Pro Tools is the standard.

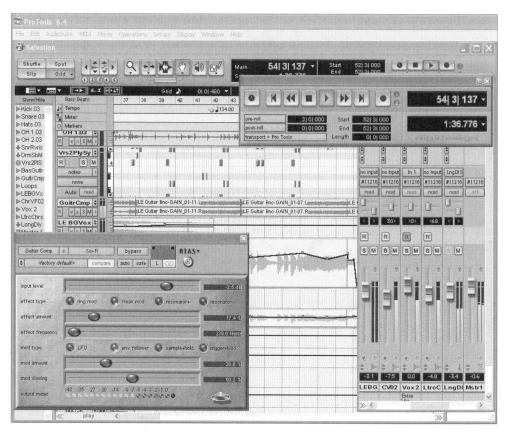

Pro Tools LE software is an affordable step into the Pro Tools world. It's bundled with Digidesign's less-expensive audio interfaces such as the Mbox. The software allows you to record and edit both audio and MIDI. (MIDI notes are represented by the tiny rectangles in the middle of this screenshot.) Note the plug-in effect controls at bottom left.

I also recommend that artists get a good front end: Buy great microphones and great microphone preamps. And record things as cleanly and professionally as possible so that the tracks you do at home are indeed useful in the studio. And most of the time, that's the case.

Bob Rock: I find that when I get demos and tracks from most people, it's usually style over substance. What I like to hear is a great song, and, really, a great song can be played fairly simply. It's amazing what people *can* do with computers now, in their home. But if there are any mistakes to be made, it's usually that they just put too much on—they just overproduce it. Actually, a lot of records are that way, too, so it's not just confined to demos and people working at home.

What I hear more than anything is people doing a lot of processing and EQing rather

Mark Isham's studio is designed for film scoring. It features a custom desk containing two Macs (one dedicated to video playback), a Kurzweil PC-88 MIDI controller keyboard, and various DAT and video decks. Waldorf Wave and Access Virus synthesizers are at the left. Playback is through M-Audio Audiophile BX8 near-field monitors and two Bag End subwoofers.

than really concentrating on the source. When I was young, all I did was EQ guitars. And what you learn is it's more about mic placement, what the actual amp sounds like, and then minimal EQ.

Jimmy Jam: Whether you're working in Pro Tools, Digital Performer, or Logic, which happens to be my personal favorite, the biggest thing that people fail to do is mark their tracks. I'm involved with the Recording Academy, and more specifically the AES Producers' and Engineers' Wing, to draft some rules of etiquette, if you will.

What we're trying to do is say that when you open Pro Tools files, for instance, they should all look the same, whether you're getting it from a home studio or a studio in New York, or L.A., or wherever. So when you open it up, you don't go, "Whoa—what is *this*? It says 'Audio-1,' 'Audio-2,' 'Audio-3'; the tracks aren't marked." It sounds like a mundane thing, but it certainly makes everybody's life easier, particularly when you're at a studio and there's some *rate* happening. [*Laughs.*]

As far as techniques, I think nowadays it's pretty foolproof. There are obviously a lot of great plug-ins. I always think it's great to have some piece of analog gear—whether it's a preamp or an old microphone or something like that—for your vocals. It's fine to do tracking at home, but I think vocals are still better in a room with the correct acoustics and the right limiters and compressors. [*Limiters and compressors reduce the dynamic range of sounds, producing a consistent volume level.*]

I also think that Pro Tools is great, but *we* do vocals on [an iZ Technology] RADAR. It's a hard-disk recording system, but it has a lot more of an analog sound. There's a lot more breathiness or airiness in the vocals. I've had many people tell me they're surprised at the difference in the way the vocals sound.

At the end of the day, it all ends up in Pro Tools when we mix anyway [*laughs*], so maybe it doesn't make a big difference. But as far as home recording, I think it's pretty foolproof at this point, and it's certainly easy to fix whatever is not done correctly.

Leslie, do you have any general principles that might trickle down to people in personal studios? Obviously, they won't be able to afford the same equipment as Skywalker Sound?

Leslie Ann Jones: Sure, but I never think you should start with the lowest common denominator. Start with the highest. Try to get the best mics you can, and the best preamp and cables you can afford. And don't expect that just because you're recording at home, that's the only place you're going to be. The whole idea of being successful is that eventually you're going to get out of your living room and go to a professional studio.

So try to build up some kind of a work ethic in terms of labeling and track sheets and things like that. That way, when that time comes and somebody says, "Hey, I have the opportunity to go into a big studio and I want *you* to help me add some vocals to the track you recorded for me," all that work you've done is going to transfer well.

Alan Parsons's private studio is based around Steinberg Nuendo recording software. The Tube Traps acoustic baffles between the B&W 802 speakers help control echoes in the small room.

So you have to be very careful to keep tabs on which is the right vocal, and on making sure your tracks are clean. Don't assume that what you're working on is not going to be successful. Don't think just because it's done at your home that it's just a demo. I'm really careful when I do rough mixes to make sure that they're labeled properly, and that they're recorded at the right level, because I've *had* occasions where my rough mixes have actually been released.

Steve Horowitz: Since I got involved in doing television stuff, I started to meet some of the people who are doing that and they *all* have these big [TASCAM] GigaStudio setups. And they're running them on these custom-designed

PCs, using the sequencers on their Macs. I sold *eight* [Digidesign] SampleCell cards and I just bought two GigaStudio setups. And I have to admit, a lot of it sounds really, really good.

Douglas Morton: I work in Logic and Pro Tools, and all the external MIDI devices are pre-patched, and it's relatively ready to go. There's always the problem of running out of disk space, though. I think data housekeeping is really important so you don't have to dump something valuable when you get excited by a new idea. Keeping the valuable stuff archived is like paving the road ahead of yourself.

For backup, I use [Dantz] Retrospect and these little data DAT tapes that hold something like 25 gigs. It has a lot of integrity. A lot of the stuff that I create, like for the Monterey Bay Aquarium exhibits, we'll repurpose onto CDs or videos or DVDs or whatever. So I often have to go back. And I found that Retrospect with data DAT tapes works great. I have stuff from ten years ago that I'm able to reload.

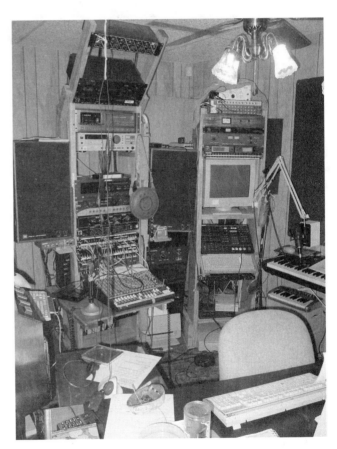

I also think you can avoid some common computer crashes by having voltage conditioners. I spent about fifteen hundred bucks on this really nice power conditioner, and since I got that the system's been incredibly stable. We have a bunch of computers, and since I cleaned up the power we don't get a lot of the freakish crashes.

Jimmy Jam: For arranging and MIDI, I think Logic is by far the better way to compose than Pro Tools. But at the end of the day, man, you just gotta do what feels good to you. There's a lot less *right* and *wrong* now.

The MPC3000 [Akai/Linn drum machine and sequencer] is still a staple around our place. We have three or four of them. And we have the 2000, which I never particularly liked, and we have the 4000, too. I don't deal with it, but one of our programmers loves it.

The Linn Drum for us goes back to the original LM-1 Linn, which we used

"I believe that people outfit their studios in a manner that is driven by fear of being thought an amateur," says the Fat Man, who has produced hundreds of successful video game soundtracks in his efficient home studio. The raw-lumber racks are dirt cheap, hold lots of equipment, and are easily modifiable. Note the radio-style mic boom at right and the headphones and telephone headset hanging from the ceiling, where they're always in reach.

The venerable Akai MPC3000, designed by Roger Linn, is a sampling drum machine and MIDI sequencer. The 16 large rubber pads respond to both velocity (how hard you hit) and pressure.

on all the Time records in '80 and '81. And then there was the Linn 9000, which was notorious for locking up. As a matter of fact, it was *so* bad working with that machine that we had a saying: If somebody did something wrong, we would say they locked up like a Linn 9000. It became part of our vocabulary.

But the MPC3000 is a staple. There's nothing like it. I've had a chance to work with a lot of the hip-hop producers of today, and when you get their list of what equipment they want, that's always the first thing. There's a few that still work with the E-mu SP-1200, and we have one of those around, too. But the MPC3000 is still the machine *du jour*.

Scott Kirkland: The most important thing is just to get good at what you do. If you're going to focus on creating with [Sony] Acid, just get in there and really learn all the tricks of Acid. Each program has little things that separate it from all the others. And over the last five years, all the subpar, inadequate sequencing programs have been weeded out. In the Mac world, you have two or three choices: Steinberg's Cubase, Emagic's Logic, and Digital Performer from Mark of the Unicorn. So if you're going to go in that direction, get a sequencing program; if you're going in a loop-based direction, get a program like Acid or [Ableton] Live.

Live is a really impressive program. The advances they've made in the few years it's been out are incredible. Along with Propellerheads and their Reason program, they've really taken that whole thing to the next level.

But just get good at what you have. If you only have a $1,000 sampler, then just get in there and work with what it has. Sometimes you can get into the going-after-whatever's-new trap. To be frank, we've fallen into that trap a few times, where we would focus too much on what's about to come out and not on what's already in existence. You spend too much time learning a new program every time something comes out and not making music. That can be a big setback to the creative process. But there's enough stuff out there for everybody.

Nile Rodgers: My former partner Bernard Edwards, who had an amazing bass sound, was being interviewed by some guitar-player or bass-player magazine and they said, "You have *such* a fantastic, original sound. What kind of strings do you use?" And he stared at the bass and said, "I don't know. What kind of strings come on a Music Man?" [*Laughs.*] Which meant to me that it was all about his powers of interpretation. It's like my guitar sounds a certain way, but if I pick up another guitar and it doesn't sound like that, then I'm going to change the way that I play it. I'm going to change my approach so that it sounds *pleasurable* to my ears. You work on it.

Don Was: I'm sure many people can relate to the notion of having *everything* set up perfectly. You're finally ergonomically correct. It's taken weeks to fine-tune this one little setup you've got, and you've got the keyboard in the right place, the speakers sounding right, everything's working . . . and you haven't got a fucking idea in your head. [*Laughs.*] There's no "incoming." It's certainly happened to me a number of times, and I would guess it's happened to everybody. And that's the point when you realize that you would trade all of this stuff—give me back my old 7 ¾ inches-per-second, mono Wollensak—for one good idea.

Do you do any tricks when that happens?

Don Was: I've tried 'em all. If it were just as simple as lighting one more joint [*laughs*], it'd be so *easy*. And *everybody* would be Peter Gabriel. Everyone would be writing "Michelle" every night.

Support Our Loops

Secrets of sampling, looping, layering, and warping digital audio

Samples and loops are an enormously fertile resource for musicians, but used lazily they can be deadly boring. Here the virtual panel discusses aesthetic and technical approaches to making better music through layering, looping, and warping short sections of digital audio.

Now that it's so easy to combine samples and grooves, what tips do you have for doing it effectively?

Douglas Morton: I try to create some kind of common environment—whether it's through EQ or compression or maybe just by running everything through a chorus or reverb to put a little *glaze* on it. A sample is like a piece of cold meat sitting there until you cook it and dice it up and throw a little seasoning on it.

BT: My technique is *really* old-school. Everything lives in a very specific part of the frequency spectrum, and I'll *write* to specific parts of the frequency spectrum. I'll listen to a song and be like, "There's no line in there at 700Hz, and that space feels empty." I'm not filling stuff just because it's empty. But when something actually *does* feel empty. . . .

Obviously, there's lot of overlap between something that holds a broad part of the spectrum, like pianos and certain kinds of guitars and vocals. But even amongst them, I do tons of notch filtering, bandpass filtering, shelving, and highpass filtering so that things live in their own space.

Robert Henke: Well, I have to admit that I would rather create stuff out of single sine waves than use *any* sample. But when you try to put your stuff on stage, it's always a good approach to find a significant phrase of something and combine it with a *less-significant* phrase of something else.

Gerhard Behles: As in real life. [*Both laugh.*]

Robert Henke: Because if you have two significant things, they're always fighting each other. It doesn't make sense to layer two bass drums, because the risk of phase cancellation is pretty high. So in that case, I would suggest taking a filter and getting rid of the low frequencies from one side—the usual DJ technologies. Everything a good DJ does is a good approach for mixing stuff in [Ableton] Live.

But with a typical DJ-turntable setup, you have just two sources to worry about. With Live, you have many more.

Robert Henke: Well, if you want to. A typical situation is combining basic *enhancement* loops with existing things: adding an extra bass drum, adding an extra hi-hat, adding a simple snare pattern.

For instance, suppose you have two tracks with complicated bass-drum patterns. The bass drums just will not blend nicely. So you superimpose a really stupid [*i.e., simple*] bass-drum pattern at the end of the first track. The audience will like it, because it's a stupid pattern. [*Gerhard laughs.*] Then you get rid of the original pattern by highpass-filtering it, so the track moves smoothly into a straighter version, which is always good for dancers. And then you get complex again by getting rid of the straight bass-drum loop and adding the second complicated track.

So with three or four tracks you can do a tremendous performance. The more tracks you have, the less you do with each.

Don Was: One of the more beautiful combinations of technology and music is probably Peter Gabriel's *So.* I remember when it came out, I just sat there shaking my head and thinking, "How does he *think* of this, putting this one sound in the middle of a song?" But after talking with him and some of the other people involved in the making of the record, it's clear that he sometimes cut *200 tracks* on a song. And for one of those sounds where you think, "How did he dream this up?", it's just that that's the only time he used track 167. A lot of the arrangement was an editing endeavor, and he had this wealth of great stuff to choose from.

Dr. Fiorella Terenzi: Before I pick *any* sound—not only a galactic sound, a pulsar, or an x-ray black hole—I go through maybe 300 or 400 sounds. I hear them, I clash them, I let them talk to me. I tend to pick sounds that are very

The Gibson Echoplex Digital Pro Plus is one of the premier live looping tools. Realtime controls let you layer and reverse loops, sync to MIDI tempo, and even replace sections of individual loops as they play.

strong in emotional impact if the song is toward that. Or maybe sounds that are very ethereal, a little bit unusual, a little bit spacey. These are my favorite for juxtaposing: one sound very hard, very violent, very clashed; and the other very ethereal.

But then, if you want to give uniqueness, you have to elaborate on that sound. You can smooth the attack or give it more impact. Maybe you can emphasize some lower frequencies.

Steve, your piece "City Life" grew out of walking around Manhattan with a DAT recorder. What types of sounds do you find especially evocative?

Steve Reich: For that piece, I sampled a lot of things I *hated.* [*Laughs.*] I mean, I *never* leave home without my earplugs. But for that piece, I recorded car alarms, which I loathe, and air brakes—*pit-tishhhhhh.* And door slams of all sorts. Actually, the kind of sound I *do* like is the huge whistle on the Staten Island ferry. And then there were police sirens and fire-engine air horns—the usual suspects.

The idea was to marry them off to the right instruments. So door slams became bass drums and snare drums, and the *tishhhhhh* became a crash cymbal. The boat horns became low clarinets, because I wasn't using brass. I also added some speech, like "Check it out" and things you hear in New York.

It was a way of dealing with those things and literally turning them into music.

Apple GarageBand can automatically conform audio loops to the same tempo and key. Its built-in database makes finding loops much easier than with the typical hunt-through-folders approach of similar programs.

That's an old tradition—composers have always had an ear out for, say, storms, which they would imitate with bell sounds. That's how the glockenspiel got into the orchestra, and tubular bells.

In the 20th century, you have Gershwin with the taxi horns, and Varèse with the sirens, and Cage with the radio. And rock and roll has been totally into that, even way back with Pink Floyd and the cash register. So "City Life" was another step in that direction.

How did you combine those ugly sounds to make them harmonize?

Steve Reich: Aesthetically, I started by trying to ascertain the pitch of anything that *was* pitched. I remember I had a Porsche horn—very nice; it goes very well with the oboe. The idea was to integrate these sounds into a musical ensemble so that they become part of the *music.*

One thing I particularly wanted to ask you about was the fine line between repetition and boredom. How do you make phrases evolve?

Steve Reich: Ha ha! That's a *very* good question. In "Come Out," you first hear the whole sentence in which the phrase "come out to show them" appears so that you understand the context. [*The groundbreaking 1966 piece was based on a recording of a black teenager explaining how he obtained medical help after being beaten by police: "I had to, like, open the bruise up and let some of the bruise blood come out to show them."*] Once it starts, you hear the phrase over and over again, but then very slowly you hear—*what is this?* It seems like it's coming apart. And, literally, it *is* coming apart. You've got the same phrase on two channels of the stereo tape and one is moving ahead of the other ever so slowly until finally it feels like reverberation. Then it feels like it's shaking, and then it feels like "cumma-cumma, showdem-showdem." And actually, you're *never* hearing any repetition in that sense. This thing is *constantly* in motion.

Repetition by itself is a cheap trick. [*Laughs.*] It doesn't mean *anything.* It's artistically irrelevant. But it's a *gold mine* if applied with some intelligence and some added feature that will make it riveting. And there are lots of ways of doing it. Variation is one. The phase pieces [*e.g., "Come Out" and "Piano Phase"*] were simply about changing the rhythmic relationship *ever* so slowly between two or more identical phrases—either speech phrases or, later on in "Drumming" and my other pieces, musical phrases.

Later, in many of my other pieces, you hear a repeating pattern and then you hear the pattern against itself—let's say one eighth [note], two eighths, three eighths *off*, which creates this overall pattern that is *very* different from hearing the pattern by itself and that sets up many *sub*-patterns that can then be picked up. In "Drumming," the women sing them in the marimba section, and the whistle and the piccolo play them in the glockenspiel section.

These are *unison* canons playing the same thing against themselves—no change of key, no change of notes, no change of timbre. As a matter of fact, it's *necessary* to do that so that all the glockenspiels playing against each other set up this sort of web, this weaving, in

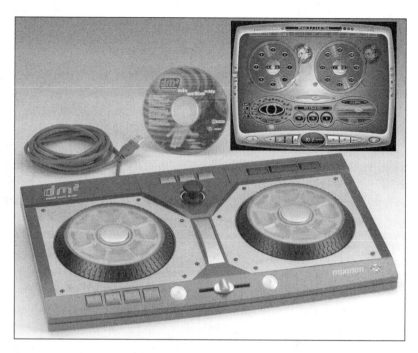

The inexpensive Mixman USB controller lets you manipulate 16 simultaneous loops with its tactile scratch rings and joystick warping effects. It works with Mixman software (inset), which automatically syncs loops to the master tempo.

which you can't really tell what any individual voice is doing but you hear an overall pattern that itself is changing.

The Fat Man: As a game composer, I spent ten years fighting the loop. And finally, I got someone to hint to me why the loop was cool. One day I was listening to [Paul] Oakenfold and drinking Dr Pepper and reading *Harry Potter* and that sound just got in my ear hole and did the sex thing that music used to do in high school. And I *got* it.

There are a lot of people who have to learn the opposite lesson, which is to respect the listener's time. In "Nowhere Man," the Beatles knock your socks off with the first couple of bars, and then they do it again and again. The Beatle Law is that no eight bars can be the same within any song. It's like another song buried inside.

And *that's* the business we're in, right? If every time you listen there's another *thing* that gives you goose bumps, that's a fabulous value. The delight that we unveil always seems to come down to this: I have a feeling in my heart and now, without any words— abracadabra: You have that feeling in your heart. That's what music does.

When you loop music, it's almost as if the *computer* is transmitting a feeling to you. And that's less interesting, because it doesn't reveal an invisible connection. It only reveals a stimulus-response manipulation.

The Primordial Loop

Although modern classical composers had been splicing analog tape recordings into rhythmic and ambient loops for decades, the distinction for the first commercial record to use a drum loop probably goes to producer Albhy Galuten. The Bee Gees' song "Stayin' Alive" used a loop of drums extracted from their song "Night Fever."

Back in 1977, when Galuten and engineer Karl Richardson made the groundbreaking loop, digital samplers and drum machines were still two years in the future. The red-hot Bee Gees were rushing to complete a recording at a remote French studio when suddenly

Karl Richardson, Albhy Galuten, and Barry Gibb (L–R) in Criteria Studio C, about one year before creating their breakthrough drum loop. Note the detented faders in this custom analog console. Each step was 1.5dB— and people complain about digital's coarse resolution!

their drummer was called away for a family emergency. As Galuten and Richardson describe in a fascinating article in *Mix* (October 2000), they copied two bars from the master tape to a four-track reel-to-reel recorder, then spliced the new recording into a loop. (The four tracks contained kick drum, snare, and a stereo room mix of the drum kit.) Because the loop was so long, they had to thread it around numerous empty tape reels gaffer-taped to mic stands to play it back. But the resulting groove worked so well that Galuten used it again on the Bee Gees' "More Than a Woman" and Barbra Streisand's "I'm a Woman in Love."

When I listen to Nirvana, it's enhanced by my knowing that Kurt Cobain died. Because it makes me wonder: *Why* did he die? When I listen to Eminem, I go, "Is the guy really going to shut the bitch in his trunk?" And I recognize a dark feeling in myself. How did he get *that* through to me?

When the computer does it. . . . Sid Meier wrote a program called CPU Bach that was meant to generate Bach-like music automatically. And it did everything but the music. It did all the *notes*. [*Laughs.*] But the thing that is the music is that *wondering* about the other guy.

Marty O'Donnell: A lot of the time in games, we're trying to recreate what nature does when you're walking around. And it used to be that to make it more interesting you had to have a longer and longer loop.

When I actually walked around, I realized the wind *basically* sounds the same every time it blows. The crow cawing essentially sounds like a crow cawing every time it crows. But I don't hear a wind gust and then a crow to my left and then a dog bark *every time* in the same exact order. So if I can randomize five or six different crow sounds and five or six different dog barks and five or six different wind sounds, and have them all playing in random orders and in random surround-sound spatializations, I can recreate essentially the way it feels when you're outside without having to have huge, long loops.

And the same thing can happen with music. You can get a lot more play out of a piece of music if you chop it into sections that can randomly play back in creative ways. And when there's a logic to the section that happens to be playing, it's pleasant to listen to. There's still something really powerful about a piece of music that has a shape to it—a beginning, a middle, and an end.

Francis Preve on Making Loops Evolve

Here are some exclusive sample-wrangling tips from Texas remixer and Keyboard magazine "Dance Mix" columnist Francis Preve. For more, check out his books Power Tools: Software for Loop Music *and* Power Tools for GarageBand, *also from Backbeat Books, or www.fap7.com.*

Temporal Warping. Now that nearly every sequencer manufacturer includes rubber-band automation tools [*i.e., the ability to draw parameter changes on a timeline*], the possibilities for realtime, reproducible audio manipulation expand almost exponentially. You can now automate ring modulation, comb filtering, phasing, distortion, or pretty much *anything* and process a simple repeating figure throughout an entire song to keep it interesting.

Before groove sequencers were available, Francis Preve developed drum machine software for the Apple Newton.

Last year, DJ Licious and I worked on a remix for Sarah Whatmore in which I took a simple vocal phrase, "it's drivin' me insane," and ran it throughout the entire track. By applying Logic's Bitcrusher to it and reducing the sample division to its lowest value, then rhythmically gating it and applying a resonant lowpass filter, I effectively converted the vocal into an aggressive, percussive synthetic texture. The real drama came when we slowly morphed the effect parameters over the course of the track, magically transforming the part back into its original unprocessed state.

Formant Shifting. This works best with monophonic passages like vocals, horns, or guitar solos. In the case of vocals, you can take a single word or phrase and adjust the formant structure with something like Steinberg's nifty Voice Machine plug-ins. [*Formants are the characteristic frequencies in a sound.*] If you start with a male vocal, you can make it more feminine or child-like and vice versa.

Resynthesizing. Apps like U&I's MetaSynth allow you to apply FFT (Fast Fourier Transform) effects to recorded audio, breaking the sound into its sine-wave components. This approach can deliver truly otherworldly effects. You can really twist the harmonics while maintaining the original phrasing and groove.

Saturating. When all else fails, you can always distort the crap out of it.

Native Instruments Intakt slices grooves into individual hits, each of which can be distorted, pitch-shifted, reversed, and otherwise creatively mangled. It also offers time compression.

Chuck D: You don't ever want to keep the same pitch and speed. I get burned out real quickly if a song is the same length time and time again. And also if it's the same tempo. That's the problem with urban music today.

Amy X Neuburg: I use the [Gibson] Echoplex looper as one of the main features of my live solo performance, but the way I use it is not typical. Most people use loopers to set up a trance-like bed of layered sounds and then noodle over the top of that. I structure my songs meticulously, with contrasting sections that require jumping from one loop to another or [that] incorporate unexpected sounds or completely different vocal styles. The songs are heavily text-based, and the looping is designed to illustrate a point or accompany it, *not* as an end in itself. And I was always fascinated by thick layers of vocal harmony, so now I can achieve that live.

Another difference is that my music is designed for a rather theatrical live performance, in which I hit MIDI drum pads to send looping commands, play synth or drum sounds, and change settings on my digital mixer. So every time a musical change occurs, the audience can *see* me doing it, which draws them into the process.

In a recording, there's really no way to capture the excitement of everything happening before your eyes, so I have to approach the songs differently. I may spend less time building up a loop, and I may incorporate sounds I can't produce live, just to add spice

ReCycle Master Class

Many interviewees recommended personalizing loops with Propellerhead Software ReCycle, which automatically slices sampled grooves into individual beats. We asked Propellerhead's'Tage Widsell to share some tips on using ReCycle and the REX files it generates.

You know, it's funny: ReCycle has been around since 1994, and we've always had trouble making people understand what to do with it. That used to be quite difficult when it was a tool to use with a hardware sampler. Someone would ask, "What does this program do?" And you start by saying, "Well, you cut a drum loop into slices. And then you export the slices to your sampler. And it maps the slices to your keyboard. And then you save a MIDI file to your hard disk. And then you take that MIDI file and open it in your sequencer. And then you can play the loop back exactly as it sounded *before* you started working with it."

And they go, "Uh, okay. Why *would* I?" [*Laughs.*] And *then* comes the big thing: Then you can start changing tempo, you can do variations of fills, you can apply different effects to the individual drum hits in a loop. But it was very hard maintaining someone's interest all the way through that chain. It's a bit easier now that there are just two steps: ReCycle it, then open it in Reason or Cubase or whatever as a REX file.

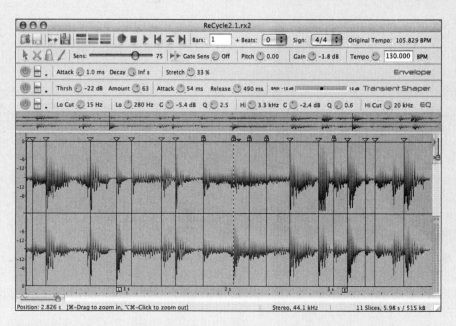

Propellerhead ReCycle automatically slices apart rhythmic audio clips on the beats. Increasing the Sensitivity parameter highlights smaller divisions.

But the power to rearrange loops to create fills—whole styles of music have emerged from that. I remember reading an interview with the Chemical Brothers in which they said they could never have done *any* of their music without the help of ReCycle.

What are some especially cool techniques in Dr. REX, the REX-file player in your Reason virtual-studio program?

One thing I really like about Dr. REX—which I didn't think about when we designed the program—is that you have realtime transpose. So a loop has a base key, and regardless of what pitch changes are going on in the loop, you can still transpose it up and down using a keyboard. That doesn't *sound* so powerful, but once you start using it in your music, you can make a loop that was recorded in one key follow through chord changes as you play. The realtime controls like filtering in the REX players are really powerful as well. So is altering the sequence of slices.

How about ReCycling something like vocals, which don't have the sharp attack transients of drums?

I do that a *lot*, and I know other people are doing it as well. It's a very powerful remix tool. You can find loads of *a cappellas* on the Net. I'm not sure how legal they are, but there are also loads of people who are *sharing* their *a cappellas*. They do songs and they say, "I'm looking for a remix. Will someone do something with this?"

It usually takes some tweaking in ReCycle to find the best slice points. But basically, you find a slice for each syllable, bring it into your software, and there you go: You can do whatever you want with it. You can use phrases of it, you can transpose it, you can take stuff out that you don't like.

and drama. I can EQ the vocal layers differently; pay a lot of attention to the stereo field, which I can't do live because the looper is a mono instrument; and add extra vocals or more intense rhythms. I end up with a different animal, but one that stands on its own musically, I think.

David Torn: I find the repetition of something beautiful is *not* boring. In fact, in my own studio, if I make a loop that I think is good, I might leave it running—just to kind of absorb it—for a couple of *hours*. I'll wander in and out of the room and see how it's affecting me, and decide if I want to fuck it up further somehow. So I never consider that line between useful repetition and boredom.

It's funny, because my own looping has become more and more manipulated. I never think of any of the loops that I'm making as static *while* I'm making them. Because each loop is a performance in itself, it seems like a very fine point on when you say, "Okay, that's good. Let's use this now."

When I got the first audio version of Logic, I started to see that you could use finer and finer grains of these samples to build rhythmic events from the textural elements. Those events would then become their own little quasi-repetitive cellular data. They're

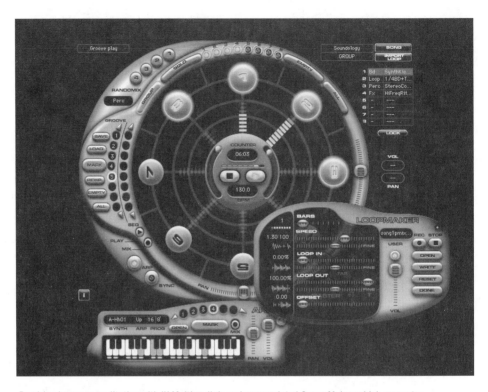

Remixing becomes meditation with IK Multimedia's underappreciated GrooveMaker, which generates semirandom combinations of up to eight stereo loops. When you hear one you like, you can mark it, and then sequence your discoveries into a continuous audio file.

not really repeating; they really are evolving. But the technology led me to a major shift where I started looking at my computer as another one of my musical instruments.

Douglas Morton: Loops caught me by surprise, man. I was a real multisample guy. People were starting to ask for loops, and I'm going, "Why? Isn't that kind of *lazy?*" I had this weird attitude about it. Then when I started working with them . . . I brought my 10-year-old nephew into my studio, and in five minutes he's got this massive piece of music going on, and I'm like, "Oh. [*Laughs.*] I think there's something to this."

Quantize THIS

Exploiting the creative tension between machine and human feel

Some of the best art arises from collisions between different cultures. And it's no different in the epic partnership (some would say battle) between musicians and machines. Here our virtual panel discusses how to harness the creative tension between quantized computer precision and swashbuckling human feel.

Today's software and grooveboxes can automatically conform sampled beats to a common tempo. How can you maintain interest when everything is chugging along in sync?

Gerhard Behles: This friend of mine, Heinrich, has a really interesting two-man band. Their setup is simple: They each have a notebook with [Ableton] Live on it, and each of them has his own set of sounds. And their rule is that they have not prepared a set. So they have a huge bag of sounds, and the artistry is that they just *know* them so well. Then they just assemble them on the fly.

I have tapes of hours of *really* cool performances that they did together. Because they have a question-and-response thing going on. One guy drops in something and the other guy comes up with a response of some kind.

Do they synchronize their computers?

Gerhard Behles: That was a good discussion I had with them. They said they tried both ways and concluded that it's much better without sync. Because computers nowadays are stable enough in terms of timing—

Robert Henke: The tempo is in sync anyway, so what they can play with is the phase. If Machine A is at 130 bpm and Machine B is at 130 bpm and you, for a short moment, go up to 131 or down to 129, it just changes the phase ratio between the two computers. So you can go from flanging to offbeat things by just slightly changing the tempo for a moment. And that somehow is way more exciting than having sample-accurate sync.

It's that wonderful randomness or imperfection creeping in.

Robert Henke: Well, it's the same as using an analog delay line, dub-style, and adjusting

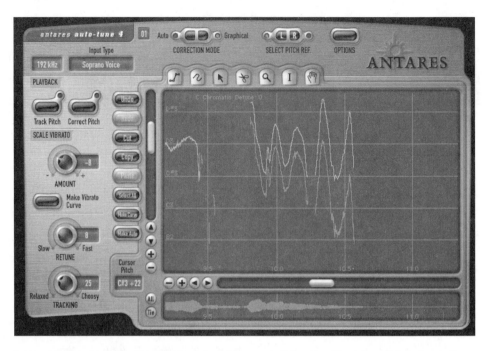

Antares Auto-Tune has been widely used (and abused) to correct pitches. Here it's moving a flat vocal up to the desired pitch while maintaining the vibrato.

it not per calculator and sample accuracy, but just until it *grooves*. It's a more musical way of thinking.

Glen Ballard: Most listeners now are accustomed to metronomic time, and so the challenge, for me, is to take real acoustic playing of interesting instruments and put that up against a grid of metronomic time. Sometimes you can go too far doing that, but I think you have to, on some level, reconcile those rhythmic elements a bit, which means sometimes correcting stuff in the live performances. And I don't even mean *correcting* it, but just kind of morphing it into [the] more metronomic stuff without *completely* quantizing it.

Almost everything people hear now, certainly in America, is quantized. And so, if you put a real drummer on, sometimes people don't get that. They don't know how to listen to that alone now. They need that extra little . . . *authority* of the regular time. So it's always how far you go with that, how far you take a conga part and turn it into a loop that's really locked down, or how much slop you allow.

I'm realizing for the first time how powerful it is to have those mistakes in there. *—Amy X Neuburg*

Nile Rodgers: Oh yeah-yeah-yeah! In other words, humans don't feel real now. I was pondering that just last night, listening to a record from an artist I want to sign. He'd given me nine tracks. The first seven were played with his band, and had a distinct quality to them. And the last two were sequenced and had a different quality. And this is really weird for me to say, but I sent him a message and said the only songs I was really into were the last two. Now, it could have been because of the composition, but a lot of it had to do with the feel. The feel of his band wasn't as good as the sequencer's. And that's *really* interesting coming from me [*laughs*], because I'm all *about* live and groove.

Musically, I imagine you can really play with that tension between the metronomic and human rhythms.

Glen Ballard: No question about it. And that can be very satisfying. On some of the best records I've made, I didn't quantize those two elements and it worked out fine. It's always sort of an innate sense of when I've gone too far. When it's stopped feeling as good as it did, you stop and go back.

Jack Blades: Sometimes you become a slave to technology and that takes the human, artistic, musician part out of it. It's good to have somebody like me who came from an analog world, who *knows* what feel is. Glen Ballard came from an analog world. Someone who hasn't come from the analog world simply doesn't know how good it *can* sound if you keep the humanistic tension and validity and volatility.

On the other hand, I know guys who are like, "I don't want to do it to grid." [*That is, record to a metronome.*] I love doing it to grid because you have the capability to fly parts around everywhere. But if you find that fine balance, that's the key. Sometimes when you double-track your voice [*i.e., record the same part twice to thicken it*], it's great to Auto-Tune one track completely and leave the other one the way it is. It just makes it really cool. It's *there,* but a little bit off.

Steve Reich: In live performance pieces where you're synched up with a tape, you would *think* the musicians would be playing the same way every night. My opera *Three Tales* is for a string quartet, four percussionists, two pianos, three tenors, two sopranos, and prerecorded sound. There *is* a click track, but *every* night is different. Whether you're pushing against that tempo, sliding *back* from that tempo, or locked *onto* that tempo, all these things are musical realities. And with good players, once they get comfortable with what they're doing, the way they play actually determines how the performance feels. They'll try different kinds of accenting, different kinds of tuning, different kinds of rhythmic stress. It makes a *huge* difference.

Roger, computer sequencers have many more quantization options than your original drum machines did. There are parameters like sensitivity, strength, randomness, and duration. Have you played much with those?

Roger Linn: Yes, and I didn't find them to be that helpful. In my earlier products, I

Swinging Machines: The Birth of Quantization

Roger Linn's discovery of quantization—or "timing correct," as he called it on his instruments—was one of the pivotal happy accidents in popular music. Today, every sequencer and drum machine can automatically move the notes you play to the correct rhythmic position, producing quartz-accurate grooves. But Linn was also the first to implement "swing" quantization (which he initially called "shuffle"), which puts a big part of the human feel back in.

As he describes the quantization breakthrough, "Memory was very expensive back then, so I needed to use it sparingly. Recognizing that most drumbeats contained only 16th-notes or 8th-note triplets, I initially created a real-time recording scheme that only allowed storage of 16th-notes. When I tested it, I quickly discovered that everything I played was being moved onto the nearest 16th-note, which had the cool effect of correcting my bad timing.

"Of course, the problem was that you couldn't record triplets, 32nd-notes, or exactly what you'd played. So I had to come up with a higher resolution. [*He used 192nd-notes, or 48 divisions per quarter-note.*] But then once I had that, I no longer had the effect of cleaning up 16th-note timing. So I ended up using high-resolution recording plus a 'funnel' that would optionally move your played notes onto 16th-notes, 8th-note triplets, or whatever timing value you wanted."

Swing quantization was another stroke of luck. While searching for a way to convert between 16th-notes and 16th-note triplets, Linn delayed the second note in each pair of 16ths so it fell on the subsequent triplet. But then he noticed that intermediate delay values produced a variety of interesting "feels." So he made that parameter accessible, and the rest is hip-hop history.

Roger Linn with his LM-1, the first programmable, sampled-sound drum machine. It has six swing settings ranging from 50 to 70 percent.

narrowed it down to what I thought were the most important things. I found that the most useful way to quantize keyboard parts is to quantize the attacks and maintain the durations of the notes. I didn't see as much need for quantization. And getting some of the less-useful settings out of the way made the product easier to use.

Jimmy Jam: I was working on a track the other day and I told the programmer, "Just set up some drum sounds for me in an [Akai/Linn] MPC3000. I'm just going to record this, and then you can fix it later. [*Laughs.*] You can grid it, you can put it in Pro Tools, and all that." But I just wanted to record the way I did in the old days, where I just put up a bunch of tracks, I recorded them, and that was it—I was done.

And when he walked into the room to transfer everything to Pro Tools, he said [*ap-*

preciatively], "Wow. This sounds like something from '88." And I said, "Good. That's what it's supposed to sound like."

Amy, you said you once tried to improve a track by compulsively snipping out all the breaths between your vocal phrases, and ended up sounding like a singing cadaver. What are some other ways you've managed to kill a track?

Amy X Neuburg: [*Laughs.*] Well, there was a particular song on my record *Utechma*—by Amy X Neuburg & Men—that was about somebody *dying*. And I took the breaths out purposefully, to give the listener, without realizing it, a sense of breathlessness. There's this *long,* flowing line of vocal that didn't have any breaths to it, and whenever *I* listened to it, I felt like I was suffocating.

So I actually did that intentionally, but there were plenty of things like that. If the Men's vocals didn't line up perfectly, I'd move them over so they'd be in perfect sync. That adds that lovely, unified, produced sound, but then the kind of beer-drinking, sloshed sound that we have on stage is gone. And there's something to be said for that raw energy.

So how else do I overwork? I used to put in gratuitous production effects that were just *cool,* like moving things from right to left for no particular reason. Or making all the pitches in a song absolutely perfect, which took some of the reality out of it, because nobody sings perfectly.

> Almost everything people hear now, certainly in America, is quantized. —*Glen Ballard*

I've been listening to Björk a lot and realizing that she doesn't do that at all. She'll double herself and just be *way* off, or she'll breathe and be about to deliver a line and realize, "Oh, wait; there's no line here," and just keep the breath in. Or the pitch just sinks into nothing and turns crackly. And it sounds like a person is singing into your ear and meaning what she says. I'm realizing for the first time how powerful it is to have those mistakes in there; in the past, I've been taking those out. And I'm going to try not to do that anymore.

Scotch Ralston was lamenting how the audio production process has become so visual. He described how bands will huddle around the computer monitor and say, "Uh-oh. My kick drum was a little bit off the grid right there. Can you shift it 10 milliseconds to the left?" He said he often wishes he could pull a sock over the screen and get them to listen again.

Bob Rock: [*Sighs.*] Yeah. The thing is, the general public is being fed music that *is* being fixed up, that *is* being homogenized, so when they hear something that isn't, it sounds odd to them. Most people don't even know *why.* Everybody's just got to lighten up on the grids and the Auto-Tune. That's why the White Stripes or the Strokes or even *St. Anger* are so abrasive to people. Because they're not actually that abrasive. Those kinds of records have been around *forever*. It's just *now,* when everything is perfectly in time and perfectly in tune, that's what people expect. So . . . turn off the monitors. [*Laughs.*]

Bob Ezrin: I completely and utterly agree with that. I *hate* having the Pro Tools in the control room. The refined manipulation shouldn't be happening at the point of performance, because they're mutually exclusive. That's why I prefer to work with artists who have developed the material completely before we ever get into the studio. You *can* manufacture performance; we do it all the time. But the difference between a manufactured performance and a real one is palpable.

The music industry has hurt itself *enormously* by trying to manufacture too much, by not allowing enough stuff to happen and grow naturally. Manufacturing is by definition artificial. And the audience isn't stupid; after a while they start to hear it.

The Fat Man: Joe McDermott [Team Fat composer and children's music performer] just did a children's song where he individually Auto-Tuned every note of a five-minute, *a cappella*, eight-part piece. And, I'll tell you what, man: He lined the Beach Boys against the wall and *fucked* them. It feels *fantastic.*

> The music industry has hurt itself enormously by trying to manufacture too much, by not allowing enough stuff to happen and grow naturally. *—Bob Ezrin*

Everyone in my circle is singing this "Baby Kangaroo" song now. And all the time he was working on it, I was yelling at him, "You are serving your computer! You are doing this wrong!"

Well, actually, I didn't. I kept it to myself this time because this has been going on for ten years, and I understand the pattern now. A guy doesn't yell at Dave Govett [Team Fat composer and GigaSampler guru] that the GigaSampler is stupid and not learn his lesson. [*Laughs.*]

Did Joe do all the vocals as well?

The Fat Man: Yeah. It's unbelievable. [*Plays "Baby Kangaroo."*] Eh? *Eh?* See what I'm talkin' about? He grabbed that thing by the balls and used it like a $20 whore and—wait, that's a mixed metaphor.

I thought he was serving Auto-Tune, but he was putting it where he needed it to do something that was on his mind.

Synth Charming

Squeezing soul out of electronic instruments

Electronic and software instruments can be very expressive if you learn to play them idiomatically. Here are some tips and insights on wringing the best performance out of them.

Mark, you've created some gorgeous electronic soundscapes. But in describing your Men of Honor *soundtrack, you wrote, "I wanted to deliver an emotional impact that still can't be created by electronic instruments." How could electronic instruments be made more musical?*

Mark Isham: Ultimately, I think it will be through detailed control of sound, and the ability to *access* that control in a performance. For instance, I have a brand-new EVI—Electronic Valve Instrument—that Nyle Steiner just made for me. [*See Steiner's site at www.patchmanmusic.com/NyleSteinerHomepage.html.*] So I figured, here's an opportunity. I've got some hybrid projects. The clients want them to feel organic, and yet they also want that sort of otherworldliness. Some new world of sound needs to be created here. And that, of course, is the beauty of electronic music—you can create a new palette of sound and then write for it.

But even with an instrument as sophisticated as Nyle's, it was like pulling teeth to get *anything* musical going in the hour and a half we spent. I actually gave up after realizing that it was going to be an entire day's project to get the right feel. Even though this instrument has a *tremendous* amount of control over parameters and was controlling an [E-mu] EIV sampler that has a tremendous number of controller inputs. Because there are no standards in these regards.

I mean, the violin has evolved over hundreds of years. There are entire buildings erected to the study of the technique used to control it. And consequently, we have an instrument that rivals pretty much anything in being able to deliver an emotional response. That's because it has *evolved.* And electronic music is still doing that.

Perhaps each patch in a synthesizer needs that amount of study and thought to really be evocative.

Mark Isham: Well, that becomes a question, doesn't it? How do we design sound-re-producing units and performance-control units so you don't have to reinvent the wheel every time you load a new patch? I mean, I can call up Sid Page, my favorite violinist, and he can play three notes that say more than *ten* notes I can play on the EVI or any electronic keyboard.

And I can say that with a great deal of authority because I'm actually a decent trumpet player, and I can pick up the trumpet and do the same thing. If the trumpet is the right instrument to use at that particular point, you can't *touch* it. [*Laughs.*]

Given that electronic instruments are still evolving, what are some ways musicians can wring more expression out of them?

Mark Isham: One thing that's really helpful is to understand how real instruments work. If you're trying to emulate a wind instrument and you never take a breath, you blow the appearance of reality right away. Whereas if you phrase as if you were breathing, a *tremendous* amount of realism comes in.

On a more general level, would you say that expression has to do with varying volume, timbre, and pitch? One telltale sign that a sound is electronic is that it never changes.

Mark Isham: Well, exactly. The truth of the matter is if you draw a bow across a violin string—even in the most rudimentary way—and then look at the waveform, there's nothing repetitive about it. It's different from the moment you start until the moment you end. And consequently, a level of randomness needs to be built into electronic sounds for them to come anywhere near the complexity of organic sounds. That's why struck and plucked instruments are easier to emulate—because they're momentary.

The only way you're ever going to get a synthesizer to sound exactly like a violin would be to have four strings on a little box with a bow that interconnects with your synthesizer. *—Dave Smith*

Scott, what parameters have you found especially expressive?

Scott Kirkland: There's a lot of little things in the Akai MPC3000 [sampling drum machine] that I just love. Just going in to the Sequence Edit mode and adjusting the filter or tuning or decay on each note can lead to some unique sounds. On our first record, *Vegas,* there's a track called "Vapor Trail" where the beginning has this very rhythmic, breathy part. That was achieved by taking a China crash cymbal and tweaking the filtering and decay on each individual note throughout that part. So it went from a "*Ch-ch-ch-ch-ch-ch-ch*" to a "*Chitty-pow! Chitty-chitty-pow-pow!*"—a really punchy, organic, breathy thing.

The Steiner EVI (Electronic Valve Instrument) converts breath pressure into as many as four simultaneous MIDI parameters. This model, Nyle Steiner's latest, can also sense bite pressure and (with a simple modification) lip pressure. The rotating barrel selects half-octaves; thumb sensors control pitch-bend and vibrato. For more information, visit www.patchmanmusic.com/NyleMIDIEVI.html.

Amy X Neuburg: *Every* parameter can be taken advantage of in a musical way: the notes you choose to use; the velocities; the durations; the dynamic shape over time; the song format; the lyrics, if there are any; the beat or lack thereof. . . . It's the very way all those things fit together that makes music musical.

If you use your tools to do something immediately gratifying or obvious, then you're likely to sound like the next person. Lots of people play the violin, but it's not too difficult to distinguish the great musicians from the ones that are simply good players. Electronics are no different.

Steve Horowitz: You know what's tweaky, thinking about that, is [Propellerhead] Reason. I've had the experience several times where I can recognize that there's a certain *sound* that Reason has. And once I started using it, I understood why. It's as if someone manufactured the same studio-in-a-box for everybody. I like it; it's like the socialist studio revolution. But it's *hard* to work in Reason and make your shit sound unique.

Because of the interface design or the sounds themselves?

Steve Horowitz: I think both. On the interface side, it's like getting a box of cookies. It's a really good box of cookies, but everyone's eating the same cookies. And then on the other side, I'm convinced there's a certain sound to the way it's processing digital audio through the [software] mixer on its output. A friend of mine was saying that he thinks it's absolutely true because he runs his outputs through Pro Tools and they sound different. And it's also because of the sequencer—it's a way of thinking about putting stuff together.

I *like* Reason. I think it's one of the coolest things that's come out in the last few years. But I don't like the sequencer in there, so I basically use it like a big drum machine. The ability to go into that thing and take 15 loops and pile them on top of each other and just

Splitting Fire

Musician and programmer Stephen Kay has created some amazing demo songs for Korg keyboards. (You can hear several on the disc.) He shared this tip.

"Here's a really useful MIDI trick you can do on almost any keyboard that has an arpeggiator: Set up a three- or four-way split, with the split points close together. Put a different instrumental sound in each zone. Then play an arpeggiator pattern so that it crosses the various split points, playing certain notes on one sound, other notes on another sound, etc. This works best if the arpeggio pattern is something with jumps and discontinuities in it.

"Also, try turning one of the zones off. That creates 'holes' in the pattern that instantly add syncopation to a boring 16th-note arpeggiator pattern. As you play notes in different areas of the keyboard, the holes will change. You can come up with a hundred different riffs quickly."

Stephen Kay developed KARMA software (onscreen) after outgrowing traditional arpeggiators.

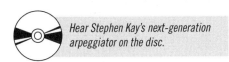

Hear Stephen Kay's next-generation arpeggiator on the disc.

come out with *amazing* drum tracks is pretty unparalleled. I just create my drum tracks and export them as audio files. And then I shoot them either into SampleCell or Pro Tools, put plug-ins on them, and go from there.

BT: For expression, I look not only to the instrument, but to the effects as a part of the instrument—and actually the most dynamic part of the instrument. The process of mixing for me is that after I've worked on each individual part, the song is mixed. So I'm often doing effects, panning, and level automation as a part of the sound itself, and that becomes a part of its voice and its unique expression.

Nine or ten years ago, when I was exclusively using MIDI, I'd be looking to things like aftertouch and breath controller and the mod wheel to control an instrument. Now I may do a realtime spectral blurring in [Symbolic Sound] Kyma, followed by automating the reverb depth and a QSound panner speed, *and* be automating the volume—all to one sound.

That's a way to make that sound speak, and actually a *much* more powerful way to make it unique than obsessively editing MIDI controllers. I'm *really* a fan of riding effects as a means for making a sound unique. Some of my heroes are guys from the dub school, like King Tubby, where they're feeding something into an effects loop and the effects loop becomes the instrument. And obviously, I make all my sounds from scratch, so that helps, too.

Are you able to use those sound-shaping techniques live as well?

BT: Oh, *absolutely,* man. Actually, I've just been coding a signature series of plug-ins. My friend Luigi [Castelli] and I made a plug-in to do live stutter edits. I used it in my set this weekend, and people who would never normally have any clue that something punk-rock was going on in the DJ booth were just standing with their mouths agape.

Right now it's got about 30 parameters; it's got LFO panning; it goes up to 1,024th notes—you grab a piece of audio and you just fuckin' freak it sideways. You can't do something offbeat, either, because it quantizes the points at which you're allowed to change the note value. It's insane-sounding, dude. You've never heard anything like it in your whole life.

Does it use automatic crossfading so you don't get clicks as you're chopping it up?

BT: [*Laughs.*] There's *no* clicks, dude. Hang on a second; while we're talking, I'll load it on my laptop and play it off headphone speakers.

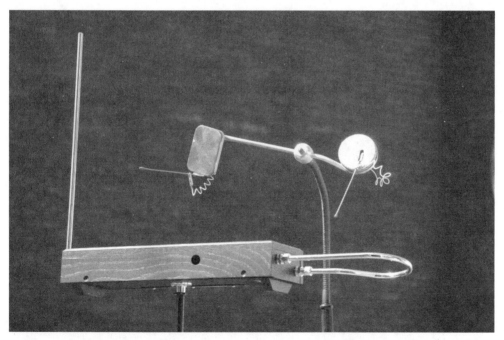

The Theremin, with continuous proximity controls for pitch and volume, can be very expressive, though perhaps not when played by a robot. Ranjit Bhatnagar built this player, "Lev," out of a floor lamp, some mint tins, and microprocessors. See www.moonmilk.com/labs/lev for more.

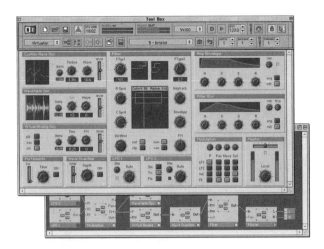

Native Instruments Reaktor is a brimming toolbox of synthesizer components you can use to build your own instrument and effects processors.

It's set up to work with four busses and the next beta of it will have four Done buttons, so when you hit one of the Done buttons, it will throw the signal into whatever effect you want.

The coolest thing is when I take it on tour, I'm going to *sing* through it. I'm going to sing a line, capture it, let the line loop around once, stutter-edit the hell out of it, and hit Done to let it go off into space in real time. That's going to blow people's minds.

Dr. Patrick Gleeson: I'm not sure that I'm the best one to speak about control because what I did a long time ago

Always Evolving

Pioneering synthesizer designer Dave Smith has made hit instruments in every phase of the electronic music revolution: analog hardware (Prophet-5), digital hardware (Prophet VS), and pure software (Reality). I asked him for the story behind his latest instrument, the Evolver, which spans those worlds.

"I was done working on software synths after sort of inventing the first ones," Smith said. "I *really* wanted nothing to do with Windows programming or computer-system programming. You spend your whole time looking up function calls, and then after you release your product, you spend most of your time updating it and porting it. If you have a software synthesizer that works great today, it won't work at all in five years. Plus, things can crash and die and burn and it's not even your *fault.*

"At about the same time, I helped Roger [Linn] on the AdrenaLinn, and it got me realizing how much fun it was to do the old embedded software/hardware projects that I hadn't done in almost 20 years. There was a period 20 years ago when a single person could design an electronic instrument. And then there was a period for about 15 years when you couldn't, because it required designing custom chips.

"But I didn't want to just do another analog synth, because that would be boring. I'm a person who likes to do things once and then move on. So since I had a lot of experience doing both analog and digital synthesis, I figured I could combine the two.

"I decided to make it monophonic just because that was going to make it cheap and much faster to design. But that ended up being a benefit, because as soon as you get rid of the polyphonic baggage, it really opens up a lot of options in the signal path and modulation. And I like to build concise instruments where you may not have every possible combination of controls, but it's limited in such a way that you can grasp it quickly.

was I gave up. I have been doing workarounds. I'll achieve the sound I want through an extraordinarily non-realtime process.

I'm doing this album with Denny Zeitlin [on which] we're taking piano pieces and basically turning them into jazz concertos with sample and synth stuff. And of course Denny wants to play real solos, and he's a wonderful instrumentalist. So we patch up the nearest bad approximation of whatever instrument he's looking for, and then after he's played it, I go back and I'll assign that one performance to maybe six or eight different MIDI channels, so that I've got six or eight different instruments playing this one instrument.

And then I take those performances, convert them to digital audio, put them through various DSP processes in [Native Instruments] Reaktor, and mix in various amounts of those Reaktor tracks to create something that really does, I think, have the nuance and the complexity of an actual physical instrument. But to do a one-minute trumpet solo, it takes probably 16 or 20 hours.

I guess everybody has accommodated to the fact that the realtime control is inade-

"The main unique feature I wanted to put in was the tuned feedback, because I've always liked feedback in instruments. The other was having everything synchronous so the LFOs synchronized with the sequencer and the delay and they all synchronized to MIDI Clock.

"It was funny how the digital oscillators came about. At first, I was thinking they could play samples. But getting back to the concise approach, I decided to use the VS single-cycle waveform oscillators just because I still had the wavetables. I even simulated the bad oscillators. As it turned out, everybody loves that part of it, as well as the interaction of the analog and digital components. You can distort the digital side and the analog will tame it nicely while still giving you outrageous sounds.

"It's funny; in Evolver I've got these 24-bit A-to-D and D-to-A's inside, but the analog filters can—on a good day—get up to 90dB signal-to-noise, which is the equivalent of, what, 14 or 15 bits? So it's put things in perspective. Chasing bits just gets silly after a while."

The Evolver is a hybrid of analog filters and digital oscillators and effects. Its four knobs offer so many sound-shaping possibilities that Dave Smith doesn't even use a MIDI keyboard to play it.

Spectrasonics Atmosphere was originally designed to make floating "pad" sounds. But the last-minute addition of another parameter completely transformed it.

quate for linear things, like a solo, because guys aren't making music on those terms. There's a lot of wonderful dance stuff going on, but it has little if anything to do with a continuous, complex line. In fact, the melodic lines tend to be campy. The complexity comes in these beautiful, semi-abstract rhythm tracks.

Dave Smith: To me, the only way you're ever going to get a synthesizer to sound exactly like a violin would be to have four strings on a little box with a bow that interconnects with your synthesizer. [*Laughs.*] You can try having pads and wheels and mouthpieces and pedals and flying your hands over something, and all that stuff can be somewhat translated into things that somewhat make sense on emulative sounds, but it's never going to be quite the same.

See and hear Dave Smith play the Evolver on the disc.

That's where the expressivity in something like an Evolver is completely different, because it's oriented towards synthesis and not emulative sounds. So the expressivity comes from the step sequencer, from the synchronized LFOs and delay, from how you interconnect everything. And then it's just a matter of automating your expressivity so it becomes

> There's a lot of wonderful dance stuff going on, but it has little if anything to do with a continuous, complex line. The complexity comes in these beautiful, semi-abstract rhythm tracks. —*Dr. Patrick Gleeson*

part of the personality of the instrument and less something that requires physical coordination and training, like alternate controllers do.

Eric Persing: With the work I've done in sessions, I've learned that layering is *extremely* useful. To a software engineer, it's no big deal. But to a sound designer, the result is very different. And coming from instruments like the [Roland] D-50, [JV-]1080, and [XV-]5080 that have multiple tones, I know this layering concept is very important to be able to create expressive sounds, especially with samples.

One of the parameters we added to Atmosphere [Spectrasonics' software synthesizer] that turned out to be really cool was sample-start offset. I had tons of source sounds from different analog synths and I had sampled the real attack of each. That ramp-up is a lot of what makes you go "ooh" about a pad sound. If the attack curve is bad, you always feel like you're fighting the keyboard a bit. Analog synthesizers have a completely smooth curve because there are no steps; that's one of the things that distinguish them from digital synths.

Companies like Roland and Korg have spent a lot of time trying to get the attack curve right. And we did, too. We found a good attack curve, but it was still just that particular one. And lot of beta testers were bothered that when they would lower the attack to zero, it still wasn't fast. So we added the sample-start offset so you can move the start point to any point in the waveform.

And just that one parameter ended up changing the instrument radically. Suddenly, evolving pads could become percussive sounds. And you could take just one harmonic out of a granular sweep. So that's why we changed the name from "Dream Pad Module" to "Dream Synth Module." Because suddenly it was a full-blown synth.

Dave O'Neal: We put sample-start offset into the audio engines for the video games, and it made all the difference in the world. I used that in *Future Cop* and it was a lot of fun because all of the explosions were scripted out of basic parts like sparks and blast rings and smoke. So it was like scoring mini-animations. I could take various sounds that I had in RAM and give them different

> If you use your tools to do something immediately gratifying or obvious, then you're likely to sound like the next person. *—Amy X Neuburg*

start offsets. And with about four explosion sounds, three build-up whooshes, and a couple of other specialty things, I was able to make a spectacular array of bizarre-sounding explosions that would fit every single one.

What else makes a good pad sound?

Eric Persing: Well, there's a certain transparency. What you're really looking for is things that will sound thick in the background but not take up too much space. Even with *all* the technology we have, if you put up a [Roland] Jupiter-8 with a pad sound, it's just *amazing.* So I prefer to find the sources that have those qualities as opposed to trying to create those qualities. Because I've found that by EQing or adding effects, you can compound the problem.

Jennifer, you're an admitted texture fiend. How do you create interesting textures and ambiences?

Jennifer Hruska: All that kind of thing I still do on the Kurzweil K2500 [synthesizer], because that's how I know I can get the most interesting weird stuff the fastest. I'll create an arpeggiator pattern and a multi-layer program, and then just start adding effects to each of the individual layers and each of the individual programs. The arpeggiator acts like a slow granular synthesizer or a wave sequencer as it moves through those layers.

Another thing I've been doing a lot on the 2500 is using the KDFX effects daughterboard, which is *incredibly* interesting and powerful. It's like a whole other synthesis engine, but effects-based. And the reason it's so cool is that it's classic Kurzweil fashion where they allow you to modulate all the effects parameters with various controllers. I usually use the logical controllers like the random generators or sample-and-holds. You can start to modulate things like the algorithms that play around with pitch and the harmonic spectrum. I get some *really* interesting stuff out of that.

The ability to go into Reason and take 15 loops and pile them on top of each other and just come out with amazing drum tracks is pretty unparalleled. *—Steve Horowitz*

Doug, when you were designing the Kompakt software sampler to run the Quantum Leap Symphonic Library, how did you pick the features you felt would be most expressive?

Doug Rogers: For the orchestra, we needed legato [*the ability for a new note to start* within *the sample rather than triggering the attack portion*] and automatic alternating of samples. With strings, for example, the software automatically alternates between the up and down bow-stroke samples. That gets around the machine-gun effect that people used to hate so much, plus it makes it sound a whole lot more natural, because that's the way a string player would play.

Dave, if you were to design your own synthesizer, what types of control would you want?

Dave O'Neal: I have a Theremin, and those things are a *lot* of fun. There are only two parameters, but they're very continuous parameters. Most keyboard players are used to a discrete world; I love continuous control over things. I love playing with feedback.

I do that with telemarketers sometimes. I'll turn on the speakerphone and bring the receiver closer until it squeals. Maybe that's not music, but—

Dave O'Neal: No, it *can* be music. Just put a good drumbeat behind it. [*Laughs.*] You're figuring out your instrument. Once you get a specific setup, you play with it and say, "Okay, where are the sweet spots?" And you start playing with those different areas.

What's in the future for expressive synthesis?

Eric Persing: Right now, the limitation is that you don't have a lot of control over the timbre. There's a *big* difference between a modeled sound and a sampled sound. An [Emagic] EVP-88 sounds great, but what people really like about it is not so much the tone. It's the playa-

I'm really a fan of riding effects as a means for making a sound unique. *—BT*

bility, because you have all the dynamics and the constantly evolving tone. [*The EVP-88 is a software synth that uses physical modeling to emulate electro-acoustic keyboard sounds.*]

But if you compare that to a really great sampled Rhodes like the Scarbee Rhodes, which has something like 12 velocities, the EVP-88 sounds like a toy. But the Scarbee doesn't *quite* have the same amount of dynamics as the real sound.

So I think what you're going to see is the ability to take all those velocity layers in a sample, make models of them, and then have the software interpolate between all those layers.

That's the dream. Because when you can do that, then you'll have all the expression *and* the realistic sound. Someday there won't be sample libraries anymore; we'll basically use samples as impulses.

Phone It In

Making mobile music

The future of music may be in the palm of your hand. In recent years, there have been dramatic advances in the sound chips on cell phones and PDAs. Downloadable ringtones are a multi-billion-dollar business, artists are composing for the synthesizers in phones, and bands are releasing their music as ringtones before the CD comes out. Here are some insights on the art and science of mobile music.

So, what's so exciting about wireless?

Jim Griffin: To be totally honest, my specialty is audio, and music and audio are to the mobile person what video is to the stationary person. If you're thinking about digital music and new forms of delivery, it's best to figure out how they're going to happen without a copper cable, because the audience doesn't want to *be* at the other end of a copper cable. The digits are finding the shortest path to the recipient, and that recipient is moving around.

You said you've been intrigued by how wireless technology is transforming Finland. What's going on there?

Jim Griffin: Well, they're a laboratory for the future. If you go there, you can get a sense of what it's going to be like here two or three years from now. We *are* starting to close the gap, but the penetration rates there already reach 80 or 90 percent.

Is that figure exclusively cell phones?

Jim Griffin: I don't think they'd *call* it a phone. In fact, their phrase for it is *kännykkä*, which means "extension of the hand." So their focus is not so much on voice as on using wireless to extend your hand into the world in a significant way. And when you get that, you start to *lose* some of the functions you previously ascribed to your desktop computer.

But it's not like a desktop on wheels; it integrates into your life. I've struggled for a long time to bring my computer with me, and boy, is that a pain. Then I realized that it's not that I want to bring my computer with me, it's that I want some of that *functionality* with me. So it's not about making computers smaller. It's about making this extension of the hand more functional so that the two meet midway.

And is music a big part of the wireless experience in Finland?

Jim Griffin: Aside from ringtones, I wouldn't say music has been big *yet.* But that's part of what makes it so interesting: You *know* that it will be. I remember when I was working with computers with modems that were 300 baud [0.3kbps]; when we started to get to 9,600 [9.6kbps], it got interesting. And at 14.4kbps, you could download a song. In 1996, when I was at Geffen, we put out a full-length Aerosmith track that anybody could download. And I would say the common speed at the time was only 14.4 or 28.8.

The wireless device is now roughly there. As we move into GPRS [General Packet Radio Service] and 3G [third-generation wireless], we're talking about broadband to the hand. So we can certainly anticipate what's going to be happening.

Thomas, it seems like mobile phones are really pushing the musical frontier.

Thomas Dolby: This downloading thing is just astonishing. It's just amazing that people have seemed reluctant to spend ten dollars a month for all the music in the world, but they're very happy to spend $2.50 on a ringtone. I think it falls into a different category. It's like spending money on clothes—it's a statement. And I think young people have a different kind of budget for self-expression than they do for personal relaxation.

What's especially interesting to me is that with samples starting to come into play, now instead of just being an abstract of the song, it sounds kind of like the real thing. It's actually converging with the mainstream music business. Music publishers have been making money from ringtones for the last couple of years. But now with these real [*i.e., sampled*] ringtones, record labels are seeing the opportunity both to make some money from their recordings *and* to cross-promote their other products.

I've heard several labels refer to it as the new singles market. A seven-inch single used to be an instant, disposable unit of music that allowed the industry to quickly disseminate new releases and break new artists, but it was really a hook to get you to buy $20 worth of music on a CD. And I think the labels are fast realizing that ringtones can serve the same function.

Traditional singles on vinyl were about three minutes long. Do you think we'll start to see hits that are 15 seconds?

Thomas Dolby: [*Laughs.*] Interesting idea. But perhaps two or three minutes is the minimum amount of time needed to state a musical idea, repeat it a couple of times, and get people hooked on it. Though maybe with the famed short attention span of younger kids, two or three minutes is longer than they really *have* to concentrate on one thing.

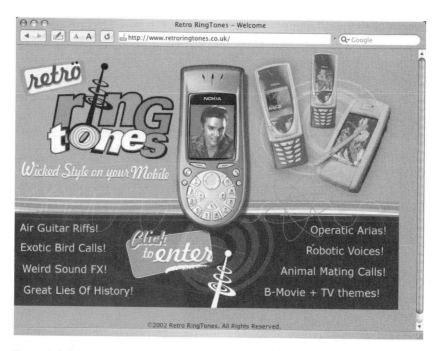

Thomas Dolby's Retro Ringtones service provides meticulously crafted ringtones to European phone companies. (Producing a good ringtone can easily take three to four hours.) The Animal Mating Calls series is especially popular.

There's a whole new aesthetic building up around phone sounds. They were originally designed to be intrusive, but now that they're more melodious, you don't necessarily want to mute them right away.

Thomas Dolby: It *is* interesting. As I'm making ringtones, I'll sometimes keep them on my phone for a day or two just to check how they're working. And it's fascinating, the range of different reactions you get.

We've just created a set of exotic bird calls. And those are actually fabulous as ringtones because they're designed by nature to emanate from a small object and carry for long distances. But they don't tick people off the way the Nokia jingle does. [*Laughs.*]

I've had one go off in a posh restaurant when it was in my coat on the back of my chair, and it took me a while to answer it. Heads turned, but they were smiling. In fact, one lady actually said, "What kind of phone *is* that? I'm in the market for a new phone." She probably didn't know about downloading ringtones, so she just assumed that if you shell out five hundred bucks for the latest Nokia smartphone, then those are the kind of ringtones you can have. So I probably helped them sell another unit that day.

But a lot of it depends on context. A very common practice has been just to take the hook from the chorus and loop two or four bars of it. But when you have full-spectrum audio, with bass and drums and vocals and everything going flat out, it fares worse coming out of a small speaker in a noisy place than if you can isolate an individual instrument or use a breakdown section.

It would be interesting to have some kind of synchronization standard for ringtones so that when multiple phones go off, they harmonize rather than clashing.

Thomas Dolby: Actually, with the exotic birds, we're thinking about doing a breakfast TV show and having a dozen or so people create a dawn chorus. And I know there have been attempts to get large groups of people to play symphonies by using the keys on their phones.

Certainly, you could do more to make the phone context-aware so that it played a harmonious sound. But in a way, that works against the need for it to jump out and be noticeable. In a club, for example, you could get it to listen to the tempo and key of the music that's playing and play something harmonious, but then you probably wouldn't hear it. [*Laughs.*]

Recently, I've been adding vibration tracks and LED tracks to our ringtones, which is a lot of fun because you get a little extra boost. I either enhance the kick drum with a short vibration or have the vibrations play a regular phone-ringing pattern—*vvvvt, vvvvt*—in counterpoint or opposition to what's going on with the music.

Do you find that composing for these extremely limited devices makes you more creative?

Thomas Dolby: Yeah. The attraction for me is sort of puzzle-like. That's coupled to the knowledge that one day this is going to go off when you're on line at Starbucks and everybody's going to turn around and go, "Whoa! Cool ringtone."

It's also challenging to see how small you can make the ringtones, because file sizes are really important. And obviously the more audio you use, the lower the sample rate has to be. So there's this constant battle to determine the minimum amount of audio you need to actually make a statement. Sometimes that means you need to get quite creative with the song. And then there's the philosophical dilemma of

> There's this constant battle to determine the minimum amount of audio you need to actually make a statement. —*Thomas Dolby*

"Would I be pissing off the artist if I made a different arrangement" versus "Well, he might be *more* pissed off if I used twice the length of audio and had to downsample it to 4kHz."

I just did a "Sex Machine" one. [*Plays a James Brown ringtone with sampled vocals; the phone's vibrating alarm hits on the downbeats.*] It's obviously restructured from the original. The horn stabs are just one horn stab being retriggered, and all the answer phrases of

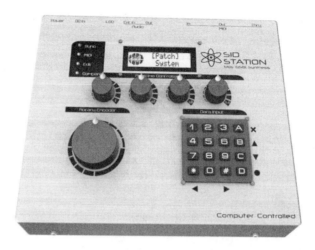

The Elektron SidStation is a modern synthesizer based on the ancient, 8-bit sound chip from the Commodore 64 personal computer. Jennifer Hruska uses its hip sound as a benchmark for her cell phone synthesizer sounds.

"Get on up!" are always the same. And then, to justify having the horn stab in at all, I wanted to come back to it more quickly.

So I'm taking quite a lot of artistic liberty with the song. And I don't know whether Mr. Brown would prefer to hear *that,* or whether he'd prefer to hear a linear section of his song, but downsampled so it's just unbelievably crunchy.

What are the typical sampling rates you use?

Thomas Dolby: Between 8 and 16kHz. We try to keep them below 30 kilobytes because that's the limit for the WAP gateways in most European territories. [*WAP gateways are computers that convert Web-based data such as ringtone files into mobile-phone format; WAP stands for Wireless Application Protocol.*] So I'll figure out what I want to do, I'll chop it up at 44kHz, and then I'll look at the file sizes. I get out my calculator and I go, "Okay, by the time I've downsampled this, what's the sample rate going to have to be to get it to under 30 kilobytes?"

It's not about making computers smaller. It's about making this extension of the hand more functional so that the two meet midway. —*Jim Griffin*

Quite often the answer will come out to 11,700 Hertz or whatever, and so I'll take that down another 500 Hertz or so just for safety. The Beatnik engine will play back any sample rate. With Yamaha chips, it's either 8kHz or 4kHz. So yeah, it's a black art [*laughs*], but it's actually quite a lot of fun.

Jennifer, your synthesizer sound banks are embedded in cell phones, so they have to fit into something like 100 kilobytes of sample memory, right?

Jennifer Hruska: Even less in some cases—one hundred kilobytes for an entire General MIDI set, which has to include all 128 instruments and a drum kit. So your individual waveforms are 1,000 bytes or less.

How do you maximize the sample memory? I assume you make only one sample per instrument and then transpose it to get new notes.

Jennifer Hruska: There *is* a lot of transposing going on, but cell-phone synthesizers start to sound pretty bad when you transpose samples too far. It takes a lot of processor power to create smooth interpolations, and phones just aren't there yet. So we try to make the individual waves small and put in a lot of 'em. One of our piano sounds uses 12 or 13 samples. Maybe the average is four or five.

Thomas Dolby was saying that working within such great limitations made him more creative.

Jennifer Hruska: Yeah. It's very akin to doing sound and music for the first PC music chips. It's like it's come full circle with cell phones, and now we're right back to doing these tiny embedded systems that definitely have their own unique challenges.

Actually, for inspiration, I think of the original Commodore 64 PC sound chip, which was recently made into a hardware synth module called the [Elektron] SidStation. Lots of techno musicians use it. It has a tiny wavetable, low bit widths, and lots of noise, but it sounds incredibly hip! So that's the trick in these cell-phone wavetables: Keep them hip-sounding even though they're small.

Hear original ringtones from Thomas Dolby and Jennifer Hruska on the disc.

But we're already starting to see the wavetables get a bit bigger, and starting to get a bit more processing power so you can do more in your cell phone synthesizer. It's starting to follow that same path that games and PCs did, and it will probably continue that way. In a couple years, we'll be back up to the PC soundcard-size sound sets and sophistication of synthesizers, and then who knows where it will go from there.

When you're demonstrating cell-phone sound sets for a client, the MIDI performances must be very important.

Jennifer Hruska: Oh yeah. It's all about the MIDI files. And the wavetable. The wavetable has to be really good. There's such an art to creating a good MIDI file, and I think there are very few people who know how to do it really well. I don't even think I'm one of them, but we've got somebody who *is*. [*Laughs.*] And I'll tell you, that guy can sequence like—he just makes stuff sound really natural and really, really good.

What do you hear in that when it moves you?

Jennifer Hruska: I don't know exactly what it is. I think it's partly his art, and partly that he's very expressive, so there's a lot of dynamics. He plays it in pretty well, so he doesn't quantize much, though he does *work* with the MIDI file after he records it. He has a technique where he creates a million tracks and then starts editing. He rips this out, rips that out, tweaks this a little bit, plays around with that. So it's a combination of being a good player and being able to play in good stuff to start with, and then just understanding MIDI well enough and having the ear to know how to tweak it after the fact.

And then you put that up with a good wavetable, where the *sound set* also has dynamic samples, where you've got a lot of movement in your samples—either through velocity-switching or filters or whatever—and you can get something that sounds really good.

Cell-phone synthesizers start to sound pretty bad when you transpose
the samples too far. So we try to make the individual waves small
and put in a lot of 'em. *—Jennifer Hruska*

George, you had a great story about how Team Fat saved a live gig with an ingenious cell-phone trick. What happened?

The Fat Man: We were stranded without any effects at a gig where the band that was supposed to leave the amps for us took off without leaving the amps for us. So we had to run all the guitars through the P.A. Well, we were pretty miserable until Kevin [Phelan] and Dave [Govett] both realized that they had free weekend minutes on their cell phones.

So one called the other, and we held one telephone up to the P.A. speaker to which my guitar had been panned, and we held the other one up to the microphone. And the sound came out the speaker, went up to the satellite in outer space, came back a little later, did some things—who knows what the phone system does—and came out the other telephone to be picked up by the microphone, which then fed it back to the speaker. And it created a lovely little slapback echo, with some repeat.

And that mysterious underwater effect.

The Fat Man: Yeah! It's the gated reverb of the '00s. It's the sound everyone will be trying to get.

Distortion Is Art

Twisting sound to your advantage

Gary Rydstrom has won seven Academy Awards for sound design, but his big contribution to this book is his wonderful quote "Distortion is art." He was talking about creating tornado sound effects, but the phrase could just as easily describe a strategy for humanizing the clinically perfect digital domain. Indeed, many interviewees seized on that idea to describe their music production techniques, from analog fuzzing to digital time compression and reverberation.

One of my favorite quotes is Gary Rydstrom's "Distortion is art." Do you agree?

Eric Persing: Oh, definitely. [*Laughs.*] Thanks to plug-ins, a lot of people have discovered how great distortion is. It used to be just the guitarist's domain. Around the time I did *Distorted Reality* [Spectrasonics' 1995 sample collection], a lot of people weren't aware that some of the great synth sounds had been processed with Marshall amps and fuzz boxes.

It's great when you can have control over whether a distortion is pre- or post-filter. That makes a very big difference. Probably my favorite analog distortion device is the GL-100, this Boss unit that very few people know about. [*At this writing, used ones were going for just $56.*] It's basically all of the Boss pedals in one rack space.

That's definitely one of my magic boxes. It's guaranteed that if I put something in that, it's going to sound interesting, and there's a good shot that the sound that comes out will be a classic.

Jimmy Jam: I totally agree with that. We always used to say hiss and distortion was our recording secret. When analog tape was out, we used to hit the tape *so hard*—we actually picked the tape we used based on which one we could hit hardest and how it would sound. That was a part of the sound of a lot of our recordings in the mid-'80s, like the [Janet Jackson] *Control* record and the Human League record.

Obviously, there will be digital equivalents of that. We've used [Empirical Labs] Distressors and all kinds of things like that to bring back that *frantic* sound—that sound where there's just a little bit of distortion that makes something sound louder than it really is.

Nile Rodgers: When I'm composing, I think in terms of purity and clarity for the most part, and then distorting it as an aftereffect. But I know a lot of people who use distortion as a construction tool, because distortion takes up a lot of space harmonically. And if it sounds happening, you have a record right there.

Alan Parsons: Well, yeah. Distortion is the very thing that makes anything interesting. But every aspect of what we combine to make music is distortion. EQ, reverbs—they're all distortions of the original.

Amy X Neuburg: I see what he's getting at—that distortion is an artistically valid way to be expressive, and it definitely is. Think of Nine Inch Nails and how much power there is in that screaming distorted vocal and the giant wall-of-distorted-guitars thing. That passion would be completely missing without the distortion. So by that token I'd say reverb is art, and volume shape is art, and contrast is art, and vocal quality is art. For me vocal quality is a big one: close-miked or not, airy or gutsy, vibrato or not, high range or low, operatic or rock. I try to choose these things so they serve the song in an expressive way.

Ken Jordan: Abso*lutely*. [*Laughs.*] Distortion *is* art. We spend most of our time getting different types of distortion and figuring out what types of distortion sound best on different things.

Scott Kirkland: I don't think there would be a Crystal Method without distortion. [*Laughs.*]

Ken Jordan: Have that guy call us!

Scott Kirkland: Yeah, distortion and all the different fuzzes and coloration—that whole process has definitely been one of the biggest sparks for us in the studio, creatively and inspirationally. Getting away from *us* for a second, yesterday I heard that Daft Punk track "Da Funk" on KROQ. And the modulated distortion on the 303 part in the middle of that just completely makes it *talk*. It gives it a human feel. I don't think there's a track on our record that doesn't have some sort of coloration on the drums, or rhythm section, or synth sound, or bass. It's what we live for.

If something says "guitar processor" on it, the *last* thing you should ever plug into it is a guitar. Use it for drum effects; put your vocal through it. *—Joe Chiccarelli*

What I really liked about the quote is that it doesn't necessarily suggest just sonic distortion. It could be distortion of an idea, or a tempo, or lots of things.

Ken Jordan: Yeah, I think for us it's . . . distortion of a sound. [*Both laugh.*]

Steve Horowitz: Are you familiar with this whole suite of Pluggo plug-ins? Those guys [Cycling '74] are doing great stuff. That thing they have in there [*laughs*]—I want to say the Crapalyzer—where you can change the bit rates? You take these beautiful sounds

The popular Empirical Labs Distressor is a digitally controlled analog compressor with selectable distortion. (Note the "Nuke" setting.) The distortion is designed to emulate vacuum tubes or analog tape.

down to, like, *2-bit,* and it's like, *wow.* Another thing I've been using a *ton* of is the Rappify effect in [BIAS] Peak. Essentially, it just makes it sound like crap, and it sounds *great.*

Dave O'Neal: Or better yet, play the sound through really crappy little speakers and rerecord it. It's always fun to put things on the speakers, like coins. It's also fun to tape speakers *to* things and record that. That's good for kick drums—you just take a speaker and hook it onto a big cardboard box and mic the box.

The little Marshalls [battery-powered guitar amps] are great. I stick them everywhere—in the washing machine, the closet; I even tried the fridge. And have you seen the little cigarette-box amplifiers [www.smokeyamps.com]? I ran my [Novation] Bass Station through the distortion on one, pumped it through my P.A., cranked it up *really* loud, and miked the floor.

With a contact mic?

Dave O'Neal: No, just a [Shure SM]57 aimed at the floor. So you're actually picking up a lot more bass from the floor; it's shaking. And then I stacked three different layers of that. It was one of the most monstrous sounds I've ever come up with. It's on the *Future Cop* soundtrack.

Joe Chiccarelli: I love a lot of the cheap stuff. I find that guitar stomp boxes and old effects boxes have more personality than a lot of the new things that sacrifice character for pristine audio quality. Recently, we found something at a toy store called the Space Phone

Dave O'Neal creates enormous distortion sounds by miking a palm-size Marshall amp and processing the result in the computer.

[www.damert.com], which is basically a Slinky with cups on it. You could attach a speaker to one end and a microphone down at the other end, and there's so much metal in the thing that it just made the tracks sound like they were coming from Mars. I used it on vocals; I used it on a bunch of things. There are $3,000 effects boxes that can't do anything like that.

Often it seems like pushing things beyond their limits is what generates the killer sounds. And maybe that's where cheap stuff excels, because professional gear is designed not to break.

Joe Chiccarelli: Exactly. Plugging a few effects boxes into each other and seeing what you get is great. A lot of guitar stomp boxes were meant to work with a full 8 or 9 volts. But when you substitute a low-voltage battery and run them at 3 volts or 1 ½ volts, they start to do some pretty weird things. The normal distortion turns into this totally destroyed hyper fuzz. So usually if something says "guitar processor" on it, the *last* thing you should ever plug into it is a guitar. Use it for drum effects; put your vocal through it. [*Laughs.*]

David Zicarelli: There used to be this assumption that sound quality could be objectively compared, that you could say one thing was "higher quality" than another.

Curtis Roads, who is a very active author and experimenter in computer music, said that he really liked these photographers—the Starn twins [www.starnstudio.com]. The thing that really inspired him about their work was that he realized that quality was a parameter. That was a profound statement for me. And in fact, you *hear* this now in electronic music. It's very obvious that people have figured out that you can create a subjective effect of presenting something that's higher quality versus something that's lower quality.

This whole idea of quality as a parameter is exactly the continuum between electronic music that attempts to be about the machine operating properly—in genres like techno—and the machine breaking down, which you see in genres like glitch and IDM [intelligent dance music].

Before quality was a parameter, there were some people who still had the balls to use it as a parameter. We're in an analogous situation now. —*The Fat Man*

Thomas Dolby: That's an interesting take on it. Actually, one of my favorite illustrations of that is on the latest Björk album. There's one song that ends up with this repeating acoustic guitar pattern. It's like somebody gradually wound down the bit rate. It becomes lower- and lower-res and starts to introduce these artifacts until there is almost no signal there at all. It's a rather wonderful way to fade a song.

Pieces of 8

Three good places to hear the wonders of 8-bit music are www.8bitweapon.com, www.chiptune.com, and www.micromusic.net.

The Fat Man: Okay—yes! And *furthermore,* before quality was a parameter, there were some people who still had the balls to *use* it as a parameter. In other words, when people were trying to build undistorted amps, there were other people distorting them and saying, "*There. That's fine. I like that.*"

We're in an analogous situation now. In game audio, a lot of attention gets paid to having an orchestral sound. Frankly, I have *one* friend—Dave Govett [Team Fat composer and GigaSampler guru]—who listens to orchestral stuff for fun. Orchestral sound is something to strive for. But it's like weightlifter mentality: Part of being healthy is having strong muscles; therefore, to be *really* healthy, I'm going to pump up my muscles to the size of SUVs. In order to make *good* music, I'm going to put a whole orchestra on there.

But there *are* a few game music fans who are adamant about what they like. And what they like is 8-bit sound. [*See the "Pieces of 8" sidebar.*]

It's funny—every year at Project Bar-B-Q we have this discussion: "What is good sound?" And we keep wanting to measure it. We keep wanting to have somebody come out and define it for us. And I keep coming back to Jim Reekes's definition of good: whatever makes your dick hard. [*Laughs.*] Because that's what sound *is.* And *nothing else matters.*

> Hiss and distortion was our recording secret. That was a part of the sound of a lot of our recordings in the mid-'80s, like the [Janet Jackson] *Control* record and the Human League record. —*Jimmy Jam*

Technology is eight thousand rungs down the ladder compared to what sounds good. There are times you're going to want to hear a bird singing outside. And there are times you're going to want to hear your child breathing, because you thought he'd stopped. That's going to be what sounds good. And *that* is what audio artists do.

Leslie, do you ever think that people just stress too much about audio quality?

Leslie Ann Jones: No. Here at Skywalker, of course, we spend a *lot* of time dealing with audio quality, particularly on the scoring stage. We've spent a lot of time and money for that critical listening path. But the room we have to record in is so incredible-sounding that we're actually able to *hear* that stuff. I think the people who record in spaces where they might not be able to hear the difference, and still obsess about it, that's something else entirely. But here, if you change a mic cable or move a mic a quarter of an inch, you can really hear it.

Bob Ezrin: Pablo Picasso illustrated better than almost anybody that distortion was art, because he made it an evocative, editorial comment. Music has gone through that transition, too. Initially, music was simply expository—a guy walking through the town singing, "The prince has died, the prince has died." [*Laughs.*] *Rarely* was it about philosophy or social commentary.

It was only when instrumental music became more refined that, through a non-verbal part of musical communication, people were able to editorialize. And it was *fascinating* to

Distortion Is Science

Joe Bryan developed breakthrough hardware and signal-processing algorithms as a staff engineer at Ensoniq and Korg. He's now vice president of engineering and technology for Universal Audio, where he develops products like the Nigel guitar-amp plug-in. (He even coined the name.) I forwarded him producer Bob Rock's comment about encountering horrible distortion when trying to squeeze Metallica's 24-bit, 192kHz audio files onto a standard CD. (See the "Bad Audio Habits" chapter.)

I also mentioned an article at TLLabs.com that says a primary reason CDs sound bad when the levels are maximized during mastering is that many digital-to-analog converters (DACs) clip even when the signal is lower than 100 percent. According to the article, the meters in most audio software measure the level of the highest sample, whereas the peak of the analog waveform that's derived from two adjacent samples could be higher than either point. (It should be noted that TL Labs sells a meter designed to detect those peaks.) Bryan replied with this informative treatise on distortion. —David Battino

Distortion is poorly understood by most people. Clipping isn't as bad as you'd think, and there are several limiters that use clipping effectively (*e.g.*, Aphex).

First, a little background: VU meters were designed to represent the apparent loudness of a signal, not the signal level. The ballistics and integration times were chosen to match as closely as possible the human hearing system. Most analog VU meters have an integration time of about 6ms, which means the signal is averaged over that interval. (It's more complicated than that, but that's the idea.) It turns out that this experimentally obtained interval corresponds to results obtained from psycho-

The Nigel guitar effects plug-in, for Universal Audio's UAD-1 processor card, allows you to morph between amp models with a slider.

the audiences. Sometimes it was almost physically repulsive. Think about the stories of people fainting in the aisles at the playing of "Bolero": The music was so evocative of something that they just couldn't put their fingers on. Obviously what Ravel was going after was that carnal part of the human nature that came from a very tribal place. And he *touched* it with that material. He made people *feel* things they hadn't felt before.

So distortion of ideas has become the best way for artists to comment on the human condition. When they just tell the story, it's sometimes dangerous, but more often it's just plain bland. But when they use hyperbole, synecdoche, relativism—any of those artistic devices that takes something, stands it on its head, and then shows it back to the audience—they *very* often touch the nerve in a much more profound way.

Steve Reich: I don't know if you saw *Three Tales*, my opera about technology in the

---

acoustic tests of clipped waveforms. Clipping durations under 6ms are not perceived as distortion, but rather as compression with harmonic enhancement. The added harmonics are correlated in time with the original signal, which actually improves clarity and definition for some signals because the brain has more information to help identify the signal.

It's true that the digital reconstruction filters in a DAC can create peaks higher than two adjacent samples, and some DACs (most in fact) will clip this signal. But as I pointed out, those peaks aren't usually perceived as distortion. What *is* perceived as distortion is hard clipping over intervals longer than a few milliseconds. You can grab most any nu-metal or hard hip-hop recording to see what I mean.

Universal Audio's Joe Bryan has been twisting sound into new shapes for years; he devised the audio input for the revered Korg Wavestation A/D.

Several of the mastering guys I know are constantly complaining about people demanding CDs that are as loud as possible. Their customers don't listen on $25,000 mastering setups; they listen in their cars and on boom boxes where their ears are expecting this distortion. Ultramaximizers aren't the problem; studio clients and their fans are. Blame Sony for making the boom box, if you will. In the golden days of analog recording, when all the beloved classic rock songs were made, people beat the living shit out of their mixers and tape decks to get that distorted tone everyone's been pining for since the first digital recordings showed up.

The main problem with digital distortion is not the actual clipping; it's the bogus harmonics that get introduced by aliasing due to the low relative sampling rate. These are not musical harmonics, and the ear rejects them as noise. A lot of the discussion these days about the merits of higher sampling rates could very well be due to the smaller number of aliasing artifacts caused by digital overs. At a high enough sampling rate, digital distortion starts to behave like analog distortion again. Analog distortion is like the flaw in the diamond that makes it sparkle.

By the way, now you know what our parents were thinking about all that racket.

20th century. The three tales are "Hindenburg," in the early part of the century; "Bikini," as in the atom-bomb tests in the '40s and early '50s; and "Dolly," the cloned sheep.

In that I used a couple of techniques I had thought about in the 1960s but which were impossible to do back then. One of them was slow-motion sound—*sssslooooowing* down a voice *without* changing its pitch. And what you discover is that basically every vowel is a glissando. You know, "*Zerooooo.*" You never say a vowel by just hitting a pitch. If you slow a voice down on any speaker, you will hear that they either start below it and rise up or start above it and slide down to the next sound.

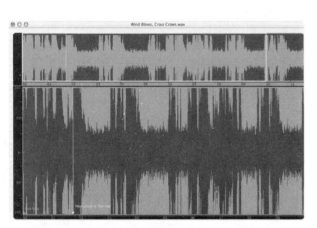

Notice the flat tops of the peaks in this waveform. It has been boosted so much that it's clipping. Digital clipping is a particularly unpleasant type of distortion.

The other technique was another sort of analogy to film: Just freeze the frame. I'd always thought, "Hey, wouldn't it be great if you could literally just say, '*Ze-rooooooo*' and have that held tone go on as long as you like?" Well, it was only possible just recently; it's called granular synthesis. And a friend of mine, Ben Rubin, gave me a piece of software to do both the slowing down and the stopping. It was written in Max, and Ben put a front end on it so I could handle it relatively easily.

In "Dolly," every speaker's vowels are extended so that when the next speaker comes along, that thought and that sound are still going on, and they become part of the harmony. It's going inside the minutiae of what happens to us every day and magnifying it, slowing it down, and sometimes just stopping it.

Aesthetically, what approaches work well when you're processing sound?

Douglas Morton: I'm a total reverb freak. I have a Lexicon 300. Everything you put through it just sounds . . . *sparkly.* And I *love* echo. A lot of times I'll put something through the [Lexicon] Jam Man and send the output into a reverb to make it *really* stereo. I put flutes through it, everything. But I don't use a whole bunch of different reverbs on one piece of music. It gets a little messy and muddy. I tend to try to get a common ambience and send little bits from each instrument to it for overall brightening.

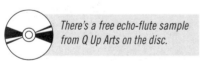

There's a free echo-flute sample from Q Up Arts on the disc.

Dave O'Neal: Digital reverbs, as much as they try to do cool stuff, you can hear them everywhere. I like natural reverb—burning a CD, blaring it out of my car speakers into a parking garage, and rerecording that. Once I started doing that, I got hooked. The sound just has elbows sticking out. It has personality.

Doug Rogers: There's really *no* reverb that sounds as good as a natural concert hall. I know there are reverbs like [Audio Ease] Altiverb—convolution programs—but for them to work properly, there's got to be enough information from the source instrument. Firing a gun in a hall and capturing the response and then applying that to a violin is not the same as capturing that violin in the hall.

The sound of a violin from behind the instrument is completely different from what it is in front. What the hall actually captures is a combination of [those] reflections, and that depends totally on the source material. So it's not something that you can successfully duplicate with any kind of convolution program, and they [Audio Ease] are the best in the market. We have a lot of very expensive reverbs here.

Hear a demonstration of EastWest's multisampled reverb on the disc. The DVD-ROM side has a 24-bit version. Try it with headphones.

We have a [Sony] DRE-777, which is like $10,000—we have them all. And we've tried applying them to the close mics from the [Quantum Leap] orchestral library, and they just don't sound anything like the hall mics.

For that product, we recorded with three stereo mics for each sample. So the user can literally zoom in or zoom out in a concert hall by changing the balance between samples.

What are some other exotic things to do with effects?

Dave O'Neal: I always like to do tape-stops, especially on drumbeats. [*Imitates sound of analog audio tape stopping.*] When one instrument does the tape-stop and everything else is cruising along, it's like, "What the hell's going on with *that?*"

Do you use actual tape or an interpolating digital delay?

Dave O'Neal: Both. A couple of times I tried to do tape. But it's just . . . messy. Which is *fun,* because if you get some old analog gear and build up this huge patch for something and make one glorious sound out of it, you get some really authentic things that people can't quite approximate on the computer. But it's a tremendous waste of time when you've got a deadline. [*Laughs.*] So other times I just draw the line for the pitch-bend [on the screen].

The Fat Man's paint-can Leslie speaker simulator *guarantees* a unique sound. He's planning a ceiling-fan version.

Bad Audio Habits

Avoiding digital downfalls

I t's easier to work the way the machines want us to work, which can lead to bad audio habits and dull music. Here, the virtual panel explores some clever approaches to recording, mixing, and mastering that can help you bust out of the rut.

Joe, in your ArtistPro.com forum, you wrote, "My New Year's resolution was to never use the solo function when I mix." How did that work out?

Joe Chiccarelli: Oh, that's really funny. I still don't use solo. I try to just put up the faders and go. And occasionally I'll take stuff out and mix *around* it, but yeah, I find that people can really get bogged down in mixing, trying to get every little element perfect.

Alan Parsons: I don't think there's anything essentially wrong with using the solo button, but I think it's important to put things into perspective and have their role in each mix defined. One way I work differently to most people—especially with *band* recordings as opposed to electronic recordings—is regarding the emphasis on the drums. Most mixers get their perfect drum sound first, and then add everything else to it. What I tend to do is get everything *else* right first and then add the drums. That was a trick taught to me by [Beatles engineer] Geoff Emerick many years ago.

Bob Rock: Joe is a man who's been around for a long time, and he's probably going through the same thing that so many people are. It's time and experience that really show the people who know what they're doing, and it *is* about the overall thing; it's not about the snare drum. That's why these guys are so good at mixing and why everybody goes to them. And that's why they can mix so fast. Part of the reason some mixes take so long is

Treat your speakers well, treat your console with respect, treat the musical *people* around you with respect, and playing into a computer can be just as passionate as playing in a giant acoustic environment. *–Phil Ramone*

The Yamaha DM2000, preferred by Phil Ramone for its tactile feel, was also one of the first digital mixers to support 96kHz, 24-bit audio and surround-sound mixing.

because people think they have to isolate everything. But really, it's about the song and the vocal; and then you bring out the best quality, and that's it.

Leslie Ann Jones: I can certainly understand why Joe might feel that way. In many cases if I'm given something to mix that is new to me, I'll put up all the faders first so I can hear what the whole thing sounds like instead of starting from a vacuum. If there's one sound that makes a record, it's a vocal. The rest of it is *important* to the record, but I don't think it's something that anybody should obsess about.

Jack Blades: The solo button is fine. I just make sure there are no pops and clicks from when you're punching in and combining. As long as the track feels good, I don't care. I learned that a long time ago singing harmonies: If it sounds right, I don't care if there's a weird part buried deep down in there. That just makes it sound that much better. My goal is not to make life perfect. Someone else can do that.

Are there any other bad computer-audio habits—not necessarily yours—that you'd like to break?

Jack Blades: Duplicating one chorus so everything sounds the same. Like on "Fly Away" by Lenny Kravitz—I mean, that's the same *one* over and over! [*Laughs.*] I do fly things around when I make demos, because it's easier. But when you're making records, you've got to have a chorus where the endings don't sound exactly the same. That's lame.

I always sing the second chorus first. And then I go sing the first chorus. Because once you get warmed up, then the first chorus comes *blasting* in. And if the second chorus is not good enough, you can sing *that* again.

There's also the recent, ugly phenomenon of dynamics being hyper-compressed.

Alan Parsons: Yes. I'm against compression and I'm against the level battle. I was playing a CD the other day and literally the overload lights were permanently on. [*Laughs.*] History tells us that louder is better, but I always try to preserve dynamics as much as possible, because light and shade are an expression of emotion.

People are often surprised when I tell them that I don't compress my mixes. I compress vocals and I compress bass guitars and occasionally acoustic guitars, but I try to steer clear of compressors on mixes, even though I realize that my mix is going to be perceived as being quieter than the next man's. The integrity of the original recording is preserved in my version much better than theirs, I think.

Bob Rock: Personally, I like the sound back; I don't like it maxed out. Really, it comes down to the artist. They just don't want somebody else to be louder than them. I would say the majority of the records you hear on the radio now are distorting incredibly. And nobody seems to care.

An interesting thing, technically: I did *St. Anger* all digitally. So we record it to 24-bit, 96k [Pro Tools] HD, we mix, and we go to master it. Now, of course, everybody these days is running at such elevated levels, it's unbelievable. So we tried to master it, and it was *horrible.* We couldn't get a CD to play it back properly. So after *all* that stuff we did, we had to put it to half-inch analog tape, just to get rid of the artifacts. That's *so* bizarre. Here I thought we were doing something really wonderful, and we had to go back to analog, because CDs can't handle what everybody's doing.

I've heard a lot of people master CDs a bit short of the maximum level, because the digital-to-analog converters on cheap CD players will crap out when they get hit with full code.

Bob Rock: Well, we did. But the problem is, especially in rock, there's the macho "We gotta be as loud as the next guy" attitude. That probably has as much to do with the sound as anything. It's all just learning. And it's kind of silly that we spend all this time getting these wonderful-sounding digital machines and then we go down to a 44.1/16-bit format. [*Laughs.*] It's insane, really.

Marty O'Donnell: I've noticed that as we have these visual representations of sound files, unless they're filling up the *screen* from top to bottom, we feel like it's not a powerful sound. I think that's why we're losing dynamic range, because we're saying, "Wait a minute—I can't *see* that waveform there. It must be too soft."

I'm like, "Well, can you *hear* it? But people are always compressing things dynamically, because visually it seems safer. It's the same with the performance. Just *listen* to the feel. If the whole band started speeding up just a little bit, maybe it was *okay*.

Any other bad habits?

Bob Rock: The only thing that I'm becoming less and less a fan of is Auto-Tune. I appreciate when they use Auto-Tune as an effect; I think that's pretty cool. But the whole premise of taking someone who's horrible and tuning them up, and then you see them on David Letterman and they're not even in the same key as the rest of the band. . . . [*Laughs.*] And I'm not pointing fingers at anybody; I've

If it sounds right, I don't care if there's a weird part buried deep down in there. That just makes it sound that much better. My goal is not to make life perfect. *—Jack Blades*

been guilty of that, too. It's just, really, to help the whole industry, everybody should have a degree of talent. [*Laughs.*] That's all I'm saying.

Do you ever notice that if you're adjusting something that has digital controls, you'll just move it to the next round number, not necessarily to where it sounds better?

Marty O'Donnell: [*Laughs.*] Right. There's no doubt in my mind that if I want to make something a little bit louder and I have the choice of somewhere between 32 and 43, I'll probably end up on 35 or 40 simply because it just looks neater. And I totally agree: That shouldn't be the approach. It should be based on what we're hearing. What we're talking about is the digital tyranny on an analog world, and I really want to get back to that analog feel. That was actually one of the things I liked most about Opcode Vision. I think they called it Vision because it was a more visual sequencer; you could draw shapes for volume and controllers.

We tend to blame the tools, but is there a way that musicians could be more creative in their approach to computers?

Amy X Neuburg: Yes! Musicians can be *so* much more creative. You don't *need* to stick to your sequencer's metronome. Your sounds can be lush and romantic if that's what you want, you can work with huge dynamic range, drama, rubato—all those things that give music shape and passion. I think the software and other tools now available provide as much possibility for creativity and expression as an acoustic orchestra, if not more, because we have such an infinite palette of sounds to work with. Whatever creativity computer music may lack, it's not the fault of the computers.

If there's one sound that makes a record, it's a vocal.
The rest of it is important to the record, but I don't think it's something
that anybody should obsess about. *—Leslie Ann Jones*

Phil Ramone: I feel a lot of that has to do with treating your computer more like an instrument. I see guys *slamming* their computer keyboard and I say to them, "Have you ever thought of treating it a little more gently? Then maybe it won't crash as much."

But all of it has to do with touch. *Mixing* has to do with touch. That's why I don't mix with a trackball; I use the DM2000 [Yamaha digital mixer] because it gives me at least 50 or 60 faders to move around.

It's just attitude. If you treat the machinery around you as musical, you'd be amazed how different it becomes. Treat your speakers well, treat your console with respect, treat the musical *people* around you with respect, and playing into a computer can be just as passionate as playing in a giant acoustic environment.

Jack Blades: That's interesting how he relates the computer to being that guy's instrument. Well, you know what? I've been known to pound on my fuckin' *guitar.* I've been known to kick an amp over when the amp didn't work. So what's the difference? As musicians, we're passionate people.

Philosophy

Producing in the Digital Domain

Benefits and perils of cranking it up to "1"

Internet pioneer Vinton Cerf once quipped, *"Power corrupts. PowerPoint corrupts absolutely."* Although digital tools can help produce great art, they can more easily overwhelm it. In this chapter, some top producers explain how they use technology on their own terms to enhance the musical message.

Bob, you did drastic Pro Tools editing to produce Metallica's St. Anger. *But that album has an extraordinarily direct sound. How did you overcome the computer user's tendency to polish the music to a slick shine?*

Bob Rock: I don't want to say I was getting bored with it, but it just seemed to have become too much of a job, too much of a technique, too much of a craft instead of the way music has always been to me.

For so long I kept saying, "What I try to use computers for is to capture a moment and *keep* it. Whereas before, I'd have to erase and rerecord it on a tape machine." But really what I kept doing was keeping that moment and then putting it in tune and in time [*laughs*]. It was kind of hypocritical of me. So for me to be excited about recording and music, it's almost like I went back to the beginnings of our musical style, which was Sam Phillips and some of those recordings.

Because there's such a *sheen* on so much music these days—though I've been partly responsible for it, too. For many years, I've been using technology to try to make things sound great. And recently I just thought I would consciously try to make records that have character to them and not be so concerned with fidelity.

The funny thing is, *St. Anger* is really the instruments being captured through great microphones, put on [Pro Tools] HD, and balanced. It's virtually flat—a little top [*i.e., treble boost*], a little bottom. So it's kind of odd that some of the reactions I've had to the

The breakthrough Alesis ADAT, introduced in 1991, brought multitrack digital recording to the masses. It recorded eight tracks of 16-bit, 44.1kHz audio on dirt-cheap VHS cassettes. (This more recent model has 20-bit resolution.) Multiple ADATs could be synced easily to deliver more tracks.

album are like, "Oh my *God,* have you lost it, Bob? How could you guys put out such a raw album?" And the fact is, that's actually how Metallica sounds. [*Laughs.*] There's no theater in it; there's no façade. Nothing's been fixed up. And I guess some people consider that ugly and kind of scary.

With the Black Album [aka *Metallica,* the band's 1991 album], there were a lot of sonics involved. And that's maybe why it's taken me to this new place with them where it's more about the moment and the true essence of what rock music is. The Black Album was probably one of the last albums ever done *without* Pro Tools. [*Laughs.*] And that was *unbelievable.* That was Steely Dan territory—trying to get the *best* performances and spending *hours* over certain guitar tracks, and *days* on snare-drum sounds.

I have always believed that the *sound* aspect of recordings was by far the least important. Otherwise we wouldn't have "Louie Louie.". *—Todd Rundgren*

Nile Rodgers: I have to say that I *love* organic sounds. Kids *never* ask me questions about technology; usually the things that are most fascinating to them are the things they can't figure out. Things like, "What was that sound in [David Bowie's] 'Let's Dance,' those things that are just clicking?" And I go, "They were just temple blocks." [*Laughs.*] And they'll go, "What's that?" They don't know.

When I started producing, when a percussion case was delivered to a recording studio for a session, all of that shit was in there. But a lot of kids have never even heard something like that. They don't even understand how *hard* a person would work to use the space around the instrument to affect the sound. And that's the thing: A lot of times people—especially people growing up today—don't understand that recording an instrument is not just recording the instrument *per se;* it's recording how the instrument is *functioning* in that environment.

And that's a lot of what makes records. At least, that's how *I* grew up. It's not the sound of the drum; it's the sound of the drum in that space, being hit by that person. Now a person just turns on a machine and thinks, "Okay, this drum sounds like this and that drum sounds like that," without thinking that same drum would sound totally different when played by another person, in another room, with another head, or another mic, on another day.

Don Was: I've got to tell you, being able to capture the *moment* of creation for an artist or a songwriter on a high-fidelity recording has had a *major* impact on making records. Because once that moment's gone, you're basically practicing re-creation, which is a whole different set of neurological functions, and you never quite get back to that one moment.

But it opens up a myriad of complications, the most significant one being the producer's ego. [*Laughs.*] The producers feel that they have to leave their thumbprint somewhere, and if someone's been able to capture it at home, why should they pay you $200,000 an album to validate their work?

The answer became really clear to me when we were doing a Paul Westerberg record. Paul had created *amazing* demos at his house, and the record company gave it to me on a second-generation analog cassette. And just by the sound of it, I assumed that they were not usable as masters. So we came up with a whole plan: [drummer] Jim Keltner and I flew to New York, Paul flew to New York, and we paid a lot of money for a big studio there, hotels. . . .

But some of the things he'd done at home, you just couldn't re-create. The drum parts weren't like human parts; they were cool parts that a guy with a drum machine would do. But they *worked* like crazy. And then someone made a passing comment like, "Man, I wish we had multitracks of this stuff, because I don't know how we're ever going to beat these demos." And Paul said, "I *do* have multitracks." He had cut it on two ADATs [Alesis digital 8-track tape recorders] he had at home.

We ended up using his ADAT demos for 75 percent of the record. Subsequently when that's come up, I've been asked to justify my presence on the recording. And I use the example of Sonny Rollins: Many people say that in Sonny Rollins's solos, the space he leaves is as important as the notes he plays. I think it's the same with a producer—just having the clearness of judgment to be able to say, "The demo is *it*. Let's go with that."

I think the artist kind of thinks that anyway, but they're waiting for someone to give them that vote of confidence. So when you throw your support behind that, you're saving a tremendous amount of money—and you're making a record that's got more honesty in it.

We're entering a weird period now where the money is not flowin' from the fountain [*laughs*] of the major labels like it used to, and where everybody's got a laptop and can make a record. And I think you'll see a little period here where everyone thinks that they can self-produce.

Yeah, you *can*, but Stevie Wonder is really the only guy I can think of who had a decent run producing himself. And then even he hit a wall at some point where he needed someone to sit there and say, "You play drums with a lot more soul than that Linn drum's ever going to do, so why don't you go back out there and set up the kit?"

I've produced a lot of records, and I'm working on my own stuff—I'm working on a Was (Not Was) record that we've been dabbling with for about a decade. [*Laughs.*] That is the *height* of the integration of mental illness and music: to take ten years to wrestle for control or perspective on *your* album. And we still don't have it. We're truly lost and we really need an objective person sitting in the room.

If you have a really distinctive voice and rhythm, you can make your point. And then the fun is what you put around that. —*Glen Ballard*

Do you ever run into problems with sonics when you decide to use the artist's demos?

Don Was: All the time. But it *doesn't matter.* To me, the feel, the integrity of intention, and the excitement of being present at the moment of creation have far greater value than any little bits of distortion can take away. You talked about recording this interview on MP2; I *like* the sound of MP3. I grew up listening to AM radio, so you've got to go a long way to convince me that something that may have a highpass filter set at 1k [*laughs*] doesn't have feel or validity. I don't really care about a "broad spectrum of frequency response." That's for *stereo* buffs [*laughs*] and *audio*philes.

I think creative people were misled down the road of hi-fi multitracking 30 years ago. No one's ever established that the ability to do that has been good for music. I think you can actually chart a real *nadir* in creativity correlating with the ability to defer decision-making and to separate musicians from each other, both in time and location in the room. *Sgt. Pepper* is still probably the crowning glory of technology as musical texture, and that was a 4-track recording.

The reality is that *nobody* puts their ear an inch from the head of a drum. It's a stupid place to mic drum sets. Sometimes, yeah, you want to bring a little more snare into the mix, but in the theoretical world, if you put one microphone where the drummer's head is, if the guy's any good, he should be getting the *right sound.*

And if he's playing the hi-hat too loud, someone should say, "Don't play the hi-hat so loud." You don't just go for maximum saturation of the tape with levels to be determined later by an engineer who may not even have been present on the live date—who may not even have a conversation with the *artist* about what's going on.

Jim Keltner told me that when they used to have 20 guys in Studio 3 at United Western, if you were playing too loud, everyone else would glare at you, because they couldn't hear themselves and they couldn't hear anybody else. So there was a mutually assured volume regulator. [*Laughs.*]

And there was a premium placed on dynamics. Now the dynamics are often deferred; you achieve dynamics by muting 30 of your 48 channels at some point in the verse. But what you really can't do is go back with mutes and create the effect of someone playing lighter on their instrument. So it's an artificial dynamic.

Whenever any new recording technology comes out, from the Victrola to metal cassette tape to SACDs, the manufacturers will get these effusive testimonials from artists saying, "It sounds just like me!"

Glen Ballard: That's true. Someone said there's nothing so dated as yesterday's view of the future. But I *totally* agree with you in the sense that when I listen to records that were cut in the '70s and '60s, they sound *really* dull. They sound thumpy and sort of *flat*.

I think they sounded *better* in the '50s in some respect, because there was more ambient sound in there. They weren't recorded in these hermetically sealed rooms where you hit a drum and it goes, *"Doop."* Drums don't sound like that. They have a whole other character—that sweet distortion we spoke about. [*Ballard had compared guitar-amp distortion to toasting bread, calling it "one of the sweetest sounds I know."*]

So how do we know what we're hearing now is perfect?

Glen Ballard: I don't know if human hearing really can accommodate too much more than what's happening. So I doubt it will be *hugely* different in the future. Digital recording is beginning to sound like one-to-one verisimilitude. If you have the right speakers, it's pretty remarkable.

Todd Rundgren: Well, that's an area in which I try to diminish expectations when I work with artists. Sound is an extremely subjective area, and I have always believed that the *sound* aspect of recordings was by far the least important. Otherwise we wouldn't have "Louie Louie"—people can't even understand the words in that song. [*Laughs.*] The guy's so far off mic that people don't even know what the hell he's singing.

So there is obviously something else. It was some basic quality in the song and the way that they performed it. I think it was the *abandon* with which they did it: the drummer doing fills every two bars instead of just sitting back there keeping time. Stuff like that made all the difference in the world.

Mixing for Your Inner Child

"Let's say you're recording children's music," said the Fat Man, when asked about unusual ways Team Fat was using technology. "So you know your audience is going to be listening on Fisher-Price cassette decks. Well, Joe [McDermott, Team Fat member and children's music composer] figured out that if you play your bass track back through a three-inch speaker and then mic it, the resulting track will have the exact frequencies that like to come out of a three-inch speaker.

"Then you do your final mix while listening on three-inch speakers, and you bring in just enough of the additional bass track that you can hear your bass again. You won't hear the difference on normal speakers, but on kids' speakers it makes all the difference in the world. You can use this technique to target boom boxes and car speakers. You can use it in a million different ways."

So I try to get all of the acts I work with to make sure they've done everything they possibly can to make the music they're about to record ready for performance. We go through all the lyrics and we say, "It sounds funny to sing that particular phrase; can we change the words here?" Or, "The lyrics here don't *mean* anything; how can you convey them with sincerity?"

So you go through and do all the work you can on the material first, because that is the most important thing: You can do a sloppy performance, but if it's of a great song, people will still respond.

Jimmy Jam: One of the things we've always tried to do is make songs that don't just stay in the same place. They *build*. I knew that was something we consciously did; we always thought that a song should start at one place and end in another place, whether it was slightly faster, whether it was louder, whether there was more energy. . . .

A good example of that is the song we did with Mary J. Blige recently, "No More Drama," which starts off very quiet. It starts with a sample of the *Young and the Restless* theme and then it explodes into a full-blown, almost gospel, refrain and then goes right back down and ends where it started, with the piano part. It's a song that takes you on a journey.

And when you have a vocalist like Mary J. Blige, that's the perfect kind of song, because that's the way she sings. She never sings anything in a static way. It always has a lot of dynamics. So if you make the music dynamic, then you bring the best out of someone like her.

One of our programmers said that when you open one of our song files and look at the tracks, the waveforms get bigger and bigger. I thought that was an interesting observation because I don't even think of opening a song and looking at the wave files [*laughs*]. But since he said that, and this was probably six years ago, I've had other engineers say the same thing.

It took me quite a while to get over the wow factor of actually looking at the music. It is an interesting thing, because you definitely get into that. Whereas you used to just listen, now all of a sudden you're actually looking at something that *is* the song, and it's a weird sensation. Now I don't even look anymore, but I used to be so fascinated: "What does this look like? What did we do?"

In the last few years, the technology baseline has gone up so much that now nearly everyone has access to world-class sound. How can individual artists make their own music stand out sonically?

Glen Ballard: Well, I think someone's voice is the fingerprint that can't be duplicated. If you have a really distinctive voice and rhythm, you can make your point. And then the fun is what you put around that. But to me the secret is always understanding how much support a voice needs in a track.

So I'm always trying to make sure that's the distinctive feature. I spend a lot of time trying to get the right vocal sound. The right vocal mic makes a *huge* difference. And I spend a lot of time getting the right key for people to sing in. Key, tempo, and the right microphone are fundamental to every decision I make about a song. Then it's the right beat, and then you build around that.

Jimmy Jam: A lot of artists we work with feel like we get the best vocals out of them somehow. The biggest thing I listen to with vocals is the performance. I don't really care about the notes—I mean, nowadays, you can literally fix the notes anyway, so it really doesn't matter. But even before you could do that effectively, the one thing I would always tell singers was, "Don't worry about the notes." The notes will come because I'm meticulous about comping vocals and really pulling out each little bit of something, whether it's a breath, a half a word, a quarter word, or whatever. I was always good at picking out the best little parts to put together, and enjoyed doing that.

But the thing I always told people was that I can't create *feel.* If you don't put feel and personality and energy into it, there's nothing I can do. But if you give me the energy and the feel, I can find the note somewhere.

Glen Ballard: If I'm recording a singer, I can give them four, five, six, ten tracks in a row, and just let 'em get warmed up and not even worry about punching in. And then in two minutes, edit it. I think I capture more of *their* juice and energy that way, and I don't have to *worry* about tracks. And yet, if I were too neurotic about it, I would make a singer do it a hundred times, when probably the best one was number 5.

I've worked with singers all my life. Some people need two hours of warm-up, but most people need more like 30 minutes. So it's those kinds of things that you're [now] able to capture lightning fast, then do a quick comp, give it back to the singer, and let them fix whatever they need to fix. In the analog days, it would take you hours just to comp a vocal. And with every bounce, you'd lose quality.

So there's been a huge revolution in that respect, because it's made it easier for me to record. That lets the process be built around the singer's emotional state and where they're peaking. Everything's gotten easier—on *that* level. It's still as hard as ever to make something brilliant. [*Laughs.*]

It strikes me that many musical instruments strive to sound as expressive as the human voice. We often talk about wailing saxes, screaming guitars, and singing sustains.

The Fat Man: True, but not all the time. To me, the voice is like the eyes in a painting. That's the thing your viewer is going to stare at. As soon as you have voice in your production, *boom*—the ear goes to it. But once you've got the vocal going on, are the saxes still wailing? They'd better not be.

I like that you see the good instrument as wanting to create the voice-like sounds, because for a while we were stuck with instruments that tried to sound like "real instruments" and ended up ignoring the voice-y aspects of them.

Too Many Notes

Overcoming option paralysis

The number of amazing musical tools at our fingertips defies comprehension. Legions of new software synthesizers and effects hit the Net daily. Sequencers come with 700-page manuals. There are now countless ways to attack any musical task, each webbing out into a maze of new possibilities. In this chapter, the virtual panel explains how it avoids option paralysis and gets things done.

Herbie, you have a trail of synthesizers and computers and gear stretching back for decades. How do you stay focused on developing a musical idea in the face of all those choices?

Herbie Hancock: Well, it's gotten to the point where sometimes there are *so* many options that I don't even know that certain options exist. [*Laughs.*] I don't read all the manuals all the way through like I used to. Usually there's a particular thing that I'm going for, and I just try to find *that* and try not to get bogged down by all the options. I may glance at them to see what they are, but I try not to use them just because they're *there*. They *are* options. [*Laughs.*]

Sometimes options *can* stimulate you. You'll see a new way to do something, and then that can conjure up other things that could be very creative. But I try to make a distinction between being controlled by the possibilities and *controlling* the possibilities.

Ken Jordan: I don't think anyone who's consistently making good music is constantly sampling all of the different software. It's pointless. That's like saying that before sequencers and Pro Tools, producers and engineers would continually try out different [mixing] boards and recorders. Whatever worked for them, they got to learn really well, and then they stuck with it.

David Mash: Well, as somebody whose first sequencer was a 16-step, analog ARP, I was really *happy* to see the capabilities expand. And I think that was great through the '80s. But then, I think you're right: Starting in the '90s, when we had a small number of competing companies trying to out-feature each other, you ended up getting these programs that do so much more than most people ever need, to the point that they're actually making it hard for what people *really* want to do, which is to produce their music.

There needs to be recognition of the various processes: I'm inspired; I hear this music in my mind; I want to capture that. I want to capture it as fast as possible, because it's fleeting. Those pocket digital studios are very popular just because of that: Somebody's in a hotel room, has an idea, plays it on a guitar, records it right in, and they don't forget it. They're little digital notepads.

Then there's the process of, "Okay, I've captured the idea; now I need to develop it." It was the same when I was writing on paper. You had that inspiration and there was the perspiration that got it from that initial idea to a completed musical piece, complete with the parts being extracted and the musicians who were playing it.

And the great thing about sequencers was that they could shorten that long time between the inspiration and the execution. The perspiration now is in the very complex set of editing and mastering tools. And they're all in the same software and all available at the same time, which is very confusing.

I think in the next few years—we're already starting to see it happen with the new versions of Logic and Digital Performer—people will recognize that there *are* steps in the process. And they'll work the software to the point where they say, "I work in *this* environment when I'm capturing my ideas, I work in *this* environment in when I'm producing the ideas, and I work in *this* environment when I'm mastering them." It may all be in the same software package, but there will be different screensets or sets of tools.

In the late '80s and '90s, there was a movement away from that modality; the philosophy was, "I want all my tools available to me at all times because I never know when I'm going to feel inspired." And of course, the result was that we got so many tools that we can't figure out how to get to the things that we need.

Roger Linn: A great example is the huge choice we have in music today. How do *you* buy music? I certainly don't go down to Tower Records and browse through the CDs until I find one that looks right. I let some friend or trusted advisor tell me what they think is good. I try it out, and if I like it, I steal it! [*Laughs.*] Well, actually, I will buy it. The times I steal it are when no one will allow me to buy it.

The greatest skill we all must master is the ability to adapt to change continuously. I find that in my workday, I spend half the time being productive and half the time learning new tools. If we can all learn to

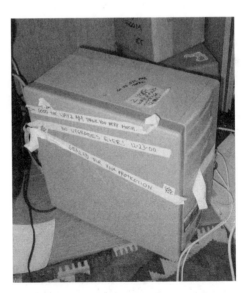

"Once your computer is operating well, wrap three layers of duct tape around it, and mark, 'No upgrades ever,'" jokes the Fat Man.

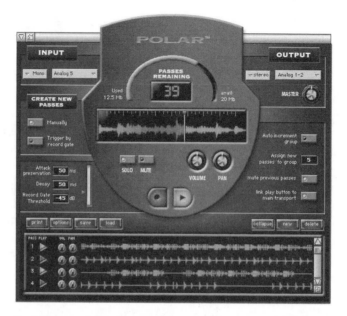

The Performance-Oriented Loop Audio Recording (POLAR) window in MOTU Digital Performer follows David Mash's goal of making the interface fit the task. Each time POLAR loops, it automatically records incoming audio to a new track and mutes the previous one, so you can focus on playing, not mousing. You can quickly lay down multiple versions of a solo or (with muting disabled) build harmonies.

adapt to change as a continuous way of life, then we get the option of *having* all these new ideas to use.

Robert Henke: I try to master one thing. So I do maybe 90 percent of my work in [Cycling '74] Max/MSP. I'm not using any VST plug-ins—with very rare exceptions—or any soft synths. And the only reason is that I know that Max/MSP basically allows me to do everything. So why not use the one way I know best and try to figure out what the *music* is like behind it instead of wasting all my time learning a new tool every day?

The same thing is true for my whole studio setup. I keep it small. I figured out that the secret of being happy while making music is having a small setup you can master.

A lot of music has been done by people with small setups. And a lot of boring records have been made when those people came into money and bought huge studios, because they spend all their time optimizing the studio. For instance, I had a big studio with the biggest and most expensive Genelec speakers available. The result was that I ended up thinking for half a day about the sound of my bass drum sample. How ridiculous! That won't change *anything*. Now I've sold the big Genelecs and I have my small ones again. And if the bass drum sounds good on my small Genelecs, it sounds good. And *that's it*. Then I go make *music*.

So reduction is always a good thing. And reduction starts with making a decision about the instruments you use.

Eric Persing: It's nice to have "seasons." I'll say, "For this season I'm going to do everything with the [Native Instruments] Pro-53 and [U&I] MetaSynth." And another day I'll go, "Okay, now I'm going to create sounds only with acoustic sources and processing." All those techniques keep your chops up. And there's the realtime aspect, too. Sometimes when you work with a computer, you just forget that live attitude because a lot of programs don't let you work in real time. So it does help if you can set up some systems and then *perform* with them a little bit, even if you don't have an audience.

Jimmy Jam: I love playing around with some of the plug-ins, but for some reason, if I start playing with plug-ins, I get stuck playing with the *plug-ins.* I don't really find that I'm creating anything great. But if I just record and then I leave it to someone else to mess with some things, it usually turns out a lot better. Because I grew up in the era when you just put the music on the tape, you know? [*Laughs.*] The first time I sequenced a song, it was probably ten years after everybody else did it. And I thought, "Okay, this is kind of cool, but now I have to think about the process of doing *this* instead of just thinking about the creative process."

Douglas Morton: Well, I love all this gear and the whole process. But I guess the most frustrating part is when you're in that creative frenzy and suddenly you have to switch into professor mode and debug something, or when something just freezes up. And that's why we still have grand pianos in our studios. [*Laughs.*] When I get frustrated with the computer stuff, I'll just play around on the piano to clear my palate. It's a really nice anchor.

But those complexities and crashes definitely drive you to get your studio hooked up so that when you're in a creative state, all the gear becomes invisible to you. People tend to go with the flavor of the month in DAWs [digital audio workstations] and sequencers, and I think it's a little dangerous to keep jumping around. There's a lot to be said for having a system that you have *moves* on.

How do you focus on finishing something—and then know when you're done?

Amy X Neuburg: You're never done. You just have to give up at some point. [*Laughs.*] You set a deadline for yourself. My problem is I've got my own studio, so I can just sit there tweaking for days without paying somebody else. Now that I can fix pitches, choose from 100 different reverbs, EQ until the cows come home, move notes around until every-

> *The most* important thing in my life in terms of creativity is finishing *absolutely* everything. —BT

thing is synced up nicely . . . well, I do. And then if I find I've worked the life out of it, I have to spend just as much time working the life back into it artificially.

So I tend to lose perspective on my work, and I can never seem to figure out when I'm done. If I don't actually set myself a deadline, I'll just spend another three years making the record. I keep telling myself, "Next time I'm getting a producer to work with—an experienced pair of ears to put things in perspective and keep the process moving along," but it never seems to happen. So I need to learn when to let go and stop futzing.

Alan Parsons: I think it's the role of any responsible producer to know when you've reached the stage where you have to make a commitment to a particular track. That's what a producer is *for*. I've seen a lot of people get bogged down with making choices on sounds [*laughs*], or recording everything as MIDI instead of audio because it's another way of making an endless number of choices possible even at the very last moment.

So I like to use MIDI to get all the performance parameters sorted out, and then find a sound that works, and then commit it as audio. You *can* change your mind and go back to the MIDI and change it. But more often than not, I've found that once I've committed something to audio, I leave it there.

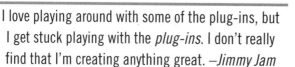

I love playing around with some of the plug-ins, but I get stuck playing with the *plug-ins*. I don't really find that I'm creating anything great. —*Jimmy Jam*

BT: To be honest, I look to my friends who *don't* finish things for inspiration. I have some friends who are *so* gifted and don't know when something's done and will mess around with it so long that they lose perspective. And then, at the *last* minute, when they're in the final stretch, they won't finish. So I finish what I work on, even if it sucks.

And if it sucks, you don't put it out. You obviously have to quality-control what you do. I feel like a really important part of the creative process is follow-through. It *nurtures* your creative energy and says, "Hey, we're capable of having an idea and actualizing it." If you let yourself off the hook, it deters you from finishing anything. So *the most* important thing in my life in terms of creativity is finishing *absolutely* everything.

Another part of actualizing your ideas is to limit the tools that you're working with. I recently pared down my studio to two computers, hardly any outboard gear—I mean, literally, the only outboard gear that I have is a really nice EAR [Esoteric Audio Research] compressor and a Neve EQ module. I got rid of my [Digidesign] Pro Controller. What else have I got in my racks? A [Kurzweil] K2000. . . .

There's hardly anything there because I found myself very confused by having so many awesome tools at hand, and just remembering what it was like to be frustrated because you only had three pieces of gear, and so digging in and learning that gear *so* well that you were doing things with it that really shouldn't be done. I totally agree with what you're saying: Some of the best music has been born out of frustration with having limited tools.

David Torn: In fact, [Marcel] Duchamp and the Dadaists set up something called "systems work," in which they would say, "You will now make a piece, and here are the

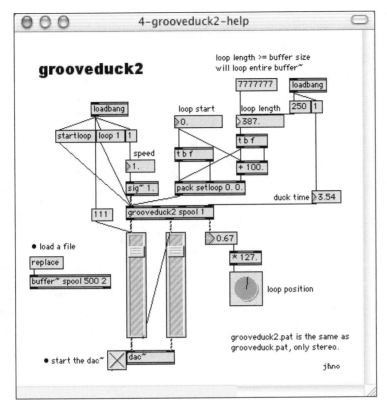

Developer David Zicarelli describes Max/MSP as an infinitely recombinable language. But he says that artists who use it don't suffer from option paralysis. The software's lack of constraints fosters a playful, exploratory approach to making music. This patch, by the author of RadiaL, loops an audio file.

materials. And you must do it within 15 minutes." And those very goal-oriented, limited pictures are *really* good exercises for people who work with computers, where the option anxiety can become the most strongly influential element that compromises creativity.

Actually, I'm remixing this Jeff Beck song right now. He sent me these tracks and said, "Do whatever you want." There are about 50 tracks. And I'm looking at it and going, "Okay. I'm not going to use all the tracks even if I like them." [*Laughs.*] I'm setting myself a limit already.

BT: I *try* to limit myself by time, but what I do more than that is make a lot of lists. Some of the songs from my album [*Emotional Technology*] took two months to complete. On "Dark Heart Dawning,"

> Sometimes options can stimulate you. But I try to make a distinction between being controlled by the possibilities and *controlling* the possibilities. —*Herbie Hancock*

Playing with U&I Software MetaSynth will change the way you think about music. The program generates sounds from pictures, and your audio-editing controls resemble Photoshop filters rather than standard waveform tools. In MetaSynth, pixel colors determine stereo position, vertical position determines pitch, and brightness determines volume.

my friends Mike and Carlos and I spent *six weeks* time-correcting a live bass, drums, and guitar. It's an *insanely* tedious process, but the payoff was that all the breaks meld *seamlessly* with the acoustic instruments. And it sounds pretty fuckin' awesome, man. It's actually my favorite song from the record.

The most frustrating part is when you're in that creative frenzy and suddenly you have to switch into professor mode and debug something. And that's why we still have grand pianos in our studios. —*Douglas Morton*

But it's really hard to go, "I'm going to work on this song for six weeks, and then by the time I'm done time-correcting it and just sick of it. . . ." You have to keep the goalpost always in sight.

The way that I do that is by making myself a lot of lists. Every night, the last thing I do—before I go and eat dinner and hang out with my girlfriend and stuff—is make myself a list. I'll listen to the song a couple of times; I'll print a mix and take it into my car. And instead of rushing back and going, "Okay, I'm going to do all this stuff right now," I'll sleep on it.

The list will be like, "Compress the kick drum a little harder; turn up 200Hz in one of the bass lines; the vocal EQ needs work and the compression is not high enough and it needs de-essing; the strings in the B section need editing"; blah, blah, blah. I'll make myself like a 20-bullet-point list. Then the first thing in the morning, I'll take the mix out in my car and listen to it, and I'll look at my list and see if it still makes sense. Usually about 90 percent of it does. And then I start on my day. It just keeps you really focused.

And when I start writing myself notes like, "Are you sure you want to use the word *such-and-such* in the lyric?" [*laughs*], I know I'm close to being finished. When your list starts getting irrelevant, you know you're close to being done. And then it gets to a point where I start playing it to my friends and they can't hear what the hell I've been doing for the last *month,* and I go, "All right; this song's done."

We're so supersaturated with such amazing technologies for the creation and offering of music that the people who rise to the top are the ones who rise to the task of conquering the technologies. And not just conquering the technologies on a fluidity type of level and on a command level, where you're able to get what you want out of them, but when you're able to know when to stop *using* them.

David Zicarelli: As far as when something is done, my own experience with recordings was *always* unsatisfying for that very reason. Because you might make something you're really excited about, and then when you listen to it a month later, little details start to come out where the performance is less than perfect. So to me the best way to think about a recording is as a performance that's been screwed up in time.

One of my favorite records is *The Mix* by Kraftwerk. They remixed songs from their previous albums, and for some reason, the remixes to me are so much better than the originals. That made me realize recordings are not fixed things. They are malleable work that you can continue to mess with forever.

One-Man Banned

Getting the band mentality—solo

Thanks to technology, it's never been easier to be a one-man band. But when you conceive and perform all the parts yourself, you lose the creative dialog between actual band members. Here, the virtual panel discusses how—and if—to recreate that collaborative mentality.

How can you replace the synergistic dialog that happens between human players when you're doing everything by yourself?

Chuck D: I'm training my staff to be totally against a one-person operation. I think the best music of our times comes from the collaboration of a lot of different minds. Yes, one person could come up with something, but in my experience, that way of looking at things leads to diminishing returns. Many people are satisfied with a loop and don't go any further with it. Many people are satisfied with a song just because they wrote it, without understanding that there are other aspects that make people *feel* music.

In the '60s, because you had a lot musicians recording with each other and trying not to get shown up, they put their heart and soul into it. And therefore, a whole bunch of simultaneous abilities floated to the top. And because so much went into it, I think people *felt* that music. It's almost like going into an old house. You kind of feel it—the spirit of the house.

Today, you can *really* get deep analog with some digital equipment, but it requires a meshing of different minds figuring it out instead of just saying, "Well, this one person in their little sterile existence is going to make this happen."

Doug Rogers: I could also take the opposite viewpoint that the whole concept of sampling is putting that dialog back. Because if you're using bits and pieces from different sample libraries, then you're also using bits and pieces of different people's ideas. And if you put those ideas together skillfully, then you more or less *have* created a virtual band.

And in many cases, sample libraries provide opportunities that just don't exist in the real world. For example, most people couldn't get Joey Kramer to play drums on their track, because Aerosmith wouldn't let him. So the next option is to use a Joey Kramer sample collection.

There is a certain interaction that happens when you get four or five people playing in a room together. Some great things can come out of that. I don't think anybody's really created a realistic sample-based jazz style, because so much of it depends on the moment.

But talk about things like dance music: It just wouldn't exist without samples. Probably 70 or 80 percent of the music that you hear in commercials and films these days is created from sample collections.

If we were to watch one of EastWest's composers creating an orchestral demo, how many fingers would he have flying around on the faders and mod wheels to get the necessary expression?

Doug Rogers: Well, it depends on the complexity of the demos. We have a MIDI composer working with us who created some of the most popular demos—Thomas Bergersen. He's a Norwegian in his early 20s, and he's very talented. He would use up something like a hundred tracks to create a demo.

When an orchestra is playing, each person in the orchestra is contributing quite a minor part to the overall sound. So if one person is going to become a hundred people [*laughs*], they're going to need a hundred tracks. And it can take quite a while, though Thomas says that he typically wouldn't spend more than four or five hours putting together a one- or two-minute piece.

Hear an EastWest sampled orchestra demo on the disc.

Stephen Kay: If you're going to program all the parts yourself, you have to learn to "be" the various musicians. Try to program little improvisational aspects into each of your parts, and then try to simulate interactivity between the parts. One way of doing that is to program a little "hop" or fill into a drum part—a quick snare accent off the beat, for example—but do it twice in a row. The second time, have the bass do something to go along with it. That simulates the live interaction of a bass player who heard the drummer's little "thing" the first time, anticipated that he might do it again, and laid his own thing on top of it.

And this is really important: There's a tendency to make each part too busy, like the drummer is playing the best shit he ever thought of in every single bar, and so is the bass player, and so is the keyboard player. You need to allow each musician to have some space. They don't all need to be brilliant at the same time!

Alan Parsons: Because the mouse is for one human hand, you can't really have more than one operator at

Beethoven didn't create the group scenario in his head when he was writing his symphonies. He simply imagined what it would all sound like. *—Bob Ezrin*

any given time. I found working with the Crystal Method an amazing experience because they just take it in turns. Ken will sit down for, say, 45 minutes and click around, manipulate a few things, introduce a few new loops. And he'll go off and get a cup of tea or something and then Scott will go and do his thing. They work so well together. They don't seem to disagree with anything that the other *does,* but they each have their areas of expertise. It's like playing a game of chess with yourself; it's just that you're both on the same side. [*Laughs.*]

> If you're going to be a one-man band, you'd better develop an additional personality to respond to. You have to develop that happy-accident guy. —*David Torn*

Ken Jordan: We know a couple of one-man-band people, and I don't know how they do it. I envy them and also I'm glad I'm not them [*laughs*], because I think they go crazy trying to figure out "Is this good?" or "Am I doing the right thing?" We've got a friend, Überzone [www.uberzone.net], who's constantly struggling with that. So I think always having a person to bounce it off is really important—for us, especially. Sometimes having *more* than one extra person will cause problems with the internal dialog—having too many cooks in the kitchen and all that. But with two people, things work out pretty well.

Don Was: I don't see anything really healthy in trying to emulate the feeling of people playing together—unless in misstating the sound, the texture, you land on something that's wrong . . . which is essentially what I think happened in hip-hop. With the Roland [TR-]808, they were *trying* to get real drum sounds. [*Laughs.*] They missed it by a mile, but landed on something that was, in its coldness, as evocative as Django Reinhardt in his humanity.

It's very hard to have live people play hip-hop and have it sound authentic. A lot of it is clearly digitally sampled and a little bit dissonant. If there's music that requires textures that are exclusive to the computer domain to be evocative, then obviously you can't do it without computers.

David Torn: I got hooked on digital audio when Logic Audio first came out. I got hooked on my capability of manipulating things right then. But I did realize pretty soon that it's boring to be a one-man band. So if you're going to be a one-man band, you'd better develop an additional personality to respond to. You have to develop that happy-accident guy, because these are completely produced works in which no other person is ever going to play anything or respond to it.

So there's got to be the ability to inject some feeling of give and take, a real response with the electronics. And that seems to be one of the small motivating things that drives me when I'm working by myself. I often do things on purpose that I *cannot* undo. I will make very harsh decisions very quickly—for example, destructively altering an audio file without making a backup copy. Or cutting a non-rhythmic audio file into hundreds of semi-rhythmic bits and not maintaining the original file.

I find that sometimes setting restrictions on an unrestricted workplace—setting up a system within which to work—actually gives a little bit more of the "Uh-oh . . . I shouldn't have done that. Now what am I going to do?" effect. And that's just another form of the happy accident.

Glen, do you have any tips for maintaining the synergistic dialog that happens between band members when you're doing everything by yourself?

Glen Ballard: I do. It's something that I do every day because I almost invariably start a track by playing everything myself. But I usually bring in other musicians very quickly if I feel it's necessary. That happens maybe 50 percent of the time. It's a little dangerous for me, because I can do it quickly and reasonably well. It's like an actor directing his own movie. So I have to make calculated judgments about my own playing. And I'm usually brutally hard on myself. [*Laughs.*]

I think the most satisfying records for me have been the ones where I'm collaborating with someone. So I usually have a large measure of the musical input, and the singer ends up writing the lyrics, or writing them with me. It's really organic. Working with a collaborator who's tuned in to what you want just expands who you are as an artist. So I'm always trying to be a medium for artists on some level.

Jack Blades: I've always been in bands, so that's a hard question for me. Of course, with Todd Rundgren in the old days, he would just record everything on his machine at home, and he made some great records that way. So it depends on the artist. I mean, Trent Reznor just blows my mind sometimes. And I'm sure he plays pretty much everything.

Bob Ezrin: You can't replicate a group situation all by yourself unless you have multiple personalities. But there's a long history of solo artists with a vision and a unique approach to creating all by themselves. Music is perceived as a collaborative medium because it's usually played by a large group of people. But *Beethoven* didn't create the group scenario in his head when he was writing his symphonies. He simply imagined what it would all sound like.

The thing I miss the most about the Time isn't really playing the concerts, it's just hanging out with the guys. —*Jimmy Jam*

What I would highly recommend to solo artists is that once they even *think* they know where they're going, *turn it off* and imagine the rest. If you can imagine the sound and the feel and the message you want to portray, then the one-man-band process is simply one of realization; it doesn't require a bunch of people working on it. *Hone* your vision and then *express* your vision using all the tools at your disposal.

Jimmy Jam: I've played in bands all my life, and I had a chance to play with what was, to me, the best band ever, the Time. Sometimes I miss just jamming with people. We try to do that in the studio a lot. We have a lot of musicians in our organization [with whom] we jam, and we record the stuff, and sometimes it actually makes it onto records, which is kind of fun.

You pull loops out of the jam-session recordings?

Jimmy Jam: Yeah. Exactly right. I enjoy the camaraderie of it. The thing I miss the most about the Time isn't really playing the concerts, it's just hanging out with the guys.

LTJ Bukem: Because of my love for the '70s music and the whole '40s, '50s, '60s, and beyond jazz and soul, I like the mix of electronica and the earthy kind of thing. And I know so many guys who play instruments so wonderfully well. I think it's so beautiful to combine that with your electronic bits and pieces. I have so much fun with it, because you get the main core of your track, and then you call the guys in. You get a saxophone,

 If you're using bits and pieces from different sample libraries, then you're also using bits and pieces of different people's ideas. *—Doug Rogers*

a trumpet, you get some strings or whatever, and then you can sit there and have a jam, and I totally love that.

There's nothing like feeding off of two or three people in the same room, just playing for an hour and then going, "*Ahhh* yeah! I like this little bit here. Give me that bit again." Then you stop and record something, and then you can carry on. But most of the time spent with those guys, interacting, is having fun as opposed to writing the music. [*Laughs.*] The music comes out of the fun.

Playing Games

Insights from the interactive-music world

Videogame soundtracks are perhaps the purest form of computer music—they're performed on (and often by) computers. They also present a huge creative challenge to the composer. Modern games frequently take 40 hours to complete, yet budget for less than an hour of music. The Fat Man, who's contributed scores to more than 200 games, compares the effect to driving across the country with one cassette tape that you didn't choose. But through clever composing and programming, game-music composers have risen to the challenge, developing techniques that can help even "linear" musicians make better music. Here are some insights from our virtual panel.

Marty, your Halo *music adapts to what a player is doing. How do you make interactive music effective?*

Marty O'Donnell: At the simplest level, it involves controlling how a piece of music will start, how it will stop, and how it becomes more or less intense. If I'm scoring a story-driven game, the music should work the way it does in movies, where it helps you know how you're supposed to be feeling at any given time.

Say you run down the beach, meet the enemy, and then defeat the enemy. If that were shot as a movie, I would know that I had 37 seconds of beach-running, 12 seconds of battle, and then a heroic finale. But if it's in a game, the player might be on the beach for two minutes and in battle for 59 seconds. So I have to be able to make something that will adapt to hit all those high points in a way that makes the player feel as though somebody had scored *their* performance.

Do you employ randomization techniques to make that work?

Marty O'Donnell: Exactly. We do that for all the audio, from the dialog to the sound design to the music. And it's surprising how much I can use the same tools. I like to give almost everything a beginning, a middle, and an end. If I know what the beginning is and I know what the end is, and I have a seamless way to get into the middle, then it's just a matter of figuring out how to make the middle malleable.

A scene from *Halo 2*, scored by Marty O'Donnell.

It's much easier to do that with ambient sounds or music, where it's just layers of moody loops. If I have a playback engine that plays those loops in random order, and maybe weights them so that most of the time you'll be hearing, say, loops 1, 5, and 7, you can spin out that material over a much greater time without being repetitive.

For thematic music that has sections like an "A" theme, a "B" theme, and rhythm only, I can do the same thing, and maybe have a more intense section that's only called when something intense happens.

To make those transitions work, aren't you pretty limited in terms of tempo and key?

Marty O'Donnell: Yeah. So that's the other part of the puzzle—how granular you think it's important to be. If you want to change the *note* you're playing as soon as something happens on the screen, that demands a MIDI-like approach, and some people are doing it that way.

I don't need to be that far down. If I'm in the middle of a phrase and something important happens, I can just have the playback engine make an instantaneous transition. If the new section starts with a cymbal crash and a tympani hit, who cares what was just playing? Because I know you can get away with doing stuff like that in film; it's the surprise change.

Transitions Are for the Weak

"People pay a *lot* of attention to having smooth transitions in game music," agrees the Fat Man, "whereas there's a lot to be said for having a sound happen *immediately*, with no regard to what happened before. In other words, a game player pulls the trigger and kills the giant flesh-eating gerbil, and suddenly you hear all the oppressed—what do gerbils eat? Say, mealworms—singing their song of joy. You don't need a transition, because when that gerbil's dead, he's dead."

If you've scored a film scene so it's perfectly synchronized, and then the director decides to re-cut the scene, often a creative music editor can figure out a nice way to edit it and still fit the scene. That might even change your melody, but it's amazing how malleable music really is. Sometimes those drastic edits actually turn it into a cooler piece. [*Laughs.*]

And to some extent, you can have the game playback engine make those decisions, too. If you want an interruption, who cares if there's an abrupt change of key? If a player is just crossing from one state of game play to another, I can wait until I'm done with the loop I'm playing, and then seamlessly go into the new section.

You've also talked about using a "boredom button" technique, where if a player never advances, you don't torment him with the loop.

Marty O'Donnell: That's something I've always felt pretty strongly about: Not everybody plays games the same way, and you don't want to torture them. They're already torturing themselves by being bad. So you don't want to play the same music over and over and make them really ticked off.

In *Halo* there is this "bored now" switch, which is, "If you haven't reached the part where you're supposed to go into the alternative piece, and five minutes have gone by, just have a nice fadeout." And then it'll fade into the background sound. People don't necessarily get the entire impact of what we were trying to do, but at least they're not getting annoyed.

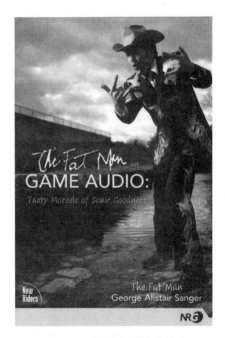

And the music will then have more impact because it doesn't just become annoying wallpaper. Especially when you're playing a game for 40 or 50 hours, I think that the majority of the time, you shouldn't be hearing music at all.

I would rather play a game where most of the time it's just really rich sound design and dialog and background ambience, so when the music comes in it's signifying something. And that way I can use something very simple—like a string sustain or a flute solo—and it still has impact, rather than having to pile more notes onto a piece of music that's already been playing for the last hour.

For a truly entertaining and insightful look at succeeding in computer game music, read *The Fat Man on Game Audio: Tasty Morsels of Sonic Goodness.*

Dave, what did working on video games teach you about making transitions in linear music?

Flashing MP3s

Composer and recording engineer Steve Horowitz has worked on numerous Macromedia Flash games for Nick.com. With online games, file size is a big issue, so Horowitz converts his soundtracks to MP3 format. Here's how he prepares his audio files so they sound good after the conversion.

"To tell you the absolute truth," says Horowitz, "I just want a good, clean file that's as noise-free as possible. And then usually it's just a matter of a bit of [dynamic] compression [*i.e., smoothing out the volume peaks*]. If I'm doing voice files, I put a tiny bit of reverb on the files—I'm talking a *really* small amount, and usually not a big hall algorithm, but just a small, almost gated, reverb. And then it's just a matter of making sure nothing exceeds 90 percent amplitude [maximum level]. Because if it gets over that, it can cause clicks and crunches in Flash.

"I know there's a lot of debate about preprocessing techniques, but I've run test after test and it just doesn't seem to make that much difference. The worst thing that will happen is if you have a lot of noise. A lot of people like to convert their original audio files to 22.05kHz first, but I don't do that. I leave them at 44.1, and the results are better or worse depending on what compression ratio you're using.

"Our standard bit rate for sound effects is 32kbps. Occasionally with music, I can bump it up to 56kbps. And sometimes with effects, we'll even go down to 8 or 16kbps. Sometimes if you really want something to sound crunchy and have that techno effect, you can crunch it down that way."

Dave O'Neal: How to build up to a transition. In linear music it was like [*lugubriously*], "Okaaaay, sssswellll," and then we'd come into the new section. Interactive music is like, "Okay, swell, *swell*, *SWELL*—" "We're at *11*, man!" "But we've got to keep swelling!"

So you learn a bit of temperance. You always have to keep a bit of headroom. One of the things [Electronic Arts'] Don Veca told me—he's a very talented sound person—was [*solemnly*], "To have something, you must first *not* have it." For me, the dive-into-it person, it was always, "We've got to start out the song with a really cool groove." Don was like, "No. If you hit that groove about two minutes into the song, everybody is going to go totally nuts."

A lot of things you do in interactive music are helpful for linear music, because we're basically trying to create ten minutes' worth of music with one patch. Often when you're trying to make a piece of linear music, you also have limited tools—a drum line, a bass riff, and a keyboard line. So what you're doing in Acid or something like that is very analogous to what we were doing in the interactive realm. If we were to come up with a better interactive interface, people might be able to create linear music with that really well.

Steve, how do you keep loops from getting annoying? You must have some special techniques.

Steve Horowitz: It's a *constant* fight. I can remember some of the games I worked on where I thought, "This is great," but when I go back and listen to them I want to put a *bullet* in my head. Because the *hardest* thing to do when you're creating these small loops is to create something that doesn't have too much melody in it.

Can you have multiple loops of different lengths that play simultaneously?

Steve Horowitz: Not really well advised in [Macromedia] Flash to do that—if you're looking for sync. If you're not looking for sync, it's fine. If you're in a game where there are a lot of ambient areas and stuff doesn't have to be so well synced up, that's okay.

Dave O'Neal: It's not so much the special techniques as the art. It's trying to find out what is *just* attractive enough to catch your attention, but banal enough to fade into the background.

There are a bunch of ways to do that technically. Actually the driving force behind our interactive music engine [at EA] was not so much how to make music respond to the activity; it was more how to make something jam on its own so you didn't hear the same thing twice.

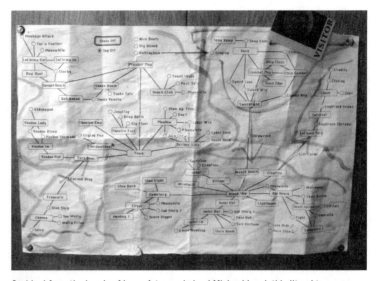

Grabbed from the hands of LucasArts music lead Michael Land, this literal treasure map of interactive music design for *Monkey Island III* now lives in the bathroom at the Fat Man's Abbey Trails Studios.

A lot of guys will layer a bunch of different loops with different intensities and cross-fade between them. And that's actually pretty effective. We tried to do more of, "Here's my improvisational groove, and as things get more intense, start hitting *these* improvs a bit more." We were working on that for a couple of years, and it got to be really responsive. But it also required people to implement it in the game properly, by deriving intensity information in a meaningful way.

The classic problem was flying over a fence, because for a while the game programmers were summing up the number of objects on the screen and considering that to be the level of intensity. But the way they constructed a fence, it had different objects for each of the fenceposts and such. So you're out in the middle of nowhere and you fly over a fence, and suddenly all hell would break loose sonically. It couldn't distinguish between fenceposts and enemies.

One of the joys of doing interactive music was being able to view the game as your instrument. So we would build our instrument first and then we had to learn how to play it. And that's where we ended up sitting down with the game implementers—the people who put the objects on the screen and make everything happen.

We could sit down and say, "Hmm, that doesn't quite feel right. What if we set the boundary for this hotspot a bit wider so you're able to build up the intensity before you come to it?"

The Future of Interactive Audio

At the 2003 Texas Interactive Music Conference and BBQ, better known as Project Bar-B-Q, one of the brainstorming groups set out to define what interactive audio is and what it should be. Participants included Clint Bajakian, winner of the GANG award for Best Interactive Score for *Indiana Jones and the Emperor's Tomb;* Dr. Mad, the inventor of the wonderful "generactive" MadPlayer (www.madwaves.com); and provocateurs from Texas Instruments, Creative Labs, LucasArts, Line 6, and Associated Production Music. I was in the group, too.

Dr. Mad, inventor of the MadPlayer, a handheld algorithmic music synthesizer, leads the interactive music working group at Project Bar-B-Q 2003.

You can read our entire report at www.project barbq.com, but here's the gist: Interactive audio is sound produced by a system whose predetermined sonic behavior is influenced by realtime events. Not all systems that respond to input are interactive, however. A doorbell, for example, simply plays back static audio events without any adaptation to input stimulus.

The panel identified 16 features a successful interactive audio system of the future needs, including environmental awareness; flexibility in input, output, and data; and peer-to-peer capabilities. To learn more about this evolving field, visit www.iasig.org, the home of the Interactive Audio Special Interest Group. *—David Battino*

So you're designing an interface to the instrument?

Dave O'Neal: Right. And that was a lot more of the magic in what made the game *good*. It didn't matter if you were using a god-awful 10-kilobyte violin sample as much as how well it responded to what you were doing.

Steve, on the sound-effects side, what are some things you do to warp sounds and make them more distinctive?

Steve Horowitz: Mostly I try to do as much custom stuff as I can—actual recording, not using sample libraries. The other thing I like to do—and I have the benefit of doing it here at Nickelodeon Online, because I'm doing a lot of stuff for kids—is use musical elements. I'll use music phrases instead of sound effects—guitar slides, little clarinet runs, stuff like that. That works well for kids, but it doesn't work so well for "kill" games. People don't like the sound of a clarinet *flooping* while they're trying to kill people.

Hands On

Designing interfaces that facilitate creativity

How do you play a computer when it can be a recording studio one moment and a saxophone or electric piano—or something far more exotic—the next? In this chapter, designers and musicians discuss how to get "hands on" with the virtual world.

INTERFACE DESIGN

Ernst, you've said the ReBirth interface enabled new people to get into music-making. What's the Propellerhead philosophy of user-interface design?

Ernst Nathorst-Böös: An example of that is the cables in Reason. Everybody loves the cables because they look cool. But some people say, "Why did you do that? This is a *computer*. That doesn't make sense. Why would you go through all this trouble to create virtual cables when there are standard interface widgets that you can use?"

There are two aspects to it. One is that everyone understands a cable. And since what they *do* in the program is exactly what a cable does in real life, you don't run into any problems. Everyone understands that a cable has only one plug on one end and one plug on the other, and if you need to go two places, you would need a splitter. When you try to transform the functionality into another user interface—dream up a new one—you always run into problems. So it's the simplest way for us to do it anyway.

Do you feel limited by that, though?

Ernst Nathorst-Böös: We only do it when it makes sense. We have pop-ups for MIDI routing in the program. We wouldn't use cables there because it wouldn't make sense.

I imagine the biggest request from Reason users is digital audio tracks.

Tage Widsell: The biggest requests are audio tracks, VST plug-in support, and MIDI output. And none of those requests goes quite well with what we want to do with Reason. [*Laughs.*] Product design isn't so much about democracy. We can't design a product that is everything for everybody. Marcus, our head of development, has this favorite catch

phrase: "Why make a Swiss Army knife when you can make a machete?" And we'll try to stay true to that statement, because I think it's really important to stay with your vision.

One of the visions with Reason is that you should be able to create full tracks with it—your entire production. If we were to add MIDI outs, then we'd have to add audio input in order for people to use their outboard gear. And putting audio in seems like not the biggest thing on earth, but really, adding some not-so-good audio recording would make Reason a less-capable Cubase instead of being a cutting-edge software-synth workstation.

It would also tamper with the stability of the platform and the self-contained concept. One of the good things about Reason is the interface. We couldn't possibly squeeze other people's VST instruments into that environment.

Why do so many music programs look like spreadsheets? It seems like that unnecessarily boxes us in, much the way that approaching a synthesizer as a keyboard instrument limits the type of music you come up with.

Stephen Kay: I might ask: Why does almost every review in a magazine about software that is a bit adventurous with its GUI [graphical user interface] include a comment such as "Cons: non-standard user interface"?

Also, why do OS developers try to force programmers to make all software as generic as possible? It's much more difficult and time-consuming to program something that doesn't look like a gray Microsoft spreadsheet or the Apple "Aqua experience" because Apple and Microsoft have whole teams of human-interface people making it difficult to step outside of the boundaries they've defined. For me, that approach takes a lot of the joy and creativity out of programming.

I *love* software that looks and acts unique, such as Kai Krause's work. [*Krause created the otherworldly interfaces for a series of innovative graphics programs; see www.byteburg.de.*] In fact, when it doesn't look the same, it may force you to work in a way that achieves results that you wouldn't have come up with. You don't

Propellerhead Reason sates the musician's fantasy of having an infinitely tall rack of gear, and this virtual studio program has been wildly popular. But emulating physical interfaces onscreen can compromise usability.

want the uniqueness to get in the way, but I like the idea that when you work with a piece of software, you can enter a unique world that transports you somewhere else.

Do you think there is a way computers themselves could be redesigned to be friendlier to artists?

Joe Chiccarelli: I think the *biggest* thing is interchangeability, coming up with a standard for file sharing—not only PC to Mac and vice versa, but for every program. It's frustrating that there are plenty of programs I would like to use, but they won't work in the environment I work in.

I wish it could all be there in one file so you could easily take the sequence you did in Logic and just drag it over to your Pro Tools session. And if you decided that you wanted to steal some drum samples from Reason, you could just go over and do that. [*See the "Flying by ReWire" sidebar.*]

I'd also like computers to start having auto-backup systems. I don't want to have to *think* to back up; I want the computer to do it for me. It's those mundane, computer-related tasks that should go away.

Thomas Dolby: To put that in context, when I started out 25 years ago, a musician was *very* unlikely to know how to work a recording studio. That whole left-brain thing of knowing what the signal path was, and how a compressor works, and what frequency to boost to make the hi-hat a little brighter—that whole vocabulary of music technology was the responsibility of an engineer. So as a musician, you might have said, "I want a bit more reverb on this" or "I want this a bit brighter," but you generally would talk in descriptive terms, not technical terms.

Eventually, machines came along that did away with the need for a studio and an engineer. But what they gave us instead was a 3D graphical representation of the *tools that he was using,* which presupposes that those are the skills you want to replace. What you really want is to be able to talk to your computer in the way that you used to talk to the engineer—to keep it creative, keep it in descriptive terms, and have the technology be there to translate that into numbers for you.

So to an extent, I feel a bit uncomfortable being forced to constantly get analytical and constantly use my brain when I'm really trying to be

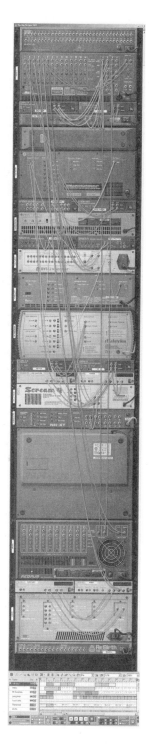

Pressing the Tab key spins Reason's rack around, exposing swinging cables. Unlike real-world ones, these don't get tangled, and they can stretch. For MIDI routing, Reason uses computer-style menus.

creative. You want to let go of all of that and just go with the flow. Of course, there's nothing to stop you from having somebody else operate the computer for you. And maybe that's the answer for me.

Marty O'Donnell: The biggest downfall for me is that a lot of the programs tend to be really good at steady tempos and rock-solid quantized feels. That can make really great music that needs to *be* that way, but there's a lot of other music that has feel and rubato and flow and emotions. And that doesn't work as well in those snap-to-grid recording environments. So I would love to see more of that performance aspect in software, so you can be more improvisatory and have feel without being penalized for it.

It's not that you *can't* do it, but the programs tend to say, "Wait a minute. You said you were going to be in 4/4 at 99 bpm—now what are you doing?" If you want a ritard or an accelerando or rubato, you have to *tell* it everything. So often it's just easier to say, "Okay, I'll just stay locked to that tempo." And suddenly everything sounds like techno.

Amy X Neuburg: The real bane of my existence is my giant Yamaha ProMix 01 digital mixer. It does *exactly* what I want: It's got moving faders, it's got built-in effects, it's automated, and it stores patches digitally so I can just call up a patch for each song instantly by changing the setup on my DrumKat. But it's a pain in the butt to carry around, so whenever I tour, I have to *ship* it.

Everybody says, "Why don't you just go to a laptop?" I have a lot of reasons for that. One is that the *only* thing that exists right now that does what I want to do is Max/MSP, and I could spend two years of my life learning how to program in that thing. And computers always *crash*. For me, it's great to have my Gibson Echoplex looper on stage because it's got these giant LEDs and red means I'm looping, green means I'm done with my loop [*laughs*]. I can just glance over and know everything's working. And if I have to stare into a computer screen, I'll be like, "Weeeeell, I can't find what I'm looking for."

I talked to a performer who said he hated the physical wall that the screen put between him and the audience.

Amy X Neuburg: That's actually a huge part of it. And the psychological component of having a laptop there, from the audience's perspective, is a little off-putting. Because they look at a computer and go, "Okay, that's

Flying by ReWire

In the quest for universal software harmony, Propellerhead ReWire (see www.propellerheads.se) is a giant leap forward. Like a virtual cable, the ReWire software routes audio, MIDI, and synchronization data between compatible programs on the same computer. That lets you, for example, control playback of Reason or Logic sequences from Pro Tools while processing the slave programs' audio through the Pro Tools mixer. ReWire streams up to 256 channels of audio and 4,080 channels of MIDI, and can even share text information such as track names. Best of all, there's nothing to buy or install; the ReWire technology is built into numerous music programs. But Joe Chiccarelli's dream of dragging samples and sequences directly between different programs is still a ways off as of this writing.

a magic thing with a brain of its own, and who knows what the human being's really doing?" And that's not what I want to get across.

Tage Widsell: I used to say that as well—I *never* wanted a computer screen between my audience and me. Now that I've switched—I recently did a series of gigs with my bandmate Stefan, using only PowerBooks, a MIDI controller each, and a DJ mixer—I find that the computer screen is not *between* my audience and me. It allows me to *have* an audience in the first place. I could never have come from Sweden to the States to do a gig without heavy financial backing if I had to pack down the whole studio. Now I have my backpack and that's all. I don't need anything more.

Dr. Fiorella Terenzi: I wish there could be some program that could give me six or seven alternatives while I'm composing. When I was at the Center for Music Experiment at UCSD, I was doing more experimental music, more like John Cage or Karlheinz Stockhausen. In that case, it's vice versa: The machine and the sound synthesis are very powerful, and sometimes you really do *not* know what you are going to get. So sometimes, the composition you have in mind comes out to be totally different and actually much better.

Those algorithmic compositions typically strike me as audible equations—conceptually interesting, perhaps, but removed from the passionate side of music.

Dr. Fiorella Terenzi: True. At the same time, the more you do that kind of music, the more you start to understand it. It's like a door opening into a new universe. I went to see Stockhausen and all those composers when I was a student in Milan, and I remember for years it was like, "I don't get what they're doing." I found the music unpleasant and nasty. Eventually your brain starts to understand and you get passionate about that music. So it's a totally different connection with a machine than doing popular music.

KNOBS AND SHADOWS

Programmers lavish attention on creating photorealistic knobs and other physical devices on-screen. Is there a more idiomatic musical interface for the computer?

David Mash: Well, we're in a transition period. It's almost ironic that we're emulating the physical world. In the physical world, we built these devices that have all these obstacles. It costs *money* to put knobs on a hardware device, so we made these user interfaces that are clunky and cumbersome to use because physically they must fit in a 19-inch rack and only cost this amount of money to do.

The instruments have *many* more capabilities than those interfaces provide. So now we go to the virtual world where *anything* is possible, and we emulate those restrictive, physical interfaces in software.

Then you move to a software synthesizer like the Emagic ES2 that looks *nothing* like any other synthesizer you've ever used. The user interface wasn't designed to look like a

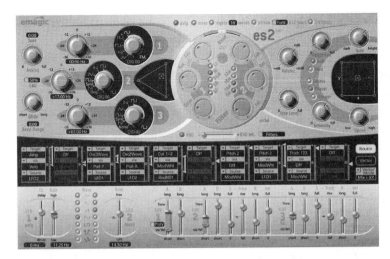

The interface of the Emagic ES2 software synthesizer resembles a signal-flow chart more than a real-world instrument. Future software instruments will undoubtedly have similar idiomatic designs.

hardware synthesizer; it was designed to allow you to make music electronically. You can actually see the block diagram for how the signals are flowing through the synthesizer.

I'd like to see the transition move more in that direction, which is to find new ways of expressing user interface that allow people better access to the tools that *make* that music happen.

Roger Linn: Whenever somebody complains about rolling a little bar of soap around to move a picture of a knob or a fader, the other side is that that malleability is allowing musical instruments to evolve far faster. You can do whatever you want and it's cheap, so ideas are popping up like crazy.

At the same time, a lot of people need an interface they're familiar with. Propellerhead Reason is a great example. The last thing I want to see on a high-resolution computer screen is a simulated LED display with those horrible fonts. But it's an excellent way for someone who's used to hardware to feel comfortable with computers— and it sounds great.

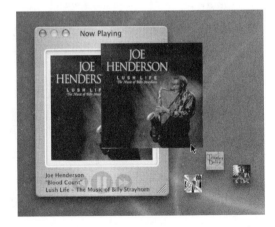

Clutter, a free iTunes companion program, helps restore the experience of holding a record album while you listen to an intangible audio file. It grabs album covers from Amazon and lets you pile them up on the Mac desktop.

BT: There's this sort of nostalgic part of me that makes me really happy when I see retro designs. I just got this program for the Mac called Clutter [www.sprote.com] that goes onto Amazon, downloads the cover for the record you're listening to in iTunes, and throws it on your desktop, like all messy. And I was like, "Wow. This is the shit." Especially for a whole generation of kids who are 14, 15 years old and never *will* buy an album, and don't know the tactile sensation of holding one in their hands for the first time. But I've got *no* complaints about Reason. That program is just *astonishing*. I *still* can't believe that a tool that powerful has been actualized. It's unbelievable.

PHYSICAL CONTROLLERS

Companies have developed untold numbers of hardware controllers to make computers more musical. There are USB MIDI keyboards, turntable simulators, knob and fader boxes; I even saw a guy using a Wacom graphics pad to control music. Where's that going?

David Zicarelli: One of the things people say about using RadiaL [Cycling '74's looping software] is that when they finally connect the fader box to the computer they suddenly have a radically different experience. When you can touch only one thing at a

Open Labs designer Craig Negoescu demonstrates a prototype of the OpenSynth neKo, a keyboard built around a powerful Windows computer. The instrument is highly customizable; each of the four controller panels can contain various knob and slider modules, and the computer components themselves can be upgraded.

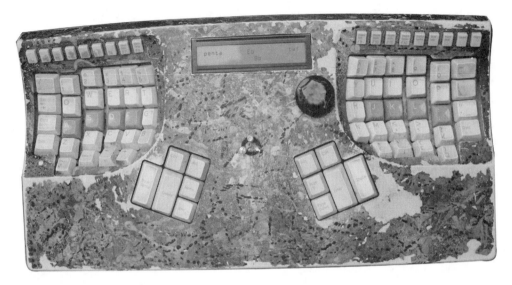

The patented Samchillian Tip Tip Tip Cheeepeeeee (www.samchillian.com) is a keyboard controller that transmits relative pitches rather than absolute ones. For example, the J key might trigger the next higher note in the scale, whereas the D key might trigger the note that's two places down. Playing them alternately would generate a spiraling flurry of notes.

time, the resulting music is more linear than you could get from a real instrument. I heard someone say once that playing ReBirth was like operating a TB-303 with a stick. [*Laughs.*]

Read David Zicarelli's "Interactive Music: Standing Up or Sitting Down?" on the disc. In it, he explains his philosophy of building musical construction kits rather than instruments.

My company once sponsored a concert by people using our software and they set up five laptops in a row on a long table. I looked at that and thought, "Boy, those people are just setting up an office." No matter what you're doing with music software, if you're just using a computer, it's office work. And it has the same gestures and assumptions as office work.

Roger Linn: One problem with using the computer as a musical instrument is that few people have developed the "human interface" skills that most traditional musicians already have in terms of vibrato, dynamics, nuance, and the like. I recently had a great conversation with Jaron Lanier, who's most famous for his work in virtual reality. But he's also worked on a number of things as a musician, so we were talking about new musical instrument designs. And he mentioned a project he was working on for controlling music through computer recognition of facial expressions.

People are trained to create and recognize tremendous subtleties of movement in certain parts of the body—our hands, our face. So if you're able to harness that, you could conceivably do some very fine control of the music with your face while your hands were busy playing an instrument. That's what Jaron was trying to do. The point is that we've made tremendous advances in sound generation and software but people are still making music primarily on a typewriter keyboard. I'd like to see more creative gestural interfaces like the ones in Don Buchla's products. Then I'd like to see musicians develop proficiency at using them.

I just had this mental image of Stevie Ray Vaughan shaping his sound by sneering into a Webcam.

Roger Linn: [*Laughs.*] Yeah. Or you get Eddie Van Halen smiling the whole time. So you'd have to have a threshold control. I'd also like to see more examples of controlling multiple modes of expression with a single parameter.

Scotch Ralston: On the *creative* end, there are two things I just keep wishing for when I'm doing a lot of computer work. One is voice command—I wish you could just say, "Go to the top" or "Solo the kick," because you spend all day staring at the damn screen. It used to be 12 hours of listening to something over and over; now it's also 12 hours of staring at a computer screen. And at the end of the day, man, you're *burnt*.

My other wish—which they probably already have, I just haven't run across it yet—is wireless remote control for the transport functions and some of the things that you do most often. [*See the "Pass the Remote" sidebar.*]

Ray Kurzweil: I'm involved with a company called NeuroSonics [www.neurosonics.com] that uses brainwaves. You hook the system up with three leads, placing one of them near the auditory cortex. It's designed to encourage alpha waves, the deeper, more tranquil rhythms of the brain that become predominant when you meditate.

Whenever your brain generates an alpha wave, the NeuroSonics system creates much more pleasant music that has a certain textural richness and some very interesting rhythms. It creates less-pleasant music when you're creating delta waves, which are the higher-frequency waves that reflect more routine kinds of thoughts.

Don Buchla's Marimba Lumina uses radio waves to identify each mallet for unique expressive possibilities. (Each mallet could trigger a different sound, for example.) The pads also sense the force and location of each strike.

The Audiopad projects its ever-changing interface onto a tabletop. You play it by sliding electronically tagged discs on the surface. Hear it in action at http://web.media.mit.edu/~jpatten/audiopad.

You can actually watch a readout and see the alpha waves grow, because they're being encouraged through this feedback mechanism. Your brainwaves are creating the music, and the music in turn is affecting your brainwaves. It's a very profound feeling. You really feel like the music's coming out of your head.

You do *not* get that feeling by watching and listening to someone else hooked up to the machine. And you also don't get the feeling by listening to your own brain-generated music as a recording. You only get it if it's actually happening when you're hooked up to the machine.

By the end of this decade, we'll have images written directly to our retinas from our eyeglasses and contact lenses. All the computational resources will be so tiny they'll be in your eyeglasses and in your clothing. And we'll have extremely high-bandwidth connections to the Internet at all times.

You'll be able to go into virtual reality environments with one other person or multiple other people. It'll pick up your own movement through electronics. And you'll be able to project yourself, but you don't have to project the same person. You could project both your appearance and the sound of your voice as being a different person.

See Ray Kurzweil's virtual-reality musical performance on the disc.

That's what I was demonstrating at TED [the Technology Entertainment Design conference]. As I moved my arm, Ramona [Kurzweil's virtual counterpart] moved her arm. And as I looked at myself in the display, it was like I was looking in a mirror, except I was a different person—which is really quite a startling experience. And I believe this will be ubiquitous by 2010.

Did changing your identity inspire you musically, encouraging you to try new techniques and directions?

Ray Kurzweil: Yes. It was quite interesting to be able to be somebody completely different both visually and sonically. I actually have a very deep voice, and here I was singing as a young woman. And it was actually then easy to get into the kinds of musical gesturing that would be appropriate for that singer—the visual appearance affects you.

I suppose you could extend that concept, becoming, say, a guitar or a drum kit instead of an android.

Ray Kurzweil: Yeah. There's a whole set of activity centered around people using motion-capture devices to become an instrument, basically converting dance moves into musical sounds. You can do that as an expert, someone who really trains themselves to dance and control music in a musically sophisticated way, or you can have a certain aspect of the music triggered by arbitrary people who are just dancing at a club. Or you can have the whole group affect the music. None of them may be professional musicians, but that group as a whole has musical intelligence in the way they respond to the music.

Pass the Remote

Salling Clicker, from www.salling.com, converts a Bluetooth phone or PDA into a Macintosh remote control. Free scripts allow Clicker to control music programs including Cubase, Logic, Apple GarageBand, and Digital Performer. For Windows, see Rip Rowan's entertaining tutorial at ProRec.com. Rowan explains how to configure a cheap laptop computer with a Wi-Fi card to control a Windows digital audio workstation (DAW). His technique, based on a built-in Windows XP feature called Pro Remote Desktop Connection, actually echoes the remote computer's screen on the laptop's screen, making it the world's most informative remote control.

Success Through Failure

Making the most of happy accidents

The very first interview for this book was prophetic, as Ableton Software's Robert Henke (aka Monolake), told a wonderful story about overcoming a show-stopping computer crash onstage. (He'd been performing solo with a laptop as his only sound source.) I found Henke's approach so inspiring that I retold his story to many of the subsequent interviewees, who added their own tales of "success through failure"—the happy accidents that occur when equipment malfunctions but ends up leading you in a great new direction.

Robert, do you do things to inject randomness in your performances?

Robert Henke: Well, there are lots of unwanted adventures [*laughs*], because I'm not good at writing comments. But on a microsound level, I'm a friend of randomness, using a lot of granular synthesis. On a structural level, I'm a friend of trial and error, which is similar to randomness, because you've got unpredictable results.

My approach is to know my software quite well. I know what the filters do; I know what artifacts the time-stretch produces. And that freedom allows me to do things I didn't check before. So I just put something in because I have an idea that it *should* do the job. And often enough, it does something completely different.

I use that unexpected result to get further. I don't treat the unexpected as a mistake; I treat every situation as something that makes sense if you combine it with the next situation. A few years ago, if I'd introduced a clip with the wrong pitch, I would have *immediately* corrected it. My approach now is, "Okay, let's see what I can do with it." And then I leave it as long as possible and start to make sense out of it. It's rewarding for the audience; the perception is that it's a structure that grows. And it's rewarding for me, because I have to face a new situation and solve it.

 I was debugging this game crash and I locked up the game at a specific point. The audio buffer had this girl going, "*Kill, kill, kill, kill, kill.*" I stopped for a second, and I'm listening to it going, "Oh, that's *creepy.*" *–Dave O'Neal*

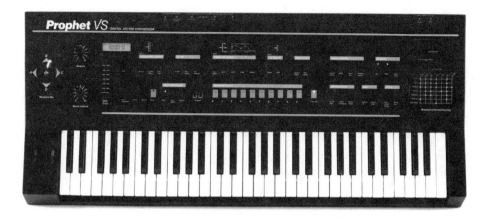

Happy accident in a box? The Sequential Prophet-VS is beloved for its digital aliasing. Golden-eared Sequential engineer Chris Meyer walked into the lab when another engineer was testing the synth with the antialiasing filters disabled—and liked the sound. The VS also sports a random patch generator.

Music is all about creating tension and relief. And the perception of failure only comes into the game once you are not able to deal with the things that are going on.

What are some tricks for exploiting those failures?

Robert Henke: Failure is great. In the studio, failure is one of the most satisfying sources of inspiration. Say your audio interface malfunctioned and produced total noise while you were recording to DAT. Calm down. You lost your piece, but you got a nice texture—take it. You can also capitalize on failure by figuring out what went wrong and making it reproducible.

One nice failure that I love to tell about was when I played [Ableton] Live in Miami in a club and the other performer had left an [Eventide] H3000 effects processor. After ten minutes, everyone was enjoying the show, including me. It was in the middle of being, "Yeah! This is getting really great." And then my Mac had a complete freeze.

In these situations, you really feel bad. It was clear I had to restart the computer. But I know the H3000 quite well, so what I did was dial up 900 seconds of reverb. I opened the aux send on the mixer, pressed Restart, and when the computer's startup sound hit the reverb, the whole club was like, *Raaaaaaaaagh!* It simply didn't stop.

I knew that the only thing now necessary to keep the audience happy was a straight bass drum. So as soon as Live was open again, the first thing I did was press Play on a bass drum sample. *Doom! Doom! Doom! Doom! Waaaaaaaaagh!* And *everyone* was crying. The place was so big that the people in the back did not realize it was a failure. And after the concert, some guy came to me and said, "That part, with the *long* chord that was slightly changing, that was *amazing.*" So this is a situation where I think failure can be so great.

Hear a live performance of Thomas Dolby's "I Love You Goodbye" (including frog samples) on the disc.

He Said Politely as He Cuffed Me

One of the things I've always liked about Thomas Dolby's music is the arrangements, especially the strange, unexpected sounds that bubble up through the other parts. I asked him if any of those were happy accidents, and got an unexpected lesson on orchestration. —David Battino

"There's nothing very accidental about my arrangements, really," Dolby said. "I sometimes think up intrusive parts or sounds. I hear them in my imagination. Very often, I'll have something fairly central and unchanging, and then weave stuff around it. It might be that the root stays the same while the chords change, as in 'Budapest by Blimp.' Or it might be that the chord stays more or less the same and the roots move around, like 'Mulu the Rainforest.'

"Or it might be just an unrelenting sound, like the anvil hit in 'Cruel,' which is quite overpowering but still leaves some space around itself to drop different things in. So quite often, there's some kind of a static element with a lot of movement around it.

"One thing that's fascinating about music is that when you juxtapose elements in different ways, they mean something completely different. Very often, there's a figure that exists in a bass part, or a riff, or a chord sequence; you can then keep that element consistent, like an ostinato, but change the weighting and the phrasing of it. So in my music, there has always been an element of repetition.

"I also try to be very evocative with arrangements, so I'll quite often use a sound that elicits a response that I think helps the mood. I suppose there are occasional accidents. In 'I Love You Goodbye,' I had these recordings of a frog colony that I wanted to use in the section that talks about the electric storm in the bayou. And a little bit hung over during the second verse, where I'm talking about the sheriff pulling me over. But in that context, it kind of sounded like his radio blurting out of his car, so I left it in."

Scott Kirkland: Mistakes in the digital world have always been the little gems for us. And with MIDI and being able to record continuous audio, you *catch* those mistakes and exploit them. You can really focus on a part that has some sort of drift or dissonant note that really takes it in a different direction. That's been a definite advantage for us.

Can you think of some recent examples?

Scott Kirkland: Well, every time we work on a track, because neither of us ever claimed to be keyboard players. I mean, we play keyboards, but we're not Paul Shaffer. We're not someone who can sit down at the piano and play a track for the family. [*Laughs.*] We have a relationship with the keyboard that works really well, but it transfers beyond that. Maybe we'll be a little late on a note, and when we quantize it, that will shift it to someplace we weren't *looking* for but that turns out to be better.

When we were working on "Trip Like I Do" [on the first Crystal Method album] we had this old tape machine that was called a—what was it called?

Ken Jordan: Wollensak.

Scott Kirkland: Wollensak. We called it the Swollen Sack. It was a really archaic-looking, heavy, reel-to-reel tape machine that had this little light on it that would tell you when you were overloading it. We would push it to the limits, and then when we stopped the tape, it would feed back. At some point we were feeding drums through it, and when we'd stop it, it would go, "Puh-*waaaaaa!*" It would just make this really *obscene* sound. And we just went crazy over that sound and exploited it and put it into the song as one of the big, dynamic moments in that track.

I think that, creatively, those sorts of things make it fun for us. They're part of reaching inside of ourselves and just spewing out stuff instead of methodically plotting something in the studio. In Digital Performer, for example, you can take a loop that's one bar and stretch that out to two bars. It still has the rhythm; it still keeps in time with the song; but it has a whole different, lazy sort of feel.

Dr. Patrick Gleeson: The accidents that happen for me now are not at the level of the equipment breaking down. I've just increasingly come to accept that when I'm hardly thinking about it and noodling away, that's probably as good as it's going to get. And I think that's true for a lot of musicians.

The first time that happened, it really awakened me. I was doing some synthesizer overdubs on a Pablo Cruise record with a really good engineer/producer named Bill Schnee. I was thinking about what I was *going* to do, so I said, "Could I hear some track?" and he played the track. Then I said, "Okay, I'm ready," and he said, "No, that's fine. I've already got it."

Hear "Void When We Want," Gleeson and Jim Lang's amazing piece that resulted from mutilating an obnoxious client's CD, on the disc.

I listened to what I had done and it was much better than what I had planned to do, because I wasn't really thinking about it. I was just . . . *being.* Because I *am* a control freak, that made me think, "Okay, you've got to figure out some ways to let go." And I'm still working on that.

Herbie Hancock: I haven't *had* any accidents. [*Laughs.*]

Why do you think that is?

Herbie Hancock: Maybe I haven't used the software they were using. We've been using [Emagic] Logic, and we haven't used a ton of software instruments at the same time. Also, we're using [Macintosh] OS X, and it's a whole lot more stable than OS 9. And if one thing crashes, it doesn't crash the whole computer.

I find that musicians have a tendency to hold on to the old technology because it's *safe.* But I'm a jazz musician. I'm used to playing it totally the opposite way. To play it safe, you might as well be in another kind of business.

The only way to be in control of the accidents is to know that they're going to happen and know what to do—to know that the stuff's not always going to work and be willing to take that chance. We carry backup computers just in case, but we haven't really had to use them.

Dave Smith: I guess the Prophet-VS [synthesizer] could be in the "happy accident" category because it had all that noise and aliasing and junk in the sound. We tried to minimize it as best we could, but then we just had to ship. As it turned out, that happened to be the sound everybody liked—the combination of all the grunge and noise and aliasing gave it a real personality. [*Laughs.*] I still hear from VS fans all the time. It was sort of a failure as far as the technical engineering side. But when you play it in context and have it programmed right, it sounds great.

Jennifer Hruska: Probably one of the most interesting pieces I ever created was "Piano Errors." I was creating a piano wavetable for a Kurzweil ROM. Something got messed up in what we used to call the sample spans, which are the start and end and loop points, and the computer put in random values for everything. All of a sudden, it just started playing this incredibly ethereal piano piece, where notes were starting in the middle of the sample and then they would leak into the next sample, and then they would jump to some other point. And it was *incredible* sounding. I had the DAT running, and I saved the mistakes as much as I could, and created a really interesting piece from it.

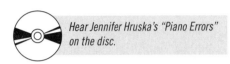

Hear Jennifer Hruska's "Piano Errors" on the disc.

I remember learning about that phenomenon in college. It was like Music Theory 102 or 103 and I had this *really* great composition teacher. She was a Zen Buddhist and she taught us about that sort of effect, that indeterminacy. I remember being *so fascinated* by that concept. And I think it changed the way that I listened from that point on. Now I'm constantly aware of sound that's happening around me. And it always is fusing together no matter what I'm doing—outside of the studio, at the dinner table. . . . There's so much *rhythm* there. And sometimes it comes together in really interesting ways.

Chuck D: I think the element of mistake is what makes human beings create art. Like when you said, "Distortion is art"? I don't think a computer agrees with that. [*Laughs.*] You know what I'm saying? Distortion means *problems.*

Some of the best things that human beings have created have come out of accidents. Not as simplistic as a Reese's Peanut Butter Cup commercial, where a cat with chocolate runs into somebody with peanut butter and all of a sudden you've got Reese's, but you know what I mean.

Everybody always asks us, "How'd you do those drum sounds?" It was totally an accident. —*Jimmy Jam*

I wonder if computers make accidents more commonplace because they're so rigid that you end up straining against them and slipping.

Bob Ezrin: Because my productions are not computer-*driven*, just computer-*assisted*, I don't find that kind of thing happens as much as *playing* accidents or *tape* accidents, which tend to occur a lot these days because people are uncomfortable with tapes. [*Laughs.*]

Mark Isham: Many years ago, when I had my very first synthesizer, I bought an old 4-track tape machine. All you could do was bounce from one track to the next. And then one day I'd saved up enough money and I said, "I'm going to buy a professional machine."

I bought myself a Revox. It was only a 2-track, but it was professional quality. So, I was going to do the same thing. I was going to bounce from one track to the other.

> At the very end of the song, you hear this little dog howl. And I thought, "Let's *keep* that." It sounded so sad and it fit into the song. —*Todd Rundgren*

Well, I flipped the switch one space over from where I was going to monitor just the other side, and I listened to both sides at the same time. And of course, what you have is the difference between the record head and the playback head—*delay* between one side and the other. And all of a sudden, there was that space. And it changed my life.

From that day on, I didn't use a single synthesizer sound without some sort of time modulation connected to it. To me, it just brought that organic, *emotional* quality that made it seem like night and day.

That was what created the sound. It wasn't the synthesizer. And you can't *buy* a synthesizer now that doesn't have a simple delay line. Why do we all crave that? Because without it, there is no sense of the sound breathing and living. There's no moment of *existence* in the air. All you have to do is stick a ten-millisecond delay on that, and all of a sudden it's, "*Ooh*—it breathed for a moment."

Stephen Kay: One of the first pieces in which I used KARMA [Kay's algorithmic music software] extensively was "The Sorcerer," a techno demo for Korg's Trinity keyboard. I created much of that piece by programming nifty effects in KARMA and letting the results drive the composition process. However, partway through [at about 2:46], I was going to have an explosion effect to move from the wild activity of the current section to a breakdown section.

Hear "The Sorcerer" on the disc.

Instead, due to accidentally using some velocity envelopes and CCs [MIDI Continuous Controller messages], I momentarily heard this "sucking" effect where everything disappeared as if a vacuum cleaner had sucked it up. It sounded so cool that I worked it into the piece as the transition, which was pretty much the exact opposite of what I had originally intended. I added the boom a few bars later, anyway [at 2:52].

And at another part, I soloed the percussion, and then I wanted to hear how much of it was going through the reverb, so I listened to only the return from the reverb. This also sounded wildly cool, so I set it up so that at two places [3:21 and 3:39] the percussion sounds are boosted and only the return from the reverb is used, not the original signal.

Dave O'Neal: One of my favorite ones was when I was working on *Soviet Strike*. I was debugging this game crash and I locked up the game at a specific point. And it kept playing through the audio buffer, which was probably about half a second. And so when I hit my breakpoint—and I'm totally focused on code—the audio buffer had this girl going, "*Kill, kill, kill, kill, kill.*" I stopped for a second, and I'm listening to it going, "Oh, that's *creepy.*"

So I ran some tape and then I spliced it over itself three times, and I had them a little bit out of sync so they all merged. So you got, "Kill-kill-kill, kill-kill-kill, Kill! Kill! Kill! KILL!" I made this total bizarre sound effect out of it. Actually, on the *Erratica* album there's a segment in "Alien Chase Scene" where that comes up in the middle of nowhere. I also used that in *Future Cop*.

Jimmy Jam: Back in the days of the old Linn drum [*i.e., the LM-1*], we had an accident that produced a huge record for us. We had come up with a song for the SOS Band—this was probably back in 1986—and one of the things about that drum machine was that it had interchangeable sound chips, and you could tune them. So we had put in these chips for a Roland 808 sound and we had cut this SOS Band song in Atlanta and never really used it.

When we got back to Minnesota, I dropped in some big rock toms, and when I turned the machine on, it was on the same sequence as the SOS Band song. I don't know how to explain it in words, but the 808 sound was this little [*sings*] *Doot-boo-doot, boo-boo boo-doo-doot.* But with these big toms in, it was like, "Boom! Dooj-dooj! Boom-boom Doo-doo-DOO-doo Dooj! And when I heard that, I said, "Ooh, I like that." And I wrote "Human." [*Laughs.*] [*The song, performed by the Human League, spent seven weeks at No. 1.*]

Everybody always asks us, "How'd you do those drum sounds?" It was totally an accident.

I remember I was in a recording studio when "Human" came out and the engineer was going, "Man, they must have spent months *on those drums."*

Jimmy Jam: [*Laughs.*] Right! *Sure* we did! I always love when people think that. But we get that a lot. There was another song that ended up like that. It was a song called "Fake" by Alexander O'Neal that was a number-one R&B record for us. It was sort of the same thing, but it was with the Oberheim DMX drum machine. The drums got tuned differently from where they were supposed to be, and then the beat got sped up.

I knew it was sounding good because there was a guy named Popeye working for us and he was asleep on the couch. And when I turned it on and it came in with this *boom-boom-boom dunga-boom ba-boom,* he literally started bouncing up and down. [*Laughs.*] And I thought, "Okay, we got something here." 'Cause you couldn't *wake* Popeye when he was out.

I suppose there's quite a few of those, but I really remember the "Human" one because I still have that SOS song that we never used, and I always laugh when I hear it because I realize that's where it came from.

I've increasingly come to accept that when I'm hardly thinking about it and noodling away, that's probably as good as it's going to get. And I think that's true for a lot of musicians. *—Dr. Patrick Gleeson*

Phil Ramone: I once made a record that started out in Michael ["She's a Maniac"] Sembello's house. And there was this little effect—we were looking to make a handclap with some slap [short echo] on it, just as a backbeat on the 4. The little Yamaha drum machine we were using started to break up and it created this sound that was almost like cracking wood. Well, it sounded great and we kept it in.

Months later, when we were trying to finish the project, that piece of gear had gone out for repair and come back in perfect shape. It took us *days* to resample what was inside that record, find that particular wonderfully distorted piece of sound, and figure out how to put it back into the record. Because it was a missing element, you know?

I used to go to the music stores almost monthly just to see what just came out. It could be an MXR [guitar effect] pedal and I'd try it on a vocal. I never put a limit on what I thought a device should be used for. And amazingly enough, you come up with something and it may lead to a hit record—like the guy who started messing with Antares Auto-Tune and created that sound for Cher.

There are some *unhappy* accidents—not recording some of the great moments that pass as you first warm up. There's no excuse for a disk recorder not to be recording *all* the time. It's just labeling, finding ways so that you can find that piece of information. That storage device is there for your brain. It's your notepad, and you'd better use it.

I find that musicians have a tendency to hold on to the old technology because it's safe. But I'm a jazz musician. I'm used to playing it totally the opposite way. *—Herbie Hancock*

Todd Rundgren: I remember we were doing a piano overdub where someone was singing with the piano, and a dog sneaked into the studio. And at the very end of the song, you hear this little dog howl. [*Laughs.*] And I thought, "Let's *keep* that." It sounded so sad and it fit into the song.

Those things happen, and you want to be open to them, which is why confidence in the material and confidence in the performance is so important; it's what enables things like that to happen. It's when you have a lack of confidence in those things that people try to *perspire* the record out. They say, "No, you couldn't possibly have gotten it on the first take; we've gotta go at least 20 takes before we even get close to it." [*Laughs.*] I'd love to get *everything* on the first take. It's when the band is the most excited about the material.

Do you set up your working environment so that accidents can happen and you can flow on from that?

David Torn: Constantly. I did it today. I'm building a new guitar amplifier with Reinhold Bogner [www.bogneramplification.com], who's a great amp maker in southern California, and we're developing some aspect of this classic tube amplifier that we call the

Surprise Mode. [*Laughs.*] Because I want to manipulate the guitar a little, and then I want the guitar and the amplifier loop to give me something back that I didn't expect that I can then manipulate further.

This is my life. I've got two microphones that are exclusively for feedback built into my current guitars. They're on momentary switches. When my playing starts to be a little too restricted by my lack of imagination, I hit this button [*laughs*], and it makes something happen—that little shock that you *must* respond to as a player, as a composer, as an organizer of sounds.

Mark Isham: Sometimes I'll turn the speakers off and just start hitting the keys. Or I'll take something that I've written that's *okay* and stick it on a completely out-there patch and see what happens. You can take something that was written on a piano patch and play it through a gamelan patch that's tuned to a completely different scale, and the next thing you know, you have something you never would have *thought* of.

LTJ Bukem: Well, I think it's more about being prepared to go that one step further and not think, "Hang on; I don't know what I'm doing here. I'll just back off and start again on something else." It's the same as when you're creating breaks. You don't really know sometimes—well, I don't, anyway—what breaks will definitely go with what other breaks. So what do you do? You sit there and gamble on this going with that, and maybe a bit of that other one, and shuffle from there.

You try so many things over two or three hours, and you might come up with nothing.

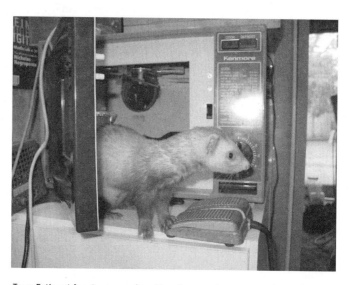

Team Fat's pet ferret emerges from the microwave to compose some more creeping music. A tube at the back of the oven leads to the Fat Man's small studio and the Ferret Man's large cage.

Then you might just get any old break from anywhere, or a break from another tune you might have started a year earlier, and there it *is*—the perfect match, sitting there, right before your eyes.

The Fat Man: We *are* set up to have accidents happen. It seems like whenever I have a sample of pizzicato up on the GigaSampler, that is the time the ferret will get up on the keyboard. So I have a few MIDI recordings of the ferret walking on the keyboard, which I *have* used in pieces. Because it just works. That's the sound you *want* for creeping around. [*Laughs.*]

Hear the Fat Man's pizzicato ferret on the disc.

We have a recording of bad singing in the GigaSampler. It's just Joe [McDermott] and me each trying to sing a *C* and a *C♯* and a *D*, and it feels *great*. It just warms the place up.

We've got bunches of old brass instruments lying around. It's become very clear that a little mediocre brass playing is a *lot* better than no brass at all in many cases. It just makes a *world* of difference to how your heart responds.

I think you can set up an atmosphere in which less is expected but more is delivered. Isn't that kind of what the Stones do? Or Beck? When you listen to their music, you're not expecting mountains of layered perfection. And that's what you *constantly* have to be doing around computers, because they're always trying to get you to do perfection.

Stephen Kay: I've tried to build the "I don't know what this does, but change it and see what happens" approach into KARMA, and quite often it results in cool musical effects.

I always keep a lot of written and audio notes while working on music projects, because often I come up with a sound or an idea that has nothing to do with what I'm searching for at the moment, yet my ear can recognize that there's something cool about it that I might want to use at another time. By "audio notes," I mean having some way to quickly record something, such as a DAT recorder hooked up to the main outs of your mixer, and perhaps a microphone plugged into a channel so that you can say something about the sound after you record it.

Of course, it doesn't have to be so high-tech—a cheap cassette recorder with a built-in microphone served me well for years. The key is to work out quick ways of recording or notating these ideas so that you don't lose the flow of what you're originally trying to do.

Nile, do you set up your environment to encourage happy accidents?
Nile Rodgers: Not at all. [*Laughs.*] I'm creative enough. I'm a big enough accident.

Business

Records: R.I.P.?

Ideas to enhance CDs and DVDs

For 20 years, the compact disc was the definitive embodiment of music—unchanging digital bits burned into a gleaming, durable disc. But the magic has worn off. CD sales are withering, and a barrage of new media formats is tempting and confusing fans with enhanced features. In this chapter, the virtual panel debates the future of the CD—and of discs themselves.

Phil, you produced the world's first CD. Where do you think the format is going?

Phil Ramone: I think there's still life in it. It's not going to go off the shelf as quickly as LPs did. The five-inch format is something we're used to. If the record business doesn't go crazy with prices, the DVD will be a very home-bound animal for the home theater.

The thing that's old-fashioned about discs that needs to be addressed is that for years and years, several of us have been after the record companies to put into a subcarrier signal all the information that was needed. Not so much for the piracy, which is bad enough, but for the retrieval of information and the possible distribution of music.

Because it's going to be distributed differently, so you have to be ready for it, and you should be offering new solutions rather than saying it's a dying force. *Nobody* predicted in the late '70s that the LP would be off the shelves. They *laughed* at people like me, running around with a five-inch format: "Do you think all of the stores in America are going to change, and get rid of that 12-inch slot?" [*Laughs.*]

I made the first pop DVD in America in 1998 and everybody said the same thing: "Where are you going to play it?" So we went to the stereo stores, where they were showing new home theaters, and we played this *West Side Story* jazz recording with both DTS and Dolby [5.1-channel digital surround sound], so people could understand it. Yes, we were two years ahead of our game. But obviously there's more to it than anyone had ever thought.

Ted, how much life do you think is left in the CD format?

Ted Cohen: I think it's got another five to ten years. If we're talking about a physical optical format, I think we've got a good 15 years, because it's just easier for a lot of people to stick a disc in a slot than to find a song on a computer.

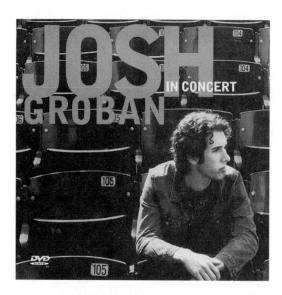

To test the appeal of DVDs, Reprise presented Josh Groban's music in two different packages—a CD with a free DVD and a DVD with a free CD. Both packages were priced the same, but one sold ten times as many copies. Which would you choose?

I think we'll end up migrating to a DVD that has some CD backward compatibility. Reprise did an interesting test with their artist Josh Groban: They offered a DVD concert video with a bonus CD and at the same time they offered the CD with the *DVD* as the bonus. One package sold 60,000; the other sold 600,000. Same price, same content, different packaging. Which sold which?

I'd guess the DVD was more popular.

Ted Cohen: No, it was the CD. *Six hundred thousand* people thought the CD with a free DVD was a better value than a DVD with a free CD. They also found it in a CD bin, whereas music video in a video store is such a narrow category that it's usually thrown into one bin rather than broken out into genres. It's a mess.

I think we're going to go through a transition where we come up with a stable enhanced CD. At EMI, we're working with Microsoft to create a very rich second session on audio CDs that will have videos and Web links, but that will play with a lot more consistency than what currently happens on enhanced CDs. I mean, I installed Windows XP on

If the record companies would use the angle that people
are enthusiasts, not pirates, we would all end up buying more music
because we'd be getting exposed to things. *–Jim Reekes*

all my machines at home, and none of my early enhanced CDs play anymore. We can't have that going forward. [*See the "How to Enhance a CD" sidebar.*]

Albhy, you and Ty Roberts developed the original enhanced CD format, as well as some highly artistic discs. Why do you think enhanced CDs never caught on?

Albhy Galuten: First of all, enhanced CDs assumed a secondary use. If you put them in your PC, you'll generally get some sort of interactive experiences that are worth viewing *once.* You generally get more mileage out of going to an artist's Web site or being on their mailing list than you do out of an enhanced CD, although some of them provide for secure access to updated content: Once you've registered as having bought the disc, then you can access a special site. But in general it hasn't been proven that adding enhancements makes the record sell any more.

What could be done to extend the CD format?

Stephen Kay: It would be cool if you could take a CD by your favorite band and somehow influence the events recorded in the audio to be different. [*Laughs.*] Suddenly the bass player is playing extra notes that weren't there the last time you listened to it and the drummer is doing a different complementary rhythm—now *that* would be interesting.

Ty Roberts: A very simple application would be that if you bought the CD, you should be able to link into the artist's online community and get special stuff. You could purchase advance tickets, receive audio streams from live shows, or do online chats. That kind of thing is certainly possible with Gracenote Link. [*The service identifies a CD in your computer and uses it as a key to unlock a private Web site.*]

But I think the labels have a problem, which is that they really only control the master recording of the artist. The movie companies have *complete* control of the movies, the Web sites, and every publicity still; they can make the movie stars go on television and talk about it.

The labels are starting to see that. But what I see more is that the artists are starting to get it. They see that it's

Herbie Hancock's *Future 2 Future* concert DVD uses innovative multiangle video playback developed by MX Entertainment. Future MX DVDs will have additional features that can be unlocked or complemented on the Web, turning a static experience into an evolving one.

worth their while to make that connection even though the record company doesn't have the rights to do all of it themselves. What the labels really need is the spirit of cooperation with their artists to say to them, "Hey, we've got a problem. And the way we can solve the problem is if we work together."

It just seems so logical that turning the CD into a subscription service in a box is the right thing to do. Most artists put out one CD a year or one every couple of years. It seems like between album A and album B, the album you bought should entitle you to access stuff.

And once we verify that consumers have the original CD—and newer drives can tell whether it's an original CD or a CD-R copy—then that user can even rip the CD and get the same experience with digital files.

What other applications do you see for Web-enhanced discs?

Ty Roberts: A good place to start is using [Gracenote] DVDKey to unlock features for music DVDs. For example, MX Entertainment has a multichannel video-switching

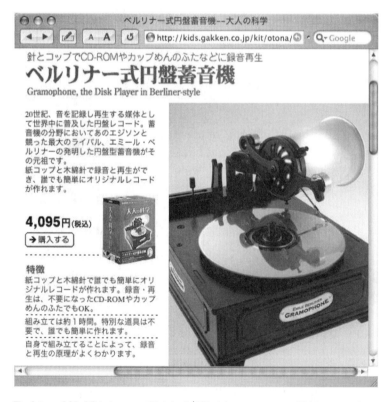

The future of CDs? This Japanese kit (about $38) etches grooves on a CD in response to incoming sound. You can then play back your recordings like vintage Gramophone records. See http://kids.gakken.co.jp/kit/otona/vol9.html.

application built into their DVDs, which they used on Herbie Hancock's *Future 2 Future* disc. Their future applications will add additional channels of video that you can unlock through the Web so the disc will live on past the thing you bought.

And community will become a part of it. There's no reason why people shouldn't be able to watch videos together even if they're not in the same home. You could have DVD players or PCs connected to the Internet and synchronize their playback—within five seconds or so—and then have a chat window so people can see what other people are saying. It's like instant messaging combined with movies. Going further, the system would be able to save those comments so that other people could see them when they play the disc.

So the disc builds up a history as people experience it?

Ty Roberts: Right. It's like blogging. That's what we're planning to do with the DVD products. But there's no reason you couldn't do it with audio CDs or concert DVDs.

How to Enhance a CD

An enhanced CD is essentially two discs in one—a standard audio CD plus a CD-ROM. To make one, you'll need a program that supports Session-at-Once mode. (A session is a block of data, much like a chapter in a book.) First you burn the audio tracks, closing the session but leaving the disc open. In some programs, you do that by clicking the Burn Session button instead of the Burn Disc one; in others, you might uncheck the Finalize checkbox.

Then you burn a second session containing the computer data—items like movies, screensavers, HTML pages, and photos—selecting Burn Disc or Finalize this time. Because audio-CD players can read only a single session, they ignore the data in the second session. Computers will see both sessions. For more detail on structuring the data session technically and aesthetically, see my eCD tutorial in the March 2002 issue of *Electronic Musician* (free at www.emusician.com).

Popular Windows programs that can create multisession CDs include Ahead Nero, Roxio Easy CD Creator Deluxe, and Steinberg WaveLab. On the Mac, there's CharisMac Discribe, Emagic WaveBurner, and Roxio Toast. —*David Battino*

In this photo of an enhanced CD, you can see the line between the two *sessions*, or data areas. The inner ring contains the audio; the outer ring contains the computer data.

Todd Rundgren's *Individualist* enhanced CD, produced by Ty Roberts in 1995, features a *Doom*-like game that's synchronized with the actual CD audio. You have the duration of the song to pop as many pundits as you can. Current enhanced CDs are much less ambitious.

Bob, from the artistic side, you said the CD format was so inflexible that it was almost like somebody had created a titanium box into which your product had to fit. What type of box would you prefer to have?

Bob Ezrin: That's a really good question. I think that because the digital genie is out of the bottle now, boxes will come in all shapes and sizes. And they probably *should.* Most products have what's called "right-sizing," which means they come in a series of sizes designed to meet the specific needs of each customer.

In music, even though the customers have indicated that they're consuming music in *many* different ways, they're still being forced to purchase it in only one way. There *have* been some moves by major labels towards an online extension of the current offline model, meaning you can buy a piece of any one of these boxes for a prorated amount, based on the labels' perceived value of the box itself. So they offer you a song for a dollar online, but it comes with certain restrictions—you can only have it if it's Tuesday at 4 o'clock and you're wearing a blue jumper. [*Laughs.*]

That's not sensitive to what the customers have indicated, which is that they want their music everywhere, *all* the time, in any format that's accessible to them. They don't want anything standing between them and it, and since *we* have not given them a satisfactory product in an easy, convenient package, they've just gone out and created one themselves.

One of the things that we have to remember as an industry is that in every other aspect of people's lives we have created a culture of consumer empowerment. Everybody gets what they want when they want it. And they get it in the most convenient way possible, because at the end of the day, content is not king; *convenience* is king. It's kind of a drag; as artists we'd really like to think that it was otherwise. But it's *not*, because people just have too many choices, too many things to do, and they don't have time to waste on our silly rules.

Jim Reekes: Copy protection is just this sick game. There's no form of copy protection that will ever work. In the worst-case scenario, if it's actually impossible to crack, I'll still stick a microphone next to the speaker and copy it.

I wonder how many R&D dollars and brains were behind the CD audio protection scheme that was defeated by a guy and a felt pen. It's such a *joke*. Now they have these Gestapo tactics like when you insert a CD in your computer, it automatically launches some application and installs some shit on your hard drive. *Radio* stations are now getting CDs that can't be played on their equipment. [*Laughs.*] Come *on*—the radio stations are the marketing arm of the record industry!

The basic philosophy should be not, "How can I lock up the content so that you can't do anything with it?" It should be, "Be willing to give music away—through airplay, downloads, fair use to friends, etc.—and help me buy more." There's a lot of music that I would like to buy, but they don't print it. There are a lot of songs that I hear on television or in movies that I would like, but they don't tell me what they were.

They do this watermarking and digital rights management. So they're trying to embed ownership into the actual content. Instead of trying to embed ownership, why don't you embed references that help me figure out what this was so I can automatically find related things?

> If you bought the CD, you should be able to link into the artist's online community and get special stuff. You could purchase advance tickets, receive audio streams from live shows, or do online chats. —*Ty Roberts*

Normally I would tell a person, "Hey, I really like Metallica," and that guy will say, "Oh, if you like Metallica, you would like—" and he names some other heavy metal band. Why do I have to ask a *person* for that? Why can't I ask the *content,* "What other content is like you?" That would be a way to help me find material that I would then go buy.

Just about anybody who even remotely thinks of jazz as pleasant would love *Kind of Blue* by Miles Davis. That is an incredible album. Yet most people don't even know about it because they're never exposed to it. That's a sin.

I want to expose other people to the experience that I get from Brian Eno's music. I want to share that experience, just like teenage girls want to share the experience of Britney Spears. So if the record companies would use the angle that people are enthusiasts, not pirates, we would all end up buying more music because we'd be getting exposed to things.

I think the record industry is concerned about offending people. And I'm passionately anti-censorship. Any time you censor something you will pervert it—and in fact you'll make it more titillating. As soon as you try to twist something, it ends up creating a market for it. Censorship is just a weird thing to me. Today's perversion is tomorrow's profits.

Dr. Elizabeth Cohen: [*Sighs.*] There's the positive side of encryption, which protects privacy. And then there's the shadow side of it, which can encourage the growth of a monoculture, because only the people with the power and the resources to create entertainment will be doing it on a certain economic scale.

You can't look at encryption in black and white terms. There are a lot of nuances that have really big impacts. We have multiple goals with encryption technology: to continue its development, to protect privacy, to protect artists' rights. But then you constantly have to ensure that it's not used to bite the hand that feeds it. Because, as we're seeing now, even though we may have thousands of channels, fewer and fewer people are *providing* media to most people.

So with the consolidation of media, it really *is* all these individual voices out there, whether it's online or in your local community club, that are creating new things, the grassroots things that are so essential for music and the arts.

Suddenly the bass player is playing extra notes that weren't there the last time you listened to it and the drummer is doing a different complementary rhythm—now *that* would be interesting. –*Stephen Kay*

Jim Griffin: Well, digital rights management is just an attempt to hang onto friction—the friction of roads and discs and all that. And who can blame them? For a blip in time, it worked. Friction had its own problems—and does.

Opportunity cost is the worst problem with friction: You forever live in this hell where you've either overproduced or underproduced. I mean, you're a record company executive; it's September. How many copies of the new Beatles compilation do you print for the holiday season? If it's a flop, you're stuck with all these records that make even a *success* unprofitable. Or do you print just a million, and then let's say the demand is for three or four million, and you left all that money on the table?

And that's just the *beginning* of the problems with those discs, because the real cost of those discs is the degree to which they disconnect you from the end user. Every time someone listens to one of those discs, they do so in isolation of *you*. So they don't know the artist is coming to town. They don't know the artist has merchandise. They don't know there are other artists that artist would recommend.

Seventy percent of the time you don't know when your very *favorite* musical artist has a new record out. And why is that? Because we give you a thing that doesn't wear out and you give us the money—good-bye. So there isn't just the opportunity cost, which is enormous, but there is this disconnection cost that I think is even greater.

Digital Distribution

Utopian and hellish predictions for online music

Some say music wants to be free. Others want to charge 99 cents a tune or ten bucks a month. One thing is sure: The record industry has failed to dam the digital stream, and the ways we find, buy, and experience recorded music will be changing drastically. Here are some utopian and hellish predictions from the virtual panel.

Where is the record business going in the digital age?

Dr. Patrick Gleeson: I think it's come to a point where we may finally go out through the asshole of Hell and into paradise. When everybody who's doing anything interesting no longer has a record contract with a major label and the small labels are collapsing as we speak, you're put back in the position of, "Okay, I'm going to make the record and release it myself." But a *sparrow* couldn't live on the income from that. Even for major artists like Prince, the numbers are quite small.

So it means that the record has been put back in the perspective where, in the sanest of all worlds, it might have stayed: as a *record* of what you've done. It's something you can sell at performances, or use for publicity, or send out to ad agencies and hope that, like Moby, they'll love it and make you a millionaire. But the last thing you'll do is try to get a deal with a major label. So in that sense it's leading toward a more music-friendly world.

Roger Linn: When I used to be a musician, I learned a healthy hatred of the record labels because they loved to water down music to fit what they thought would sell. But do labels even matter anymore? In the Internet world, where you bypass the gatekeepers, what purpose do the labels serve except to try to change our musical taste to theirs? That made sense when you had only a few radio stations and it cost a lot to get a record manufactured. But now that they're bypassed, who cares?

In 20 or 30 years, historians may look back at the latter half of the 20th century and call it the short, happy life of the music business. And they'll say that before the technology of broadcast, there *was* no music business to speak of. People played music on the side, entertained their friends, played in small venues, or were lucky enough to have

Tell Musicmatch Jukebox one song you like, and it will generate endless Internet radio playlists containing songs from other artists it believes you'll also like. The recommendations are based on surveying (with permission) the listening habits of tens of millions of other Musicmatch users.

sponsors. Nobody really got rich off it. Then broadcast allowed one voice to reach millions of people, and suddenly there was great potential for income, so business stepped in.

But now you've got narrowcast, in which every voice has the ability to reach every ear and every ear to find every voice. With all those choices, the millions of listeners have less interest in focusing in on a few hit voices. And that's a *good* thing, because everyone can find the music they really like instead of what somebody wants to sell them.

David Fagin: Now that anybody who wants to make a record *can* make a record, it's quite interesting. We've got the tools that the record company had over us—the keys to the kingdom—for so many years. You needed a record company for two things: making a record and promotion. And now half the battle is over. The Internet was the promise of the other half, but it hasn't worked out that way so far.

Ted Cohen: You still need aggregation. That's the problem. If you hang a sign up on the Internet saying, "Hi, I'm here," you're not going to get the critical mass you need to get attention. People always say, "Will record companies go away?" They *may*, but I don't think the expertise—the promotion, the marketing, the creating-critical-mass is going to go away.

A friend of mine said something once that I thought was brilliant. He said that an artist's fear of being pirated is greatly overwhelmed by his fear of never being heard. It is really important that you get something out there and *get* people exposed to your music.

And you should hope that if you're giving something away at the beginning—and you *should* give something away at the beginning—that it's not the only good thing you're ever going to do. An artist I really admire, Duncan Sheik [www.duncansheik.com], said he views a single track from his album as a trailer from his movie. And to continue the movie metaphor, you really hope that the trailer isn't the best part of the movie. [*Laughs.*]

Jim Reekes: I have an artist friend who's very prolific, and I helped him put together a Web site with MP3 samples of his songs. There are editorial comments; there are reviews by fans; there are "If you like that, you'll like this" links. So you get reference points, and then you buy the songs and he'll burn you a CD.

He's selling five to ten times fewer units than before, because the stores aren't pumping him and he gets *no* airplay. But he's actually making more money, because instead of getting less than a dollar per CD by selling through the record industry, he owns *all* of it.

So what will it take for digital music distribution to really take off?

Marc Geiger: One of the factors is just pipe—speed into the home. But if bandwidth were the only issue, then 60 *million* people wouldn't have adopted Napster in nine months. At that time, DSL and cable modem penetration was *seven* percent.

Then there are interface issues. Consumers are bombarded with pop-ups and pop-unders, interstitials, eye-blast ads, Flash, Shockwave, slow-loading graphics, etc. Yet gazillions of them use the Web every day, which shows me the strength of the demand. And the user experience will only get better.

So if you look out three to five years, the rights issues and the business issues are bigger than the technology issues. We've got to get away from unit pricing. That's the big one. On the supplier side, the label, artist, and publisher have to sort out their percentage splits, which is a *massive* issue, and that may take the longest out of everything.

The third thing is they've got to get out of the mindset of security. There is no way consumers are going to tolerate Big Brother reaching into their devices and turning off a file.

First of all, the users have always chosen what

Art and knowledge and music and speech are anarchistic. That's what makes them so valuable. You should not *want* to put an end to that. *—Jim Griffin*

software they use. It doesn't matter which is the better technology. Look at Beta [video]. And look at Windows Media: It sounds better than MP3. So it's not about that; it's about what the consumer wants. That's the first law.

The second law is that consumers don't want to be fucked with, and you *cannot* sell them a file that has *rules* around it. They will not tolerate it. Piracy would just continue then.

The only thing that needs to be secure is your credit-card payment and your identity. Now, if you're saying you want to redistribute all the music you pulled down, that's a no-no. And that would be a term of use I'd make you sign up for.

But what actually prevents me from just forwarding all the music I've bought to someone else?

Marc Geiger: It's called the carpool-lane rule. Whether it's driving in the carpool lane or using a bootleg cable box, there's got to be a substantial penalty—a monetary fine that makes it just not worth doing if you get caught. That will make you think twice.

So how do you catch and prosecute people?

Marc Geiger: You go after a few of them and publicize it enough and people will get the message. But it's bullshit—it's Prohibition if you crack down on them and don't give them a real alternative. Once you have a real digital music solution, if people still pirate, that's wrong. If people are pirating now, that's a supplier problem. You're just creating a pirate market. It's sex or drugs.

Ray Kurzweil: I've thought about this technically, and I'm convinced there's no technical solution if people are bent on breaking copy protection. It's just like there'd be no technical solution if everyone decided they wanted to loot stores. Our whole law-enforcement system relies on the fact that 99.9 percent of people aren't going to do that. If everybody decided to do it, well, then we do see examples in the world where law and order breaks down, and it's impossible to stop.

What happens is that stores quickly run out of things to loot. You might think that's not the case here, since you can make an infinite number of copies of information, but there's not an inexhaustible supply of the *creation* of this kind of intellectual property. I've been involved in creating albums; it can cost well into six figures to create a really professional album. The equipment's getting less and less expensive, but you still have to pay for the musicians and all the other talent you need.

Jim Griffin: I used to use the phrase "intellectual property" all the time, until Richard Stallman [www.stallman.org] started bugging me. [*Laughs.*] And I thought he had a point. Thomas Jefferson was right: There's nothing less susceptible of being considered property than an idea or creativity. It's dangerous when you perpetuate this illusion that we're dealing with property and that it's still stuff that we can control, because it's *not* and we *can't*. And that's a good thing, because art and knowledge and music and speech *are* anarchistic. That's what makes them so valuable. You should not *want* to put an end to that.

Ted Cohen: My dream is, I want to send you music and I want you to live with it anywhere from three days to a week. At the end of the week, it's going to say to you, "Hi! Time's up. Do you want to buy me?" And the compensation may not be money. The

compensation may be access to your usage information—what kind of music are you listening to? You may be part of some virtual A&R committee.

But I want you to have a moment where *you* have to make a decision: "Do I want to keep this or let it go?" Because the problem with peer-to-peer music distribution right now is there *is* no sense of loss. When people say that peer-to-peer creates demand for people to go out and buy the CD—*possibly.* In most cases, if you've downloaded three tracks that you like from Kazaa, and they're 128 or 192kbps encoded, and they don't clip at the beginning and the end, it's, "Sorry. I've got it."

Do I *really* need to go buy it? It's not like I'm registering it for some warranty in case it goes bad, because if something goes wrong, I'll download it again. So when people say peer-to-peer is just like radio, I respectfully disagree. On radio, if you hear a song two or three times over three or four days, you go, "Wow, I really like that. I want to get it." When you download something from Kazaa, you've *got* it.

Peter Gotcher: I'm a strong believer that over the next five to ten years you will see broad adoption of music subscription services. And my guess is it will work very similarly to cable TV: You'll pay a base rate for a whole bunch of back catalog and current non-premium content, and you'll also have pay-per-view. It will probably use an ASCAP/BMI-style model, where the company streaming the media will track playback information and then artists will be paid in proportion to what people are listening to.

For that to work, we'll need pervasive, wireless broadband. Your appliances will connect to the network and identify each other, and all the headaches of broadband in the home today will go away. That definitely will happen in the next couple of years. You'll even see devices like audio TiVos—caching devices where you'll be able to select the audio you want to have at your fingertips.

Marc Geiger: You'll also be able to subscribe to artists individually, at a much lower price. But the *big* model is the cable TV of music, or what other people call the Jukebox in the Sky. The question is how you protect against fooling those systems—where a record company has 200 kids downloading the same artist constantly. [*Laughs*] That's going to be the new payola.

Jim, you coined the phrase "celestial jukebox." How will independent artists get their music into that system?

Jim Griffin: Actually, I don't think there *is* a celestial jukebox. I think that will be the *effect*. When you look at your device, it will appear to *you* that you have a giant jukebox. For example, to a Napster user [*of the original, illegal version*], it appeared that they had the greatest jukebox in the world. It found everything—songs that were just out in garages somewhere. They end up alive again.

So you could put your song out there yourself by making it available on a peered network. You could buy software that made it possible to stream it, like Windows Media Server or Real Audio Server. You could put your stuff on services like MP3.com [*now Download.com*]. Or you could encourage your friends to put it on peered networks, because you could say, "Dudes, the more my stuff moves, the bigger a check I get. So let's have some action." [*Laughs.*]

But the truth is that it's out there already. There is nothing we can do to stop that behavior [*i.e., file sharing*]. Everything we do to stop it drives it further underground and makes it harder to even understand or address. The question is how you're going to monetize that. When you make things highly available at roughly a flat fee as cable TV does, people lose the motive to copy things at all.

But how are people going to find music they like once this firehose of audio is turned on?

Marc Geiger: *Ahhh* . . . great question. The bottom line is, when the world goes to a three million-song library, new things just get lost. Today there are a myriad of ways

May I Have a ReFill?

Sample-library developers, which supply a tech-savvy yet often underfunded audience, have been battling piracy for years. When Propellerhead Software released its hit program Reason, it introduced a file formant called the ReFill that groups hundreds of samples into a single file. The individual ReFills that come with Reason fill hundreds of megabytes. I asked Propellerheads CEO Ernst Nathorst-Böös if that had helped prevent piracy.

"It *seems* it has," he replied. "But it's really not about copy protection. We felt that some of the file sharing that's going on, especially on the Internet, is not because people are evil; sometimes it's just that they don't understand. And with a little WAV file, it's like, 'How can that be important intellectual property?'

"By doing the ReFill thing, where you put an *identity* on the whole bank—it's got this splash screen, it's got a name—I think it's more obvious that this is something that someone actually assembled. It's like a work of art, so they'll be less inclined to send it to someone else. And it seems that sound developers share this view, because there are *so* many ReFills being done."

that people can find out about music—friends, word of mouth, record stores, radio, magazines, television, etc. All of those things I call filters. And they're not going away.

Answer number two is that a whole new set of filters is going to evolve, and they will be much more like HTML newsletters. You'll subscribe and they will e-mail you things to try based on your preferences. I call those playlists.

Right now, Amazon.com has two types of filtering. One is when you buy a record and it tells you, "Here are some other records you might like." That's not just collaborative filtering, which says, "Other people who have bought this like *this*." Amazon actually curates it and says, "*You* might like this." And you can also go to their lists and ask, "What are the top 100 jazz albums?"

> [Record labels] have got to get out of the mindset of security.
> There is no way consumers are going to tolerate Big Brother
> reaching into their devices and turning off a file. —*Marc Geiger*

The next evolution will be, "I think Amazon's people are really good at filtering through all this music. I want them to tell me what albums I might want to listen to." And then your favorite radio DJ will say, "Go to our site and sign up for our playlist." And if you do, every week you'll get an e-mail of links. When you click on the links, they'll start playing the music or downloading it to your iPod or whatever.

You're going to sign up for a bunch of music newsletters, and they're going to push you stuff because you trust them; they're a trusted filter. And the digital music service itself will have a huge number of pre-programmed filters that you can access, just like TiVo. TiVo is a half step toward what we're talking about. It talks about the hottest directors and what's showing this month; you can break it down by docudrama, award-winners, and so on.

I believe the human-curated list is going to be a bigger deal than the robotic "I looked at your record collection and here's what I recommend" approach. I think there's a whole new job waiting for the music tastemakers today—the critics, the writers, the DJs, the record store clerks. They will become people you might subscribe to.

Peter Gotcher: Finding music you like is the single biggest issue. The music-discovery process is broken now. The labels are organized around the blockbuster model, in which one highly successful artist pays all the bills. But it's incredibly expensive to promote a mainstream pop artist. So a lot of interesting bands get signed but never promoted, because the price tag of any real promotion is a million bucks plus—all recoupable, of course, against the artist.

With revenues dropping, the major labels are becoming more and more risk-averse. So they're only promoting bands that look like one of the five or six profiles that have been recently successful. And it's a self-fulfilling prophecy.

And the consolidation of radio, with Clear Channel essentially managing playlists now, is making radio more narrow and pop-oriented. If you're a new band, how do you get noticed?

I'm working on a startup to do that—to try to connect independent artists to people who have been identified as having a high probability of being receptive to their type of music. The key engine for that is things like Musicmatch, where you have 25 million users, but you've also got a ton of preference information from the 70 percent of users who have opted to have their listening logs uploaded for the purposes of music recommendation.

I've heard that type of predictive modeling is frighteningly accurate.

Peter Gotcher: It really is. I've been doing venture-capital stuff for the last four years, and I looked at seven or eight companies that were taking different tactics for making music recommendations, because it's been an interest of mine for a while.

There was a company called Gigabeat [*later acquired by Napster*], whose whole approach was to take a song, do an FFT [Fast Fourier Transform analysis] of it, and then look for songs with a similar spectrum. They assumed that if you liked one you'd like the others. But a song with bass, drums, guitar, and a male singer could be a punk tune or a country tune. And so Gigabeat really didn't make useful recommendations. It used a lot of technology, though! It took a lot of DSP horsepower. [*Laughs.*]

There have been some other ones like MongoMusic [*later acquired by Microsoft*] and Savage Beast Technologies. They basically use human editorial to listen to a piece of music. They'll create a database that will have anywhere from 15 to 35 musical descriptive attributes, and then try to come up with correlations between different pieces of music using those attributes. And that actually works well. The problem is that it doesn't scale very well, because you need to have a human listen to every song.

The reasons somebody who likes Miles Davis might also like R.E.M. are incredibly complex. So there's really no substitute for just analyzing the behavior of a very large population of users. And so Musicmatch has created a very large collaborative filtering engine with some other twists that has identified these clusters of musical tastes. Maybe I'm biased [*Gotcher is on the Musicmatch board*], but I personally find *that* is the scary one. It really works well.

Of course, another great music-discovery method is simply to have a friend say, "I think you'll like this song."

Peter Gotcher: Well, exactly. The whole peer-to-peer dynamic is great. And there isn't really any kind of mechanism that mutually rewards people for forming clusters with similar tastes and recommending music to each other. [*A new service called Weed might fit the bill. See the "How Weed It Is" sidebar.*]

Future

The Future of Digital Music

Dreams and fears for tomorrow's technology

Predictions are usually more fun than accurate, because the world of music technology is moving so fast. But predictions also reflect our hopes and fears, and that offers a valuable perspective on where we've been. For this chapter, we asked the interviewees to speculate about the future of digital music, and they attacked the challenge from a variety of interesting angles.

MAKING MUSIC

As technology evolves, how will it change the way people make music?

Mark Isham: I can't help but think it's going to be more interactive. Just look at the way things are going with access through the Internet to all sorts of music, and people's interest in remixes and alternative versions, and little home programs for making your own mixes. The truth is, it's getting very easy to make music.

Pop music has always had pretty stringent rules, and it's the people who break those rules who define the next chapter. And as more people have the ability to interact and create and make their own *decisions* about music, perhaps this lowest-common-denominator concept that record companies tend to fall into will get *raised* a bit. And that's a good thing for our culture in general.

Tage Widsell: I hope the electronic live scene will grow, so that people will discover what a truly rewarding experience it is to play your music live to others. It's becoming easier and easier to do that. Now I have my PowerBook and my little keyboard, and that's all. It's so much easier to find places to play when you don't need an hour to set up and an hour to pack down.

Alan Parsons: I would like an answer to where recording will be ten years from now, and whether the music being made in people's houses and garages *now* will bear any resemblance to the music in home studios and garages ten years from now.

It will be interesting to see if it goes back towards the concept of musicians playing together and interacting with each other, or whether it will continue to be this solitary experience. So many records are the vision of one or two people now. Vocalists are

We're going to merge with the technology; we're going to be sending billions of little intelligent robots called nanobots into our brains. —*Ray Kurzweil*

brought in as almost an afterthought, and I think that's a sad day for the songwriter and a sad day for the music business as a whole.

There's nothing exciting about watching somebody set up a computer on a stage, press the space bar, and just tap his foot. I think we will always want to see musicians interacting with each other, and that means bands and that means we will *have* to get to the stage where the computer takes second place. It's very definitely in first place right now.

Ray Kurzweil: We're going to enhance human intelligence. We're going to merge with the technology; we're going to be sending billions of little intelligent robots called nanobots into our brains. They'll interact directly with our biological neurons and we'll be adding virtual connections that can operate millions of times faster.

And the ultimate implication is that we will be able to do more of what we consider quintessentially human. How many people can create music like the Rolling Stones or Beethoven? And even *those* individuals, how often can they really strive for those levels? Most people have a musical imagination but don't have the means of ever expressing it. So these are some of the possibilities that a direct, intimate merger of our biological thinking with new forms of non-biological thinking will open up.

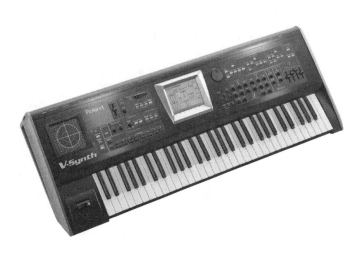

The Roland V-Synth offers a glimpse of the future; its VariPhrase technology can transpose sounds in real time without changing their durations.

Working with audio used to require a phrase-based approach to composition, whereas MIDI dictated a note-based approach. It's been fascinating in the last few years to see technologies like Celemony Melodyne, Spectrasonics Groove Control, and Roland VariPhrase start to blur that distinction. Where's it all going?

Roger Linn: I think we're going to see less dependence on deciding which way you want to go before you record. You'll just

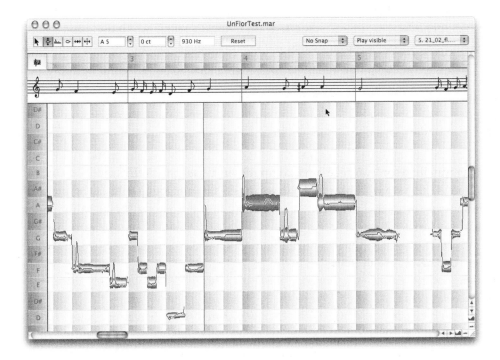

Celemony Melodyne blurs the distinction between audio and MIDI by isolating individual pitches in monophonic audio files. You can drag notes to create new melodies and rhythms. Someday, that will be possible with chords as well.

record, and the software will be able to extract pitch and other parameters from the music in the background, which you'll then manipulate.

It's like the way Adobe is blurring the line between vector and bitmap art. Adobe Illustrator includes tools for filtering vector objects, and Photoshop has tools like Magnetic Lasso that allow you to turn useful sections of bitmaps into separate objects.

> The cost of storage is dropping precipitously. By the end of the decade, you'll be able to fit all the recorded music from all the major labels on a single $100 hard drive. *—Albhy Galuten*

Eric Persing: The ultimate goal is resynthesis. We're getting closer to that with things like the [Hartmann] Neuron. And some aspects of VariPhrase work that way. But we're in a very early stage where the DSP solutions sound interesting but not terribly realistic.

A *lot* of research still has to happen, because modeling and resynthesis are based on how you measure sound, and we're a long way off from really being able to measure sound properly. There are big pieces of the puzzle that we're not able to quantify—certain things like air, and width, and separation, and warmth, and those kinds of things that musicians talk about all the time. When you talk about that to technical people, they look at you like you're insane because none of that stuff shows up on any graphs.

But the truth is that these slight differences we perceive—they're *real*. At some point somebody will figure out, "Oh! We were measuring it incorrectly." Or that there's a way to measure it in a different dimension. And then we'll have much better tools.

So when those things happen, and when we have computers that are *much* more powerful than we have now, you will start to see audio, sampling, and synthesis truly merge. You'll be able to take an audio track, hit a button, and it will be analyzed and turned into additive synthesis. And you'll have tools to be able to manipulate it that won't have *any* of that metallic, flangey sound they have now. Things will sound completely natural.

EXPERIENCING MUSIC

Albhy, you've helped define numerous music data formats. How will those formats hold up? If people call up a file ten or 20 years from now, it might not even play.

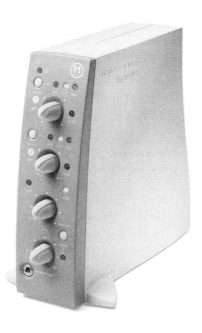

The future of music is mobile: This $500 Digidesign Mbox audio interface and a laptop computer were enough for producer Don Was to record the Rolling Stones.

Albhy Galuten: Well, it *may* not, but I have hope that, at least in the audio space, successful formats will continue to be supported. Certainly 20 years from now, there will be no technical difficulty in supporting MP3 as a format. It will be just another set of instructions the processor runs, and for which there's already mature code that costs nothing to add. The patents will already be in the public domain, so there won't be any license fees. If a format was particularly successful, there's no reason to ever exclude it. Turntables still play 78s.

You might find that your device doesn't play a TwinVQ file ten years from now. But there's a pretty good chance it will play an MP3, a WMA, and maybe an AAC file. And copy protection is just a matter of business rules and interoperability—there's no processing information in the file. Manufacturers must agree to support various legacy DRM [digital rights management]. So 30 years from now, your high-res video player will probably still have the key that lets it play today's DVDs.

But isn't it true that a lot of the enhanced CDs you made for ION in the '90s don't play anymore?

Albby Galuten: Well, that's different. That's not a format; it's an executable [*that is, the material is a program rather than a document*]. That's why we've tried to define some standards around markup languages. An executable is always going to be OS-dependent, whereas with a format that's clearly defined, there's no reason why the new OS's shouldn't support the old format.

Jeff Patterson: I just got one of those Nomad MuVos—those tiny little MP3 players. So now I take that with me on the subway and listen to that on the way to work. I was thinking how cool it would be if it had Bluetooth in it so that everybody on the subway who had a Bluetooth-enabled MP3 player could tune into each other's devices and hear what they're listening to. And you could broadcast to the rest of the subway car what you were playing.

So you'd get a performance-art effect as you walked through different cars?

Jeff Patterson: [*Laughs.*] Right. It'd be cool because it'd be totally anonymous. You could just flip through and see what else was playing. It'd actually be a cool way to meet people, too. If you liked the music you could signal something, and get into a dating page or something like that.

Albby Galuten: I think that eventually music subscription services will be a great choice for most people. But that will require some sort of intelligent mechanism. At the simplest level, it requires connectivity everywhere at high bandwidth, which is not efficient. So that's quite a ways out. But as you know, the cost of storage is dropping precipitously. By the end of the decade, you'll be able to fit *all* the recorded music from *all* the major labels on a single $100 hard drive.

I think having an MP3 as the soundtrack of your life is a step towards a chip being implanted in your head with everything on it, and just turning your neck to the side and going to whatever year you wanted to hear something. —*Chuck D*

Will people have those drives in their homes as servers?

Albby Galuten: Well, actually, you'll have it in your car. You'll have it in your home; you'll have it in your portable device. The storage will be irrelevant. What *will* be relevant, I *hope*, is your access to it. So if you have the right to subscribe to a service that gives you access to all of the music, you'll pay ten dollars a month and you can listen to *anything*.

So if I hear a new song that I like, I'll just send you a pointer to it. If you're a subscriber to a service, you'll just play it. And if you're someone who wants to buy tracks individually, you'll go, "Okay, I'll buy it." But it will already be there. *Where* the content is stored should be irrelevant. There's no reason it should matter to the consumer.

It's just like your LRU [least recently used] cache in your browser. Do you *really* know when a GIF to a page you've been to before is loaded from your cache or reloaded from the site? It doesn't make any difference. The reality is that you have the directions for how to consume that.

And in that case, you have the right to consume it and it's either paid for by the good graces of the person who made the site, or by advertising, or a subscription, or a per-unit fee. There is *some* means of exchange associated with it, just like network TV. So you'll buy a car; it's got the top 3,000 songs or 10,000 songs, which make it for most people; and then when you click on something and there's a couple seconds of delay, it means they sent it to you over the network because you didn't already have it cached.

 You'll probably be able to say, "I'd like to have a completed product of what I just enjoyed," hit the Enter button, and it will be delivered in some format, either directly to your computer or to some portable device. *—Phil Ramone*

Looking way into the future, how do you think people will experience music, say, 50 years from now?

Amy X Neuburg: Ooh, it's a scary picture. There is already too much music out there. It's no longer necessarily an art form but an expected component of our background noise, a commodity to lure people into stores, distract them at the dentist, relax them in restaurants.

Already fewer people attend concerts, and practically no one actually sits down between the speakers and listens to a CD the way I and a few of my geeky audio friends do. I don't mean to sound elitist; I'm *into* popular music. And I'm a firm believer in art as entertainment.

But my point is how we as a culture have become disengaged from our music while, at the same time, it's everywhere. So I see a future of way too much music, and music that is less interesting, with people paying less real attention to it, and an attitude that strays very far from our original spiritual connection to music. Does this sound cynical? I hope I'm wrong.

David Mash: What we *can* predict is that music will be ubiquitous. Fifty years ago, the barrier to making a record was steep. Today, most musicians who are making records have their own personal studios in their houses. The great thing about new technology is that it's all about personal expression. And if people have good tools to express themselves, there's going to be great music.

And there's no such thing as too much good music. The more people who are making music, the more opportunities there are for music that I want to listen to to be created. These technology tools have opened that world in a way that's really exciting and wonderful.

Thomas Dolby: I think that overall this is a very fertile time for music and art. In spite of the complaints you get from the music industry, it's a time that is really laden with opportunities for musicians and music fans.

I've got people who have been friends for years and years who basically consider me the lucky one. They thought they would never be able to get a record deal and never be able to make a living as a professional musician, and they have really taken heart now, because the barriers to entry are so low. They are making their own CDs, keeping mailing lists and Web sites, selling at their gigs, and so on. And they're able to make a stream of income from their music, which they never were 20 years ago. So I think that's very encouraging.

I think what's called for now is somebody who can somehow bridge the gap between the musician sitting in his shed, making his own CDs and selling them off the Web himself, and a wider audience.

Phil Ramone: I think the way we experience music in the future will be a visual combination. Your driving mechanism will be an all-engrossing combination of not just space glasses [*i.e., virtual-reality goggles*] but environmental changes. I think people, after a busy day, will want to go sit in their private little environment—it may be only a 10-by-12-foot booth in their own living space—and immerse themselves in combinations of classics and pops that they've been brought up on.

And then they might say, "Let me be educated for 20 minutes. Let me know the history of all of this." And a complete pictorial and aural history will come about. I think education will come in so many different ways—and *fun* education, not the dry who-was-born-when thing. You might want to know that Haydn had something to do with the chord structure of modern pop songs.

I also think you'll be calling it up on the Net and saying, "I'd like to pay for this experience." The word "pay" will come into a monthly or weekly subscription. You'll probably be able to say, "I'd like to have a completed product of what I just enjoyed," hit the Enter button, and it will be delivered in some format, either directly to your computer or to some portable device. We have to realize that the only antipiracy solution is to be able to charge a fair number and have people enjoy the material on *their* prescription.

I think what's called for now is somebody who can somehow bridge the gap between the musician sitting in his shed, making his own CDs and selling them off the Web himself, and a wider audience. —*Thomas Dolby*

Ted Cohen: *Totally* connected; totally wireless. You'll be able to get what you want, when you want, where you want. [Jim] Griffin calls it the celestial jukebox; I referred to it ten years ago, pre–Mr. Griffin, as "my stuff." Jim and I both agree that access to your stuff is going to be what it's going to be all about.

I walk around airports with headphones on and people are wondering why I'm smiling like a little kid. I mean, I bring home 40 or 50 CDs a week. I have realized that there is now more music in my house than I have years left to listen to it. So I'm *rapidly* trying to listen.

Chuck D: Well, I think having an MP3 as the soundtrack of your life is a step towards [*laughs*] a chip being implanted in your head with everything on it, and just turning your neck to the side and going to whatever year you wanted to hear something. People just being able to take a small pill and—I don't know if this is good or bad for society—have every song *ever made.* Within your blood system. And every *film* ever made.

Do you think people will start slipping those pills into other people's drinks?
Chuck D: Of course.

Dr. Elizabeth Cohen: [*Laughs.*] Fifty years now, if *I'm* still around, there won't *be* much of my hearing left, and I sure hope I have some sort of hearing device in my ear that allows me to tune in to what's going on. So I would definitely think that we're going to see all sorts of implantable devices or wearable devices that will allow us to both create and hear music.

I wonder if silence will become much more valued as a result. Now we have to pay for music, but in the future we might have to pay for silence.
Marc Geiger: That's so untrue it's frightening. You sound like Clifford Stoll. [*See the "High Tech Heretic" sidebar.*] You're just not able to deal with the noise. There's clearly media overload, but that's *not* what's happening. What's happening is *more choice,* and alongside of more choice—in the first phase—there's always noise.

The second phase is sophisticated filtration tools to get you what you need. When you go to a newsstand, there's noise. Most of the magazines are garbage to you. But you can pick out, say, *Time, Spin,* and the *San Jose Mercury News.* That was the old world. The new world is, "Ooh—everybody's got my e-mail address! It's all coming to my house. *Stop!*"

So the first reaction is to shut down. The second reaction is, "Aren't there really sophisticated spam filters?" Go get Matador [www.mailfrontier.com]. It's the best spam filter out there. You sound like you need it. But I don't believe anybody doesn't want the good stuff. They just don't want all the bad stuff.

 Good, soulful songs that resonate in your emotional life are what it's all about. The delivery system's going to change, but in the end, what's the difference between AM radio and MP2? It *really doesn't matter. –Don Was*

Yeah, but that still seems like a huge problem.
Marc Geiger: But it's the *same thing as TV!* What's the biggest complaint on television? "It went from seven to 500 channels and there's still nothing on." Who cancelled their cable? Nobody! One percent of the people said, "Fuck this; I'm canceling my cable." The rest of them just didn't watch it all the time. And then came TiVo.

And if you *had* a TiVo you'd know that's the way you get these 500 channels and get *exactly* what you want. I stopped watching live TV. My family does not do anything but watch TiVo, which is *exactly* only the stuff we want. And that's a filter. It happens to be hard-drive based, but it's a filter. It presents information to you in the way you want it.

Chuck, do you think we'll be paying for silence in the future?

Chuck D: Of *course.* To me, as a creator of sound and noise, silence is everything. God gives you sound, and God gives you silence. But both of those things might have to come with a price.

Dr. Elizabeth Cohen: Sooner or later, people will have to recognize the importance of silence. Our cities are too noisy, our work environments are too noisy, and the further apart you get from nature, the more limited your sonic vocabulary becomes. We've had what [ethnomusicologist] Alan Lomax referred to a long time ago as "cultural grayout." When you have Western pop music dominating the world, then it's like these ecosystems end up taking over—there's music pollution, too.

So ideally what one wants is to have very strong local artistic communities. If the local artistic community is strong, then it meets the world music community—or the western pop music community—and new forms evolve from it. And *that* becomes interesting and very worthwhile. But when local music dies out, it's tragic. You have the Mc-Donaldization of music.

It is kind of creepy that McDonald's french-fry boxes are now promoting music.

Dr. Elizabeth Cohen: Well, it's not so creepy if the music is good. If the music is good, then maybe when someone listens to it, they'll think, "Why Mickey D's?" Music by itself is subversive in nature. It *always* questions. [*Laughs.*] If it's good music.

Don, how do you think we'll be listening to music 50 years from now?

Don Was: If it's altered too much, it won't really be music. Music is still an auditory medium, and whether you're looking at videos simultaneously, or the sub-subwoofer is pushing air through your nostrils, you still have to listen to it. Good, soulful songs that

High Tech Heretic

Clifford Stoll polarized readers with his provocative books *Silicon Snake Oil* and *High Tech Heretic*. But this astrophysicist who became famous for singlehandedly nabbing an international computer spy ring is far from a Luddite. In an interview at FamilyHaven.com, Stoll says, "I love computers. Technology doesn't scare me. In fact, if anything, our problem is obsession with it. It's this idea that if you're not online, if you don't have all sorts of computers in front of you, then you are going to be left in the past. We computer jocks need to open a discussion: How much computing do we need? Do we need more channels of video, or maybe fewer?"

At Edge.org, Stoll continues, "Human kindness, warmth, interaction, friendship, and family are far more important than anything that can come across my cathode-ray tube." See his pointed home page at www.ocf.berkeley.edu/~stoll.

Brian Eno on the Distant Future of Music

Due to scheduling conflicts, we were never able to schedule a one-on-one interview with Brian Eno, the visionary artist and producer many other interviewees
cited as a huge influence. So we did the next best thing: When Eno gave a public
lecture in November 2003 for the Long Now Foundation, I showed up with my trusty
Korg PXR4 pocket digital recorder. (The audience turnout was so huge that I had to
park almost a mile away.) Eno concluded his forward-looking lecture, titled "The
Long Now," by answering written questions from the audience, and one of the
questions he picked was mine.

Brian Eno also theorizes that the
extremely high tempos in some
modern music are an attempt to
convert rhythm into ambience.

You can download the entire talk in text and audio formats at http://semi-
nars.longnow.org. The Long Now Foundation, which Eno co-founded in 1996, aims
"to promote 'slower/better' thinking and to foster creativity in the framework of the
next 10,000 years." For more on Eno, see www.enoweb.co.uk. —*David Battino*

*Fifty years from now, when we all have broadband receivers embedded in our
skulls, will we be paying for silence instead of music?*

Yes. Absolutely right. I've done my best in that respect—of making music
that has less and less sound in it. [*Laughs.*] Actually, in the 1950s, I heard, there used to be jukeboxes in America
that had one silent disc on them. So, if you wanted a bit of peace, you put your dime in and dialed up that number,
and you got three minutes of silence. I'd love to get a collection of those records. [*Audience laughs loudly.*] Wouldn't
it be fantastic? To have a jukebox where that's all you had on: different varieties of silence.

resonate in your emotional life are what it's all about. The delivery system's going to
change, but in the end, what's the difference between AM radio and MP2? It *really doesn't
matter.* Kraftwerk or Ricky Nelson—it either speaks to you or it doesn't.

I hope what I'm saying doesn't come across as negative. Digital advancements in the
technology can be extremely beneficial in capturing a moment of truth, and that's a very
positive thing. I'm sitting in a room that's got an Mbox and a Digi 001 [Digidesign computer audio interfaces]. It's just a room in my house, and it's got three different digital
recording setups. So I'm really not a Wollensak advocate, and I do recognize the positive
attributes of this movement, which are that it returns it to the realm of folk music. It's
possible to be self-contained and, for very little money, capture something that has a lot
of feeling.

Someone said the computer is the acoustic guitar of today.

Don Was: That's absolutely right. When we recorded [the Rolling Stones'] *Voodoo
Lounge,* we did a lot of it at my house on Mulholland Drive, and I probably had close to

a million dollars' worth of gear just in my house—a 72-channel Neve [mixing board] and all that. And I actually have more flexibility now with about $1,700 invested in an iBook and an Mbox. I can react quicker to things and alter things—move things around. I can do *so much more* with a tiny investment than I could pumping a million dollars into a room. So it's *fabulous,* but what does it have to do with the sources of creativity and the fundamental values of music? By nature, it neither detracts nor adds; it's simply a tool. You're either connected to something real or you're not.

About the Authors

David Battino, a lifelong musician, majored in philosophy at Oberlin College but spent most of his time tormenting synthesizers in the Oberlin Conservatory's electronic music studios. He is the founding editor of *Music & Computers* magazine and the *Desktop Music Production Guide,* and has covered music technology for *Electronic Musician, Keyboard, MacAddict, MacHome, Maximum PC,* and Productopia.com. David was also Technology Editor for *Revolution,* the biggest launch in music-magazine history, where he designed and produced the monthly CD-ROM. He is on the steering committee for the Interactive Audio Special Interest Group (www.IASIG.org) and has designed sounds for Lazer-Tron arcade games and Ray Charles's album *My World.* For links to David's articles, music, and more, visit www.batmosphere.com.

Kelli Richards, a veteran in the digital music/media arena over the past two decades, connects the dots between major content brands, established artists, dynamic technology companies, and consumer brands to create innovative and profitable alliances. She has rich experience as an executive and strategist with both mainstream entertainment (EMI, others) and technology (Apple Computer, SGI, Philips) companies, where she focused on developing traditional and digital music and entertainment initiatives for each. Kelli also pioneered the first Internet-based artist subscription service, Patro-Net, with Todd Rundgren in the mid-'90s. And she has been a producer of awards shows, digital music/media conferences, and celebrity fundraisers. Kelli recently co-authored the book *Create Business Breakthroughs You Want: Secrets and Strategies of the World's Greatest Mentors,* with notable co-authors including Mark Victor Hansen, Robert G. Allen, and Brian Tracy. You can find more details about Kelli and her company, the All Access Group, at www.allaccessgroup.com.

We amassed far more material than we could fit in these pages. Please visit www.ArtOfDigitalMusic.com for updates and bonus interviews.

Photo Credits

All photos were supplied by publicists or the authors, with the following exceptions:

Page 8: courtesy of Laika Entertainment
Page 19: Jon Silberg
Page 25: courtesy of David and Robin Thurlow and Disc Makers
Page 56: Chris Johnson
Page 66: Yolanda Accinelli
Page 67: Barbara Petersen
Page 75: Min Hee Kwak
Page 79 (Powell & Moog): Alan Blumenthal
Page 90: Wonge Bergmann
Page 94: Mark Leialoha
Page 96: courtesy of Nile Rodgers Productions
Page 107: Randi Anglin
Page 118: courtesy of *Tape Op* magazine
Page 124: courtesy of Apple Computer
Page 141: Matt Traum, Patchman Music
Page 143: Ranjit Bhatnagar, 2003
Page 206: Fadi Kheir
Page 208: Mariliana Arvelo
Page 250: Richard Dean

About the Disc

Here's what you'll find on the enhanced DVD

We asked the interviewees if they'd be interested in sharing something personal for the disc, and received *gigabytes* of fascinating songs, videos, loops, and behind-the-scenes photos. Then one interviewee remarked that she'd love to hear what everyone else sounded like. So we extracted 60 seconds of audio from each interview, cleaned up the background telephone and trade-show noise with Waves X-Noise, added some original music with Ableton Live to move things along, and synchronized everything with the photos using LQ Graphics Photo To Movie. Thanks to Tim Tully, Jim Reekes, and Roger Powell for their aesthetic and technical help.

—David Battino

DVD Contents—Video
You can view this part of the disc with any standard DVD player or a computer with a DVD drive.

- **Interview Audio Excerpts** with synchronized color photos, including many not found in the book.

- **Music Videos** from Roger Linn, Amy X Neuburg, Ty Roberts (The Residents), Todd Rundgren, Dave Smith, and Fiorella Terenzi.

DVD-ROM Contents—Computer Files
Viewing this part of the disc requires a computer with a DVD drive and a Web browser. (The contents are presented in HTML.)

Songs and Audio Examples

Thomas Dolby
"One of Our Submarines" (Live)
"I Love You Goodbye" (Live)
Ringtone Demos

The Fat Man
"Dog Eat Dog"
"No Man of Earth"
"The Hero"
"Raw Ferret Pizz" (MIDI ferret)

Dr. Patrick Gleeson & Jim Lang
"Void When We Want"

Jennifer Hruska
"Piano Errors"
"Sompassion"
Sonic Implants Sample Demos
Ringtone Demos

Stephen Kay
"The Sorcerer"
"Chemistry, vol. 1"
"PlanetKARMA"

David Mash
"Mashine Blues"

Douglas Morton
"Float Plan"
"Radial Symmetry"

Amy X Neuburg
"Every Little Stain"

Marty O'Donnell
"Halo 2 Trailer"
"Halo 2 Remembrance"

Alan Parsons
"Cloudbreak" (5.1 surround mix;
requires DTS decoder)

Jeff Patterson & the Ugly Mugs
"Abracadaver"
"Constitution 18"

Eric Persing
Sample-library demo songs

Roger Powell
"Lumia" (1973)
"Emergency Splashdown" (1980)
"Window Pane" (2003)

Scotch Ralston
"Pik Perry Pimbo"

Doug Rogers (Producer)
Quantum Leap Symphonic Orchestra:
"Cartoon" (by Dave Marsden)

Dave Smith
Evolver Demos

Dr. Fiorella Terenzi
"Sidereal Breath"
"Heavenly Bodies"

Videos

David Mash
QuickTime Virtual Reality studio tour

Dave O'Neal
Two complete episodes of *Deep Fried,
Live!*

Ray Kurzweil
Virtual-reality concert footage

Samples

All samples are licensed, not sold, to you.
You may use them for commercial music
production without paying royalties, but
you may not resell them.

BT
Ten loops from *Breakz From the Nu
Skool* (courtesy of EastWest)

Jennifer Hruska/Sonic Network
Six SoundFont banks

Stephen Kay
68 Karma loops and hits

Douglas Morton/Q Up Arts
Seven loops

Essays

Todd Rundgren (courtesy of *The
Hollywood Reporter*)
Commentary on Downloadable Music

David Zicarelli
"Interactive Music: Standing Up or
Falling Down?"

Web Links

Links for every interviewee, and
further reading

Index

Profiles of individuals are indicated by **boldface.**

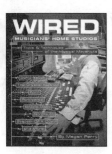

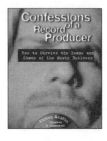